THE AFRICAN
EMPEROR

THE AFRICAN EMPEROR

The Life of Septimius Severus

SIMON ELLIOTT

ICON

Published in the UK and USA in 2025 by
Icon Books Ltd, Omnibus Business Centre,
39–41 North Road, London N7 9DP
email: info@iconbooks.com
www.iconbooks.com

ISBN: 978-183773-172-5
eBook: 978-183773-173-2

Text copyright © 2025 Simon Elliott

The author has asserted his moral rights.

No part of this book may be reproduced in any form, or by any means, without prior permission in writing from the publisher.

Typeset by SJmagic DESIGN SERVICES, India

Printed and bound in the UK

Appointed GPSR EU Representative: Easy Access System Europe Oü, 16879218
Address: Mustamäe tee 50, 10621, Tallinn, Estonia
Contact Details: gpsr.requests@easproject.com, +358 40 500 3575

*To Sara, loving wife and my partner on the Severan journey!
All my love, always!*

Contents

Introduction ix

1 Identity and Race in the Roman World 1
2 The World of Septimius Severus 17
3 Early Life and the Rise to Power 55
4 AD 193: 'The Year of the Five Emperors' 87
5 Civil War 127
6 Imperator: Severus in the East and Egypt 159
7 Imperator: Severus in Rome and North Africa 175
8 Imperator: Arrival in Britain 201
9 Imperator: The Severan Campaigns in Britain 225
Conclusion: The Severan Legacy 257

List of References 277
Bibliography 289
Index 299

Introduction

'No: we are not going to leave a single one of them alive, down to the babies in their mothers' wombs – even they must die. The whole people must be wiped out of existence, with none to shed a tear for them, leaving no trace.'[1]

Writing in the Mediterranean and after the event, these are the words contemporary historian Cassius Dio has hardman Roman Emperor Septimius Severus say before his final, apocalyptic campaign against lowland Scotland in AD 210.[2] Here, Dio, who knew Severus, paraphrases Agamemnon in Homer's *Iliad*, having the ageing emperor order a genocide. Hard data in the archaeological record from this time showing large scale settlement decline, and the abandonment of huge swathes of agricultural land in lowland Scotland, now shows this really occurred. Such was Severus' attitude to any who stood in his way, and this is his story.

Severus was the Roman Empire's African emperor, born in the heat of a Libyan spring in Leptis Magna in AD 145. His story arc is truly astonishing, ending in death in the freezing cold of a northern British winter in York in February AD 211. His career is one of superlatives. Ruling at the height of Roman military power, he commanded more legions than any other emperor. Further, under his rule, permanent Roman territory was expanded to its greatest extent. Given this martial prowess, I argue here he was the most powerful person ever born in Africa based purely on military and political agency.

The legions certainly played a key role in his story. Across its vast territory around the Mediterranean and northwestern Europe, the Roman Empire was always at war. Even in times of relative peace, which were few in Severus' reign, conflict could always be found.

He understood this better than most, in his case from the very beginning of his reign when he rose to power at the point of a sword in AD 193, last man standing in the 'Year of the Five Emperors'. Severus never forgot his military roots, famously telling his squabbling sons Caracalla and Geta on his deathbed to 'be of one mind, enrich the soldiers, and despise the rest'.³

Throughout his life, Severus stayed true to his African heritage. Dark skinned, he ensured he was portrayed this way in contemporary portraiture. While in his time this was unimportant in what was a largely Mediterranean empire, in our world today it is. I address this directly here. Further, even in politest Roman society amid the patricians of Rome, he insisted on keeping his strong Punic accent. Then, once in power, he swiftly promoted North Africans at every opportunity to key positions of authority. This is not surprising given, as I have seen in my own frequent research trips across the region, this was the richest part of the empire, with a proud cultural heritage to match anything in Rome, Athens or Alexandria. Severus used his North African upbringing as the template for what I style 'the Severan reset', which was the first major post-Augustan reformation of the Roman world. This established the Severan dynasty which lasted almost half a century. Such was the scale of this reorganisation, which some go further and call a hostile takeover, that it was not repeated again until the accession of Diocletian over 90 years after Severus became emperor, and that in extremis after the 'Crisis of the Third Century'.

Meanwhile, Severus was not a shy man, monumentalising his rule across the empire at every opportunity. He visited, and fought in, every region. When he did, he left a mighty legacy in the built environment. Many of these sites I have visited personally, following in his travels. Intriguingly, given the popular focus on the likes of Julius Caesar, Trajan and Hadrian, this urban Severan legacy often hides in plain sight, with few aware of it. Yet the high-profile examples are many in number. Think of *forum Romanum* in Rome where much is Severan, the lovely Temple of the Vesta just one example. Then, standing imposingly above the *forum*, most of the imperial palace on

INTRODUCTION

the Palatine Hill is Severan. From there, shimmering in a heat haze in summer, the distant Baths of Caracalla are also Severan, designed to be his great public legacy in the imperial capital. Elsewhere in Europe, the presence of Severus is writ large from east to west. Even in far off London, provincial capital of troublesome Britannia, the land wall that still defines the City today is Severan, while in York one can actually stand where he perished in the legionary fortress *praetorium*, now the undercroft of today's Minster. Meanwhile, in his native North Africa, every city and town I have visited has a highly visible Severan phase, whether in the soaring snow-capped Atlas Mountains or along the arid Saharan fringe.

The story of Severus also features a *dramatis personae* fit to dazzle any historical epic. Think of Marcus Aurelius, the philosopher emperor, and Commodus, his mad and bad son. Then Publius Helvius Pertinax, the son of a slave who became Roman emperor and was Severus' friend and mentor. Next, Decimus Clodius Albinus and Pescennius Niger, British and Syrian governors respectively, and Severus' former brothers in arms in the Marcomannic Wars. Both were destined to fight him tooth and nail for the throne in epic confrontations across the empire. Also, Didius Julianus and Flavius Sulpicianus, scandalous bidders for the imperial throne when auctioned by the Praetorian Guard, truly one of the lowest points in Roman history. Then, last but not least, his own family. Foremost was Julia Domna, his second wife and love of his life. She was a leading figure across the Roman world in her own right, and together they were the power couple of their age. Finally, their two sons, the psychotic Caracalla and unfortunate Geta, destined to live a spiral of bitter rivalry ending in the most sanguineous way.

SOURCE MATERIAL

In terms of the data used in the research for this book, I have accessed the widest possible range. For primary references, we are well served with three of the best available sources of the high Principate. These are

Cassius Dio with his *Roman History*, Herodian with his *History of the Roman Empire*, and the anonymous *Historia Augusta*. Although the level of detail in all is often patchy and inaccurate, their accessibility makes them invaluable here, especially when cross-referenced with each other, the work of later writers and modern archaeological research.

We also have several later Latin chroniclers who briefly mention aspects of the Severan story. These include Flavius Eutropius with his *Breviarium*, Aurelius Victor with his *De Caesaribus*, Jerome with his *Commentaries* and Paulus Orosius with his *Seven Books of History Against the Pagans*. Meanwhile, in terms of the many fine modern references, various aspects of Severus' life are well recorded. All of these works are detailed in the bibliography.

In terms of other archaeological data, much new information has emerged in recent years which significantly improves our understanding of the reign of Severus and of his many military campaigns. This is particularly the case in the east where he fought the Parthians, in North Africa where he campaigned against the Garamantes, and in Britain. Here, recent work on the indigenous Maeatae and Caledonian peoples of the far north has greatly added to our knowledge of the *expeditio felicissima Brittannica*.

CHRONOLOGY

Most of the key background information to help the reader fully engage with the story of Severus is detailed in Chapter 2. However, from the outset an understanding of the chronology of the Roman world is essential given this forms the template for the wider narrative. Here, I reference four main periods of Roman history. First, the Roman Republic, lasting from the overthrow of Rome's last king Tarquin the Proud in 509 BC to the Senate's acknowledgment of Augustus as the first emperor in 27 BC. Next, the Principate phase of the Roman Empire which lasted from Augustus' accession to that of Diocletian in AD 284. The name Principate is derived from the term *princeps* (chief or master), referencing the emperor as the leading

INTRODUCTION

citizen of the empire. While *princeps* was not an official title – emperors often assumed it was on their accession – it clearly was a conceit which allowed the empire to be explained away as a simple continuance of the preceding Republic. The Severan dynasty sits within this period of empire.

The final phase of the Principate is today called the 'Crisis of the Third Century', a time when the empire was faced with multiple external and internal threats, including the devastating plague of Cyprian. The crisis lasted from the assassination of the last of the Severan emperors, Severus Alexander in AD 235, through to Diocletian's accession. The new emperor was then faced with a series of immediate challenges, tackling them with a fundamental reform of the empire on a scale to match the earlier Severan reset. This featured a new, far more overtly imperial system of administration, which today we call the Dominate. This new title was based on the word *dominus*, or lord, with the emperor now the equivalent of an eastern potentate. The Dominate lasted through to the end of the empire in the west in AD 476, when the last western emperor Romulus Augustulus abdicated.

However, the empire in the east continued to thrive, and from that point is often called the Byzantine Empire. Some argue the name should be used earlier, some later, but I find AD 476 an elegant date to make the switch. It should be noted this is not a name the eastern Romans themselves would have recognised. As far as they were concerned, they were still Roman, even if Greek speaking. This Byzantine phase is relevant to this work given Severus' long-term legacy in the east and North Africa.

NOMENCLATURE

A final piece of housekeeping here concerns nomenclature. In the first instance, when using personal names, I have tried to keep their use as simple as possible. For example, Septimius Severus is always referred to as Severus, although when more than one member of the Septimii are referenced, I clarify which at the point of use.

Meanwhile, his eldest son was named Lucius Septimius Bassianus at birth, then later renamed Marcus Aurelius Antoninus by Severus, though he is better known by his nickname Caracalla after a type of Gallic hooded tunic he favoured. For the most part I use that here, clarifying when necessary to avoid confusion. Other personal naming issues I cover in the narrative itself.

More broadly regarding the use of classical and modern names, in the main text I have again attempted to ensure my research is as accessible as possible to the reader. For example, I have used the modern name where a place is mentioned, referencing its Roman name at that first point of use where applicable. Meanwhile, where a classical name for a position or role is well understood I use that, for example *legate* for a senior military leader. Further, when an emperor is first detailed in the main narrative, I have listed the actual dates of his reign at the point he is first mentioned.

Finally, some key definitions for readers unfamiliar with the Roman military of the Severan period:

- **Guerrilla Warfare**: irregular warfare fought by asymmetrically inferior combatants using unconventional tactics (see below).
- *Legate*: a senior Roman military officer, today of general rank, usually commanding a legion or larger formation.
- *Legion*: at the time of Severus, the premier Roman military formation, comprising 5,500 legionaries.
- *Legionaries and Auxiliaries*: for the majority of the Roman Republic, and the Principate phase of empire, the elite Roman warrior was the legionary, a heavily armed and armoured infantryman, who most often formed the main line of battle. From the time of Augustus, supporting troops were then organised into formal units known as auxiliaries, often lesser in quality to the legionaries but still a match for most opponents the Romans faced. Auxiliaries provided both foot troops and most of the cavalry in Principate Roman armies.
- A *cohort* is a sub-unit of legionaries or auxiliaries, or an entire unit of foot auxiliaries, while an *ala* is a unit of auxiliary cavalry.

INTRODUCTION

- A *vexillation* refers to a detached sub-unit of legionaries and could be any size.
- **Symmetric and Asymmetric Warfare**: in the first instance, war between evenly matched belligerents. In the second, conflict where one is so dominant that the other is forced to use unconventional strategies and tactics, for example guerrilla warfare. By way of example, Severus' conflicts with the Parthians in the east can be described as symmetrical given both sides were often evenly matched, while his campaigns against the natives in the far north of Britain forced the latter to respond asymmetrically.

ACKNOWLEDGEMENTS

Lastly, I thank the many people who have helped make this new biography of Severus possible. Specifically, I would like to thank, as always, Professor Andrew Lambert of the War Studies Department at KCL, Dr Andrew Gardner at UCL's Institute of Archaeology and Dr Steve Willis at the University of Kent for their ongoing encouragement and guidance. Also, Rebecca Jones, former Head of Archaeology and World Heritage at Historic Environment Scotland, Dr Sam Moorhead of the British Museum, Professor Sir Barry Cunliffe of the School of Archaeology at Oxford University, and Professor Martin Millett at the Faculty of Classics, Cambridge University. Next, Darius Arya for his hospitality and forensic insight into Severan Rome over a number of visits and detailed conversations. Moving on, my patient proofreaders Professor John Lambshead and my lovely wife Sara. All have contributed greatly and freely, enabling this work on Severus to reach fruition. Finally, of course, I would like to thank my family, especially my tolerant wife Sara once again and children Alex (a teacher of history) and Lizzie.

Thank you all.
Dr Simon Elliott FSA
July 2023

1

Identity and Race in the Roman World

Severus' origins are the subject of much debate today in the context of current discussions on ethnicity. This is because he was both African and dark-skinned. In that context, he is often referred to in the modern world as the 'black emperor'. Therefore, considering the subject here in the first chapter hopefully removes the issue as a point of dispute, at the very least allowing the reader to make their own minds up about his family origins when presented with the hard facts.

ROMAN SOCIETAL STRUCTURE

Given Severus' aristocratic origins and his dramatic rise to power, an understanding of the structure of Roman society is very important. At the very top were the aristocracy, comprising three broad classes, the senior being the Senatorial class. These were said to be endowed with vast wealth (with a minimum property value of 1 million *sersterces* at the time of Severus), high birth and 'moral excellence', there being around 600 senators at the time Severus became emperor. Members of this class were patricians, a social political rank, all those below including other aristocrats plebeians.

Next were the equestrian class, of which Severus' grandfather and father were members. Equestrians had slightly less wealth but usually had a reputable lineage. They numbered some 30,000 in the late second century AD. Finally, among the aristocrats were the curial class, with the bar set slightly lower again.

Below this were the freemen middle classes of the empire, who were free in the sense that they had never been slaves. Freemen included the majority of smaller scale merchants, artisans and professionals in Roman society. All of the above classes were also full *cives Romani* citizens of the Roman Empire if they came from Italy.

Freemen born outside of Italy in the imperial provinces were called *peregrini* (in Latin meaning: 'one from abroad') until Caracalla's AD 212 *constitutio Antoniniana* edict that made all freemen of the empire citizens. As such, in the late second century AD *peregrini* made up the vast majority of the empire's inhabitants.

Further down the social ladder there were freedmen, former slaves who had been manumitted by their masters either through earning enough money to buy their freedom or for good service. Providing the correct process of manumission was followed, freedmen could then become citizens/*peregrini*, though with less civic rights than a freeman, which included not being able to stand for the vast number of public offices – except one, the priestly office of *Augustalis*. Their children were freemen, as with Publius Helvius Pertinax, Severus' mentor and the first emperor in the AD 193 'Year of the Five Emperors'. His father, Helvius Successus, was a manumitted former slave who later made a fortune running a logging business in the Po Valley. Meanwhile, at the bottom of society were slaves.

RACE AND ETHNICITY IN THE ROMAN WORLD

First, a health warning. Discussing race and ethnicity in the Roman world is a divisive subject. However, it is a crucial part of the story of Severus given the modern debate (which did not exist at all in his own world) about his origins in Africa, and specifically his own ancestry as he was dark skinned. Therefore, it cannot be ignored. What I set out here are the facts as I see them based on hard data.

First, some definitions. To start, where does the word race originate as we use it to discuss ethnicity today? It is first detailed in Middle English, the version of common English used in much of Britain between 1150 AD and 1500 AD, as an appropriation of the Italian *razza*, meaning breed. Next, the word racism. Here, I define it as discrimination and prejudice (overt or otherwise) by a culture, institution, community or person against other peoples based on their membership of a particular race or ethnic group.

Finally, in terms of definitions, the word Ethiopian (in Roman vulgar Latin, *Aethiop*). The use of this term in classical and late antique literature is problematic given it has multiple meanings. To the classical Greeks it could reference either those specifically from Nubia (today, the far south of the Republic of Egypt and the Republic of Sudan), those from the Levant and anywhere to its east, or anyone not Greek, dependent on the author. To the Romans it could similarly reference anyone from Nubia, or anyone with an especially dark skin originating outside the empire, though here it was used purely as a geographic descriptor rather than a reference to Roman racial superiority based on skin colour (see below). Therefore, when I use the word Ethiopian in the book I will be very specific about its context.

That the Romans were racist is self-evident. However, racism in their world was very different to racism in ours. Today in the west we associate racism with skin colour, this through the prism of the shocking experiences of over 12 million Africans during the colonial slave trade in the period of western imperial dominance. To be sure, in the same time period slavery of many other kinds was sadly extant across the world. It still is. Racism in the Roman world was very different. There, it was not driven by skin colour. Indeed, in his wide-ranging review of the lack of colour prejudice in the ancient world, Frank M. Snowden highlights that from the third millennium BC onwards, when we have the first Egyptian references to meeting dark-skinned Nubians, there is little or no mention of any discrimination based on this difference.[1] Providing further context, he adds:[2]

> 'The very striking similarities in the total picture that emerges from an examination of the basic sources – Egyptian, Greek, Roman, and early Christian – point to a highly favourable image of blacks and to white-black relationships differing markedly from those that have developed in more colour-conscious societies.'

Simon Hornblower and Tony Spawforth reach the same conclusion:[3]

> 'It is difficult to discern any lasting ascription of general inferiority to any ethnic group in antiquity [in contemporary literature] solely on the basis of body type.'

This should come as no surprise. The Roman Empire was Mediterranean in nature, with most of its inhabitants having tanned, brown or darker skin, not white as is often portrayed today in popular culture. That is a legacy of recent western colonial history which centred on now faded empires who culturally appropriated the world of Rome to contextualise their own colonial activities around the globe. In short, if it was good for the Romans, it was good for them, though in this case with white skin being a key differentiator for their self-perceived cultural dominance. However, in this interpretation of their Roman role models, they were flat wrong. Indeed, given the fact the Roman Empire was Mediterranean-centred, the individuals who would have stood out most were those with north-European white skin. One need only note Pope Gregory I's reaction to seeing north European boys in the slave market in Rome in the late sixth century AD, as narrated by Bede:[4]

> 'We are told that one day some merchants who had recently arrived in Rome displayed their wares in the market-place. Among the crowd who thronged to buy was Gregory, who saw among other

merchandise some boys exposed for sale. These had fair complexions, fine cut features and beautiful hair [often translated as fair hair]. Looking at them with interest, he enquired from what country and what part of the world they came. "They come from the island of Britain," he was told, "where all the people have this appearance." He then asked whether the islanders were Christians, or whether they were still ignorant heathens. "They are pagans," he was informed. "Alas!" said Gregory with a heartfelt sigh: "How sad that such bright faced folk are still in the grasp of the authors of darkness, and that such graceful features conceal minds void of God's grace! What is the name of this race?" "They are called Angles," he was told. "That is appropriate, for they have angelic faces, and it is right that they should become joint-heirs with the angels in heaven."'

Notably, angels are usually portrayed in late antique art with alabaster white skin and blond hair. More importantly, it is traditionally the memory of this event that prompted the Pope to send St Augustine and his 40 companion monks to Britain in AD 597 to convert the English peoples in Britain to the Roman church.

Instead, Roman racism was driven by something very different that had nothing to do with skin colour. This was whether you were a Roman or a barbarian. No matter what your origins across the empire, if you were a Roman citizen (or *perigrini* outside of Italy until the AD 212 *constitutio Antoniniana* under Caracalla) then you were 'in'. If not, then you were 'out', often in the most dehumanising of ways. Thus, Roman racism was more akin to what we today would call xenophobia.

It is useful here in the context of Roman race and ethnicity to understand how the Romans used the word barbarian. Unsurprisingly, it was a cultural appropriation from the Greek world. The word originated as βαρ-βαρα, an onomatopoeic ancient Greek term referencing the (to them) incomprehensible 'bar bar babbling' sound made by those speaking a non-Greek language.[7] The earliest written form appeared in Mycenaean proto-Greek, where it was scripted as ρα-ρα-ro. The term then later appeared in Homer's *Iliad* as βαρβαρόφωνος in the context of the Carians, a Luwian people from south-western Anatolia fighting as Trojan allies.[5] Academically, this is called linguistic discrimination.

By the beginning of the sixth century BC, barbarian was being used by the Athenians and their Attican allies to deride their various *polis* rivals in the Peloponnese, though it soon came to be used by all Greeks as a term of abuse for the Achaemenid Persians after the onset of the Greco-Persian Wars. In this context, it is most overtly visible today through the work of the Athenian tragedian Aeschylus, in particular his *The Persians* which was first performed in 472 BC. This play, based on his own experiences fighting in the Greek naval victory at Salamis in 480 BC, is threaded with references to the Persians in a negative context. For example, in one line we have a leading protagonist say:[6]

> 'Alas! In truth a vast sea of troubles has burst upon the Persians and their entire barbarian race.'

In *The Persians*, Aeschylus extended the distinction between Greeks and Persians from the latter's lack of competence in Greek, as detailed the origin of the word barbarian, to an additional absence of moral responsibility. This included a lack of *logos* (the ability to think and speak clearly), and of control regarding cruelty, sex and food. Writing over a century later, Aristotle then made the difference between the Greeks and barbarous Persians one of the key themes in his *The Politics*.[7]

Barbarian was later adopted by the Romans as the Latin *barbarus* after their conquest of the later Hellenistic kingdoms in the eastern Mediterranean; they used it to describe all of those living outside the borders of land under Roman control. Given the Romans often portrayed such non-Romans with beards in their literature and artwork, it is from *barbarus* we have the Latin name for beard, *barba*. Meanwhile, by the mid-first century BC, the Roman statesman and scholar Cicero was using barbarian to derogatively describe those living in the mountainous interior of Sardinia, this having such an impact at the time that the region is still called Barbagia today.[8] Further, writing shortly afterwards, the Greek-speaking historian Diodorus Siculus then picked up Aeschylus' commentary on the lack of control among the barbarians, with his focus specifically on the Gallic proclivity for alcohol. In his *Library of History* he says:[9]

> 'Great drinkers are the Gauls. They drink wine at full strength: and when drunk either pass out or act crazy. Small wonder the Italian merchants rate them as their most valued customers, plying the drink upriver by the boatload and overland by the cartload. And great is their reward, for the price of one amphora is one slave.'

Barbarian was then first used by the Romans to describe the Germans at the end of the first century BC. By this time, *barbaricum* was in regular use to detail the vast tracts of dense forest north of the Rhine and Danube, and Roman commentators were describing all of those living north of the *limes* (fortified frontier) here in a similar negative way. Harry Sidebottom summarises this distinctly one-sided narrative well, saying that to the Romans:[10]

> '... northern barbarians were huge, unpleasantly pale, lazy, drunken and violent. Ferocious in the first rush of battle – lacking discipline and thus true courage – they quickly became dispirited. Their sexuality was shameless: given the chance they were dedicated gang rapists, while their wives openly coupled with other men, and youths were equally flagrant in soliciting passive male-male sex. Naturally stupid, indeed lacking rational faculties, they were incapable of improvement or civilisation.'

For this description of those living north of the Roman frontier in Europe, read a similar Roman attitude to those living to its east and south, too. For example, St Paul later employed barbarian to describe non-Greek speakers originating outside Roman territory in the New Testament,[11] while a century later Lucian of Samosata used the term to satyrically describe himself given that, as a native of Commagene in northern Syria, his family had only been 'Roman' for a few decades.[12]

A key issue to note here regarding the Roman attitude to barbarians was that they often had no voice of their own. Here, as Thomas Williams explains:[13]

> 'While the Roman Empire bequeathed words by the hundred thousand, those outside its borders left none. Nor have barbarian oral traditions survived from this time. So classical authors became the spokesmen for the barbarians by default; and it could be rightly said that they have hijacked our way of seeing their world.'

Further, as Williams continues, not only are the Roman and post-Roman sources heavily biased against the barbarians, they are often only interested in them as worthy opponents for the Romans to overcome. Thus, we usually only ever hear of their martial prowess, and very rarely of their other key behaviours. This has led to a paucity of primary source references regarding other aspects of their culture. Peter Heather picks up on this theme when considering how the behavior of barbarians in the classical and late antique world was reported at the time. He says:[14]

> 'Barbarians were expected to behave in certain ways and embody a particular range of negative characteristics, and Roman commentators went out of their way to prove this was so.'

Thus, given Roman racism was driven by cultural identity rather than skin colour, it is no surprise to see individuals of all skin tones and ethnicities thriving across the empire in all its phases. Again, one should note here this was a Mediterranean empire, so why would they not. Think of the imperial trouble-shooter Quintus Lollius Urbicus in the mid-second century AD, who played a leading role in putting down the Bar Kokhba Third Jewish Revolt in the AD 130s and was later, as governor of Britannia, to drive the frontier there north from Hadrian's Wall on the Solway Firth-Clyde line to the Antonine Wall on the Clyde-Forth line. Urbicus was a dark-skinned Numidian Berber. Meanwhile, Marcus Opellius Macrinus, the usurper who as Praetorium Prefect arranged the assassination of Severus' eldest son Caracalla and was then briefly emperor, was also a Berber. Born in Cherchell (Roman *Caesarea*) in modern Algeria, he was either Numidian or Mauritanian by origin.

For another multicultural example we can look to Philip the Arab (full name Marcus Julius Severus Philippus), who reigned from AD 244 to 249 amid the turmoil of the Crisis of the Third Century and who was indeed Arabian. He was born at the beginning of the third century AD in Shahba, now a thriving Syrian city but then a small oasis town later renamed Philippopolis after him once he became emperor. This lay 90km southeast of modern Damascus in the province of Arabia Petraea. His family were rich equestrians with long-standing links to the long distance trading networks in the region, this the source of the family wealth, with some contemporary writers also hinting at familial links with the Severans given their proximity to Julia Domna's family in Emesa to the north. Originally *perigrini*, living on the very edge of the empire, they had become full citizens after Caracalla's *constitutio Antoniniana*, with Philip taking full advantage. Although his rise through the ranks of the regional administration and military was initially steady, his career took an unlikely upward turn in AD 243 when he became Praetorian Prefect for the young Gordian III during the latter's campaign against the Sassanid Persians in the Euphrates valley. This was at the suggestion of Philip's older brother Priscus, who was an important court official. Then, when Gordian died in mysterious circumstances in February AD 244 (either assassinated, slain in battle or dying of an illness, depending on the source), Philip was quickly elevated to the throne, no doubt to his surprise.

In the modern world, Philip often gets a bad press, most frequently for the peace forced on him by the Persians at the point he became emperor. Some believe this negative view may be through the prism of antiquarian prejudice given his Arabian origins, which sadly still influence views of his rule today. However, his five-year reign was one of comparative stability. He proved to be a good administrator, who invested heavily in public building programmes, for example redeveloping the water supply system in Rome to cater for the growing population there. Further, he also showed a martial nature not often referenced, for example provoking a war with the Goths north of the Danube in AD 245 to try to attain some of the military acclaim earlier achieved by Severus, Caracalla and Maximinus Thrax. Here, he was clearly aware that while he had acquired victory epithets after his withdrawal from Persia at the beginning of his reign, and had even had medallions and coins minted celebrating success there, all were aware that was far from the case given the onerous peace agreement forced on the Romans to allow their secure withdrawal from Persian territory.

On a final note regarding Philip. Prior to his becoming emperor, the most frequent references in contemporary literature to Rome and the Arabs were in the context of their Ghassanid allies, who were frequent collaborators when fighting the Persians. The fact no ancient or late antique writer pays any attention whatsoever to Philip's Arab origins again shows the cosmopolitan, multicultural nature of the Roman Empire at the time.

This is no better illustrated than with the startlingly lifelike Fayum mummy portraits from Egypt. These are naturalistically painted funerary images rendered on wooden boards in the style of panel paintings attached to upper class inhumation burials in Roman Egypt. Dating from the first century BC to the third century AD, the largest collection to survive were found in cemeteries in the Fayum Basin, a large oasis immediately west of the Nile River 100km south of modern Cairo. These portraits are remarkable in the context of race and ethnicity in the Roman world given they feature individuals with all types of skin colour, and from many different backgrounds.

However, we have one final example of classical portraiture to consider here, and this directly related to Severus and his family. This is the astonishing Severan Tondo, a tempera egg-based painting on a 30.5cm diameter circular wooden panel (hence tondo, a renaissance name for a circular work of art). Dating to around AD 200, it depicts Severus on the viewer's right, Julia Domna the viewer's left, and below them Caracalla at right and Geta at left. All are resplendent in sumptuous ceremonial garments and regalia. In particular, Severus and his two sons hold sceptres and wear gold wreaths decorated with precious stones.

The Severan Tondo, now on display in the Altes Museum in Berlin, is noteworthy for three reasons. First, that it survived at all. The origins of the tondo are unknown, though some speculate that given the distinctive artwork it originated in the same Egyptian workshops that produced the Fayum mummy portraits. Severus certainly travelled through Egypt around the time the tondo was made while returning from his second eastern campaign against Parthia, this detailed in Chapter 6. Though its provenance is undisputed, it then only reappeared in the twentieth century AD through the antiquities trade when it became part of the Antikensammlung collection in Berlin. From there, it then eventually found its modern home in the Altes Museum.

Second, the tondo presents one of the most striking examples of *damnatio memoriae* anywhere in the Roman Empire. This was an official action by the Senate, usually on behalf of a sitting emperor, in which an individual, group, military unit or organisation was deemed never to have existed. As such, it was one of the most extreme forms of Roman punishment given it officially wiped someone's existence from memory, with their images and names being removed from any sculpture or inscription throughout the empire. In this case the subject was Severus' younger son Geta, who was murdered either by, or on the orders of, Caracalla within a year of their father's death (see Conclusion). Geta was then the subject of a particularly well observed *damnatio memoriae*, manifest on the Severan Tondo with Geta's face being systematically erased.

Finally, and most importantly for this chapter, the Severan family is shown in full life-like colour, with Severus having dark brown skin and, by way of contrast, Julia Domna having alabaster white skin, with Caracalla also shown as fair. The artist here would have gone to great lengths to make the image as accurate as possible, so there is no doubting at the very least this is what he thought Severus looked like, noting he may even have seen him in real life if this was painted at the time the emperor was travelling through Egypt.

Here we have the prime evidence often referenced when discussing Severus and his skin colour, leading to the modern debate about whether he was 'black' or not. Interestingly, our key primary sources do not mention his skin colour, despite other contemporary references to his appearance, emphasising again that this was unremarkable in his world. However, whether Severus was 'black' or not is certainly an important subject now given today's usual definition of racism based on skin colour, as I discuss above. Here, I simply set out the facts and allow people to draw their own conclusion about his origins and appearance.

Severus clearly had dark skin, based on the tondo image, and was North African given he was born in Leptis Magna in modern Libya. Further, as detailed in full in Chapter 3 where I discuss the Septimii family tree, we factually know his paternal great-grandfather was called Septimius Macer prior to the family adopting the *cognomen* Severus. Macer is a Carthaginian or Punic name, reflecting Leptis Magna's origins as a Phoenician colony. Thus, Severus' forebears on his father's side were Levantine from Phoenicia, centuries before his birth. In the generations afterwards, there is no evidence of interbreeding with the local Berbers, though given the proximity of the Garamantes to the south and Numidians to the west this cannot be ruled out. However, there is no evidence of any familial connections with sub-Saharan Africa to the south, or Nubia to the east.

We also have astonishing contemporary insight into the multicultural composition of the Roman army in the mid-third century AD, and this from the perspective of their mortal enemies. This is in the context of the conflicts along the frontier there with the Sassanid Persian king Shapur I (AD 240 to AD 270), whose lengthy monumental rock relief inscription at Naqsh-e Rostam in Fars province, Iran, records his victories over the Romans in graphic detail. Naqsh-e Rostam, 13km northwest of Persepolis, was the necropolis for the earlier Achaemenid Persian kings. Below their fine tombs near ground level are eight huge rock reliefs, most with accompanying inscriptions, featuring some of the leading Sassanid Persian kings, who, centuries later, were keen to gain legitimacy (even in death) through association with their Achaemenid forebears. The most famous shows the Shapur I in all his regal finery mounted on a huge stallion with the Roman emperor Valerian, captured in AD 260 and then brutalised by the king in the most humiliating way, bowing to him in submission. Meanwhile, Philip the Arab, earlier forced into the peace agreement detailed above after succeeding Gordian III, is shown holding Shapur's horse. Finally, to emphasise Shapur's superiority over the Romans, Gordian III himself lies beneath the figures in death.

The relief's inscription details Shapur's many achievements, and within it there is a description of the various races which comprised the eastern Roman army of Valerian when campaigning against Shapur in AD 260. It says:[15]

'When I moved against Harran [Carrhae] and Urha [Edessa] and besieged them, Valerian caesar came against me. And there were with [him] from the land of Germany, from the land of Raetia, from the land of Noricum, from the land of Dacia, from the land of Pannonia, from the land of Moesia, from the land of Spain, from the land of Africa, from the land of Thrace, from the land of Bithynia, from the land of Asia, from the land of Pamphylia, from the land of Isauria, from the land of Lyconia, from the land of Galatia, from the land of Lycia, from the land of Cilicia, from the land of Cappadocia, from the land of Phrygia, from the land of Syria, from the land of Phoenicia, from the land of Judaea, from the land of Arabia, from the land of Mauretania, from the land of Germany [again], from the land of Rhodes, from the land of Osrhoene [the eastern frontier city state], and from the land of Mesopotamia, an army of 70,000 men. And on this side of Harran and Urha there was a great battle with Valerian caesar, he being captured by my own hand, and the rest, the praetorian prefects and the Senators and the officers who were the leaders of this army, were all captured and led into Persia. And the land of Syria, the land of Cilicia, and the land of Cappadocia were burned, laid waste, and plundered.'

The level of detail here is astounding, with Roman troops originating from all parts of the empire, including in the west, the latter most likely auxiliary cavalry.

Finally, here, for completeness when considering racism in the Roman world, the origins of citizens and *perigrini* are often referenced in contemporary literature based on their place of origin within the empire, both positively and negatively. For example, Dio says of Caracalla:[16]

'... he belonged to three races and he possessed none of their virtues at all, but combined himself in all of their vices; the fickleness, cowardice and recklessness of Gaul, the harshness and cruelty of Africa, and the cunning of Syria.'

Meanwhile, the northern Roman provinces in Gaul were nicknamed *Gallia Comata*, meaning 'long haired Gaul'.

In the same context, people's appearance (or that of their forebears) was also used as a descriptor in the Roman world, including skin colour and tone, with names a prime example. Here, the *cognomen* nickname was particularly important. For example, two of the senior figures in this book, Clodius Albinus and Pescennius Niger (both key protagonists challenging Severus for the throne in the AD 193 'Year of the Five Emperors'), provide excellent examples. This is because the former name literally means white Clodius, and the latter black Pescennius.

The *Historia Augusta* says the North African Albinus was so named because of his extraordinary white complexion.[17] Meanwhile, the same source also says that the Italian-born Niger's *cognomen*, also shared with his brother, originated with their father Annius Fuscus.[18] The latter means brown, dimly lit or dark in Latin, and although Fuscus was notably white (and corpulent), he had a very red face and 'black' neck, the *cognomen* somehow translating into Niger during his sons' generation. Meanwhile, later, we also have the excellent example of Flavius Valerius Constantius Chlorus, *caesar* and *augustus* in the west a century and more later (AD 293–AD 305, and AD 305–AD 306), and father of Constantine I. Here, his *cognomen* referenced his pale skin.

Meanwhile, by way of counterpoint, other physical features could also be the source of a Roman individual's name. A prime example here can be found today in the excellent Colchester Museum and Castle where the tombstone of the first-century AD auxiliary cavalryman Longinus Sdapeze is on display. A *dupliciarus* double-paid trooper (so junior officer), his unit was raised in Thrace. Of relevance here, some believe Longinus references his height, or that of a forebear which then became part of the familial name, in the same context we today would use the nickname lofty.

However, and crucially in the context of this work, while the above name references were regarding appearance, none were in a negative and discriminatory context. It was simply a normal part of Roman nomenclature. Further, all those so described were still Roman, so far superior to anyone from outside the empire, no matter what their regional traits, appearance or social rank. Indeed, by way of example, the only time the colour black is referenced negatively in terms of skin colour or tone in contemporary literature is very occasionally in the context of superstition, with the colour sometimes (though not always) associated with death and ill favour. One famous episode here in terms of superstitious negativity involves Severus himself, as fully narrated in Chapter 8 in the context of his final campaigns in Britain.

2

The World of Septimius Severus

Septimius Severus ruled at the height of the Principate, the first phase of the Roman Empire which lasted from 27 BC, with the accession of Augustus, to AD 284, with the accession of Diocletian. Under his rule, Roman military power peaked. It also saw the empire expand to its greatest extent (except for a very short period under Trajan). With his reset of the empire, he also laid the groundwork for the later major reforms of the imperial administration in the Dominate phase of empire.

DYNASTIES OF THE PRINCIPATE

The Principate phase of the Roman Empire featured a number of distinct dynasties and phases, these being:

- The Julio-Claudian Dynasty, from the accession of Augustus in 27 BC to the death of Nero in AD 68.
- The 'Year of the Four Emperors' in AD 69, with Vespasian the ultimate victor.
- The Flavian Dynasty, from Vespasian's accession through to the death of his younger son Domitian in AD 96.
- The Nervo-Trajanic Dynasty, from the accession of Nerva in AD 96 to the death of Hadrian in AD 138.
- The Antonine Dynasty, from the accession of Antoninus Pius in AD 138 to the assassination of Commodus in AD 192.

- The 'Year of the Five Emperors' in AD 193, with Pertinax the first incumbent and Severus the ultimate victor.
- The Severan Dynasty, from the accession of Severus to the assassination of Severus Alexander in AD 235.
- The 'Crisis of the Third Century', from the death of Severus Alexander to the accession of Diocletian in AD 284. This was a period when the empire was under great stress from a multitude of issues that collectively threatened its very survival. These included civil war and multiple usurpations, the first deep and large scale incursions into imperial territory by Germans and Goths over the Rhine and Danube, the deadly Plague of Cyprian, and the emergence in the east of the Sassanid Persian Empire, which presented the Romans with a fully symmetrical threat (meaning one that could match Rome's own military might) for the first time. Collectively, they caused a major economic crash. The steps taken by Diocletian to drag the empire out of this chaos, in what is often styled his reformation, were so drastic that from that point we talk of the Dominate Empire.

THE PROVINCIAL STRUCTURE OF THE PRINCIPATE

By the time Severus became emperor in AD 193, the Roman Empire had grown to cover a vast geographic area. It encompassed the entire Mediterranean basin, much of northwestern Europe and the Levant, and was spread over three continents. It stretched all the way from Hadrian's Wall in the north of far-flung Britain to the *limes* of distant Arabia. This was a distance of around 4,200km as the crow flies. The empire's population in Severus' day was around 65 million people, some 21 per cent of the entire world's population.

At this time the empire was divided into 44 provinces of varying sizes, some huge, some far smaller. The word itself provides interesting insight into the Roman attitude to its empire, with Philip

Matyszak explaining the Latin *provincia* referenced land *'for conquering'*.[1] There were two kinds of province in the Principate. These were senatorial provinces dating back to the Roman Republic which were left to the Senate to administer, and whose governors were officially called proconsuls and remained in post for a year, and imperial provinces established with the onset of the Principate which remained under the direct supervision of the emperor. He personally chose the governors for these, they often being styled *legati Augusti pro praetor* to officially mark them out as deputies of the emperor. Senatorial provinces tended to be those deep within the empire where less trouble was expected, and these are highlighted below.

The provinces of the Principate empire broadly broke down into seven regions, namely Britannia, Gaul and Germany, Spain, the Danube and Italy, Greece and Asia Minor, the East, and North Africa. I detail them all here given each played a key role in the story of Severus.

Britannia encompassed the main island of Britain up to the line of Hadrian's Wall, built around the time of this emperor's visit in AD 122. The impressive frontier fortification ran west to east along the Solway Firth-Tyne line. For much of its 117km length, it tracked the earlier Flavian Stanegate Road. From around AD 142, the northern border actually moved further north to the line of the Clyde-Firth of Forth, the fortification built there known as the Antonine Wall. However, this was abandoned after only eight years of occupation in the early AD 160s, with the border once more moving back south to Hadrian's Wall.

Britannia was the wild west of the Roman Empire. A marginal province at best, it was always a place of difference, the never conquered far north requiring an exponentially large military presence. This was some twelve per cent of the empire's entire military complement in what was only four per cent of its geographic area. This radically altered the geography of the province, with the south and east a fully functioning part of the empire but the north and west a heavily militarised zone with the entire economy there geared to maintaining the military presence. Given Britannia was also far from Rome, the combination made the province a hotbed for usurpers and troublemakers in the later empire.

Britain was difficult to invade in the first place, with Gaius Julius Caesar himself failing (if his intention was to stay, unlikely) in 55 BC and 54 BC, and the great Augustus and mad Caligula (AD 37 to AD 41) both planning but abandoning conquest. Even the Aulus Plautius-led invasion of Claudius was problematic, the troops wary of crossing terrifying *Oceanus* until shamed into boarding the invasion fleet by one of the emperor's senior freedmen, Tiberius Claudius Narcissus. In this story, when the legionaries refused to clamber onto the invasion vessels in northwestern Gaul, the former slave himself boarded a ship. Shouting *'Io Saturnaila'*, referencing the end of year role-reversing winter festival, the chastened soldiery followed and the invasion proceeded.

The story of Roman Britain through to the time of Severus is also one of many famous individuals well recorded in the primary sources. Think Caratacus, who opposed Plautius' invasion in the reign of Claudius; Vespasian, who conquered the southwest in the late AD 40s; Boudicca, who nearly destroyed the province in AD 60–1; her nemesis Gaius Suetonius Paulinus; the Brigantian Queen Cartimandua; and the North African Berber Lollius Urbicus, who drove the border north to the Antonine Wall in the mid-second century AD. A highlight of my own travels around the Roman Empire was finding his family tomb high in the Atlas Mountains at the town of Tidis (Roman *Castellum Tidditanorum*) in modern Algeria.

By the time Severus became emperor, Roman Britain was at the height of its provincial success, such as it was. The province was threaded with a well-built system of military trunk roads linking its major settlements – these *colonia* veteran settlements, *municipium* mercantile towns and *civitas* capital county towns. A prime example was Watling Street that started at the imperial gateway of Richborough (Roman *Rutupiae*) on the east Kent coast, resplendent with its Flavian carrara marble-clad monumental arch. From there it headed west to the provincial capital of London (Roman *Londinium*, where the governor was based), then on to *municipium* of St Albans (Roman *Verulamium*) and thence to the far off *civitas* capital of Wroxeter (Roman *Viriconium*) in the Welsh Marches. Here, it branched north and south, to the legionary fortresses at Chester (Roman *Deva Victrix*) and Caerleon (*Isca Augusta*). Meanwhile, Ermine Street linked London with the *colonia* at Lincoln (Roman *Lindum Colonia*, originally a legionary fortress) and the legionary fortress and *canaba* civilian settlement at York (Roman *Eboracom*, later itself to become a *colonia* military settlement). Its extension, Dere Street, then headed even further north, through the fort and small town at Corbridge (Roman *Coria*), then through Hadrian's Wall before traversing the Scottish Borders, reaching the Firth of Forth at Inveresk. Another key route was the Fosse Way, linking Lincoln with the southwestern *civitas* capital of Exeter (Roman *Isca Dumnoniorum*, also originally a legionary fortress), passing through Cirencester (Roman *Corinium*) on the way. The Fosse Way crossed Watling Street at modern High Cross in Leicestershire, one of the major transport intersections of Roman Britain. This was a very militarised province, with its conquest and later military establishment literally etched across its landscape in the form of roads, fortifications and, in most cases, civilian settlements, which often developed into towns in their own right.

When Severus arrived in Britain in AD 208, there were three long established legions in the province. These were *legio* II *Augusta* at Caerleon in southeastern Wales, *legio* XX *Valeria Victrix* at Chester and *legio* VI *Victrix* at York, the latter replacing the earlier incumbent *legio* IX *hispana* in the early second century AD. Vexillations (companies) of each rotated through postings to the north, either along Hadrian's Wall and the Stanegate forts immediately to its rear (for example Vindolanda), or mounting incursions into the unconquered far north. They were joined on the border, and on campaign, by numerous auxiliary cavalry and infantry units. All were supported by the *Classis Britannica* provincial regional navy. This was headquartered in northwestern Gaul at Boulogne-sur-Mer (Roman *Gesoriacum*), also operating from bases around the coast of Britain including Dover (Roman *Dubris*), Caerleon and Chester on the west coast, and South Shields (Roman *Arbeia*) on the east coast.

The economy of Roman Britain was dominated by agriculture, as with the rest of the empire. Much new land was reclaimed during the occupation that helped to greatly increase agricultural output, for example in the Fenlands around The Wash on the east coast. Agricultural yield was also increased by the introduction of new farming technology and techniques. The surplus from this farming boom helped the population to grow to some 3.5 million by the time of Severus, up from around 2 million in the Late Iron Age (LIA) immediately prior to the arrival of the Romans.

Industry also featured in the province, including the iron industry in the Weald and the ragstone quarrying industry of the upper Medway Valley, both still in full production during his reign. These two vast *metalla* were among the largest industrial enterprises anywhere in the empire. The former provided all of the iron utilised by the military in the north, while the latter supplied all of the stone used to build and maintain the new urban environment in the south east, including London, where Severus later ordered the building of its land wall at the end of the second century AD. Other industries that flourished under the Roman occupation of Britain included indigenous pottery manufacturing, glass making, mosaic manufacture, brewing, mill and quern stone manufacture and textile production. It was the latter that provided the Roman world with its best-known British exports, the *birrus* rain-proofed hooded cloak and the *tapetia* fine quality woollen rug.

Compared to the rest of the empire, Britain made little contribution to its political life, except through the numerous usurpation attempts (including that of Decimus Clodius Albinus against Severus). We know of no native British senator, and indeed the most famous Romano-Britons were religious figures, namely St Alban (who may have a Severan association), St Patrick, and the controversial theologian Palagius, accused by St Augustine of Hippo of denying that good deeds required divine intervention.

As will be later seen, Severus had a problematic relationship with Britain, culminating in his shock and awe campaigns to conquer the far north in AD 209 and AD 210. It was also he who initiated the division of the province into two, Britannia Superior with its capital remaining in London, and Britannia Inferior with its new capital in York, though this was likely completed under Caracalla.

Moving on to Gaul and Germany, the rich provinces there illustrated how quickly indigenous territories could be culturally assimilated into the Roman way of life. Real Roman interest in the region began in the mid-second century BC through mercantile engagement with the Greek colony of Marseille (Greek and Roman *Massilia*), with a treaty being signed to protect the town from Gauls to the north and Carthaginians in the western Mediterranean. Further Roman interest there led to the creation of a new province in 122 BC along the Mediterranean coast called Transalpine Gaul (also called Provincia Nostra, translating as 'our province'), this later being renamed Gallia Narbonensis after its regional capital of Narbonne, founded by the Romans in 118 BC.

The province then became the springboard for Caesar's conquest of Gaul in 58 BC when he became its governor, along with Cisalpine Gaul (the far north of Italy either side of the Po River). In pursuit of glory and wealth, Caesar lost no time in campaigning north, and by the end of the decade had reduced the Gallic kingdoms there to Roman vassalage. From that time they became new Roman provinces, these revised by Augustus in 22 BC, with more territory to the north and east being added later. By the time Severus became emperor, there were nine provinces in the region, these being:

- Germania Inferior in the Rhine Delta and lower Rhine valley.
- Germania Superior in the upper Rhine valley.
- Gallia Belgica, broadly the area of modern Belgium.

- Gallia Lugdunensis, a broad strip through modern central France ranging from Brittany in the west to the provincial capital of Lyon (Roman *Lugdunum*) in the east. It was here Severus served as provincial governor, and where he also married Julia Domna and where Caracalla was born.
- Gallia Aquitania along the Bay of Biscay.
- Gallia Narbonensis in modern Provence, a Senatorial province.
- Three small provinces bordering Gallia Narbonensis and Italy, from north to south Alpes Graiae et Poeninae, Alpes Cottiae and Alpes Maritimae.

This large region featured distinct cultural and economic differences across its wide geography. The far north and east were more militarised given the provinces there featured the *limes Germanicus* separating the world of Rome from *barbaricum* (as viewed by contemporaries) to the north. Further south, the northern Gallic provinces were nicknamed Gallia Comata, meaning 'long haired Gaul'. This territory featured fine quality agricultural land heavily exploited for arable and fruit crops, including the fine quality wines associated with the region to this day. It was also the home to a dense network of *fabricae* state-run manufactories around Autun (Roman *Augustodunum*) in the Bourgogne-Franche-Comté region of modern France. These produced much of the equipment for the military in the region. By way of contrast, the far south was much more urbanised, reflecting the longevity of large-scale, stone-built settlements there dating back to the early period of Greek expansion in the western Mediterranean.

In addition to Lyon, key cities included Cologne (Roman *Colonia Agrippina*), with its legionary fortress that by the time of Severus was the provincial capital of Germania Inferior, Mainz (Roman *Mogantium*), with its legionary fortress which was the provincial capital of Germania Superior, Reims (Roman *Durocotorum*), which was the provincial capital of Gallia Belgica, Narbonne (Roman *Narbo*), which was the provincial capital of Narbonensis, and Marseille.

The Rhine frontier featured a dense chain of fortifications to maintain the northern *limes* that ran for over 570km from the Rhine Delta to the Danube. The key bases were the legionary fortresses, with sites at Nijmagen (Roman *Noviomagus*), Xanten (Roman *Vetera*) and Neuss (Roman *Novaesium*) joining those already detailed at Mainz and Cologne. A further 55 other forts of various sizes and over 1,000 watchtowers completed the defensive frontier here.

The *limes Germanicus* was divided into three sections, these being:

- The Lower Germanic *limes* extending from the North Sea coast to the Rheinbrohl municipality in the Rhineland Palatinate of modern Germany.
- The Upper Germanic *limes* from Rheinbrohl to Lorch am Rhein near Darmstadt in Hesse.
- The Rhaetian *limes*, with only the section on the Rhine detailed here, the Danubian length covered in the next section.

At the time of Severus, the *limes* of the first two sections were home to some of the crack legions of the Roman Empire. These included *legio VIII Augusta* and *legio XXII Primogenia pia fidelis* in Germania Inferior, and *legio I Minervia pia fidelis* and *legio XXX Ulpia Victrix* in Germania Superior. The military establishment here also featured the usual complement of auxiliaries, and the *Classis Germanica* regional fleet which was headquartered at Cologne. This patrolled the Rhine and the riparian zone along either bank. Together, the legions, auxiliaries and fleet faced off against multiple threats to the north, including the Germanic Saxons, Thuringii and Alamanni.

Heading to the far south, the Iberian Peninsula featured three provinces that were formed in 14 BC when Augustus reorganised the territory of his new empire. These were Hispania Tarraconensis in the northwest and east, Hispania Baetica in the south and Hispania Lusitania in the southwest. The peninsula was well known in the Roman period as an exporter of fine wine, olive oil, *garum* fish sauce (all made in industrial quantities), and precious metals and copper. The latter extractive industries featured some of the largest *metalla* operations in the entire empire, including the Rio Tinto mines in the region of modern Andalusia and the Vispaca mines in Portugal. Hispania Tarraconensis was a province of contrasts. The eastern Mediterranean seaboard was largely Punic in origin, with key towns like Cartagena (Roman *Carthago Nova*) dating back to the time of Hannibal, though the provincial capital of Tarragona (Roman *Tarraco*) was an earlier Spanish founding. Meanwhile, the mountainous north retained much of its pre-Roman Basque character. Unusually for a province away from the frontiers of empire, Hispania Tarraconensis also featured a legion. At the time of Severus, this was *legio* VII *Gemina*, based at León (Roman *Castra Legionis*) to maintain order among the troublesome native northern Lusitanians, and to ensure the smooth running of the key *metalla* operations.

Next, in the far south of the Iberian Peninsula, the Senatorial province of Hispania Baetica was one of the richest Roman provinces, featuring the key Atlantic port of Cádiz (Roman *Gades*, originally a Phoenician founding). With its provincial capital at Cordoba (Roman *Corduba*), Hispania Baetica was most notable in the Roman world for being the birthplace of the emperor Trajan.

Meanwhile, Hispania Lusitania, sitting on the Atlantic seaboard, encompassed much of the territory of modern Portugal. Its provincial capital was located at Mérida (Roman *Emerita Augusta*). The region had proved particularly difficult to defeat during the Republican wars of conquest here, with Strabo declaring that Lusitania had been '… the greatest of the Iberian nations, and … the nation against which the Romans waged war for the longest times …'[2] By the time of Severus, however, it was a sleepy backwater, not requiring the close military attention needed in northern Tarraconensis.

Moving on to the Danube frontier and Italy, at the time of Severus the former was another key military border zone while the latter was the centre of the empire, featuring the imperial capital Rome. The Danube region featured nine provinces, these being (west to east):

- Raetia, the province linking the Rhine and Danube.
- Noricum.
- Pannonia Superior.
- Pannonia Inferior.
- Dalmatia.
- Moesia Superior.
- Dacia.
- Moesia Inferior.
- Thracia.

This region of the empire was particularly complex in terms of wealth and culture, given the Danubian provinces spanned the whole range of Roman civilisation from the settled Celtic tribes in the west to the urbanised seaboard of Dalmatia, and on to the ancient Greek colonial cities along the Black Sea coast. There, the Thracian regions east of the pass of Succi were Greek-speaking and their cities had Greek names. Meanwhile, the Latinisation of Dacia after an occupation of 150 years is reflected in modern Romanian.

The key cities in the region included Augsberg (Roman *Augusta Vindelicorum*), which was the provincial capital of Raetia, Wels (Roman *Ovilava*), which was the provincial capital of Noricum, the legionary fortress and *canaba* of Vienna (Roman *Vindobona*), the legionary fortress and *canaba* of *Carnuntum*, which was the provincial capital of Pannonia Superior and where Severus was later proclaimed emperor, Split (Roman *Aspalathos*) on the Adriatic coast, where Diocletian later built has palace when he retired, Budapest (Roman *Aquincum*), which was the provincial capital of Pannonia Inferior, Kostolac (Roman *Viminacium*), which was the provincial capital of Moesia Superior, Roman *Ulpia Traiana Sarmizegetusa*, which was the provincial capital of the redoubt province of Dacia following Trajan's two wars of conquest there, Konstantsa (Roman *Tomis*), which was the provincial capital of Moesia Inferior, and Roman *Perinthus*, which was the provincial capital of Thracia.

As with the Rhine, the Danubian provinces were defined by the northern *limes* here which ran for much of the river's 2,860km length. These fortifications were divided into four sections:

- The Rhaetian *limes*, here only the section on the Danube.
- The Noric *limes* in Noricum.
- The Pannonian *limes* in Pannonia Superior and Inferior.
- The Moesian *limes* in Moesia Superior and Inferior, running down to the Black Sea. From AD 106 during the reign of Trajan (AD 98 to AD 117) to AD 275 in the reign of Aurelian (AD 270 to AD 275) this section actually ran far to the north, encompassing the salient province of Dacia standing proud of the Danube.

The Danubian *limes* at the time of Severus were also home to some of the most experienced legions of the empire, battle-hardened during the Marcomannic Wars. These were based in a string of legionary fortresses along the *limes*, ranging from Vienna in the west to *Troesmis* in the east. At this time the legions here included *legio* III *Italica concurs* in Raetia, *legio* II *Italica* in Noricum, *legio* X *Gemina*, *legio XIV Gemina Martia* (this the legion which declared him emperor) and *legio* I *Adiutrix pia fidelis* in Pannonia Superior, *legio* II *Adiutrix pia fidelis* in Pannonia inferior, *legio* IV *Flavia felix* and *legio* VII *Claudia pia fidelis* in Moesia Superior, *legio* XIII *Gemina pia fidelis* in Dacia and *legio* I *Italica*, *legio* V *Macedonia* and *legio* XI *Claudia pia fidelis* in Moesia Inferior. As with the Rhine frontier, they were joined by an equivalent number of auxiliaries, while the two regional fleets here were the *Classis Pannonica* on the upper Danube and the *Classis Flavia Moesica* on the Lower Danube.

Combined, they faced off against yet more aggressive northern neighbours at the time of Severus in the aftermath of the Marcomannic Wars. These included the remnant Marcomanni, Juthungi and Quadi, various Sarmatian tribes including the Iazyges and Roxalani, and remnant Dacians and Bastarnae, while on the horizon were the various Gothic confederations beginning to emerge in the north and east.

Moving south, the provinces of Italy were Italia itself, Sicily, and the twin island province of Corsica et Sardinia. Italia had been one political entity encompassing the whole Italian Peninsula since the incorporation of Cisapline Gaul in 42 BC. Rather than being an imperial or Senatorial province run by a governor or proconsul, it was actually administered directly by the Senate. To claim to be a Roman citizen before Caracalla's AD 212 *constitutio Antoniniana*, one had to be a freeman born in the peninsula or a former slave manumitted there. Across Italy, nearly all roads literally did lead to Rome, including the *via Appia* to Capua and then Brindisi (Roman *Brindisium*), the *via Aurelia* to Pisa (Roman *Pisae*), and the *via Cassia* to Genoa (Roman *Genua*). By the time Severus became emperor Rome had grown to an immense size, with a population of nearly one million. It was easily the Roman world's largest city, by at least 50 per cent in terms of population. Its twin ports of Ostia and Portus were fully occupied importing vast quantities of grain from Egypt, North Africa and Sicily to feed its bourgeoning population. Severus and Julia Domna were to leave a lasting legacy in the built environment in Rome during their time as emperor and empress, and this is fully detailed in Chapter 7.

In terms of a military presence, aside from the Praetorian Guard there was no significant land-based military unit in Italia until Septimius Severus established the newly raised *legio* II *Parthica* in *Albanum* 34km from Rome in the late AD 190s to keep an eye on the elite classes there. Interestingly, it was commanded by an equestrian, not a senator. However, the province did feature the two most prominent regional fleets of the empire. These were the *Classis Ravennas* based at Ravenna in the northeast with responsibility for the Adriatic Sea, and the *Classis Misenensis* based at Miseno (Roman *Misenum*) on the northwestern tip of the Bay of Naples with responsibility for the Tyrrhenian Sea.

Moving further south, Sicilia was one of the wealthiest provinces in the empire and was for most of the Principate peaceful and so little mentioned by primary sources. As detailed above, it was one of the key sources of grain for Rome, featuring an intensive agricultural economy that included many huge imperial estates owned by the emperor. Meanwhile, the Senatorial province of Corsica et Sardinia is similarly little mentioned by contemporary sources, being equally peaceful and agrarian in nature. Corsica was famed at the time for its wax exports, while Sardinia was a major supplier of lead and silver to the western Empire.

Further east, in Greece and Anatolia were located some of the most important provinces of the empire. The former was divided into four provinces, Macedonia in the north, including the broad plains of Thessaly, Achaia (including the Peloponnese, Euboea and Boetia), Epirus to the west on the Adriatic coast, and Thracia to the east stretching to the Black Sea.

Macedonia was one of the larger Roman provinces, and Senatorial in nature. It was also one of the earliest created, in 146 BC after the final destruction of the preceding Hellenistic kingdom. Except for its eastern seaboard, it was rather remote and agrarian, with a social structure based on its many villages. The provincial capital Thessalonica was a striking exception, the city prospering as it sat astride the *via Egnatia* major trunk road which linked the Adriatic coast of the Balkans with the Bosporus. After the time of the Severans, it rose to even greater prominence as an imperial capital in the east when Diocletian (AD 286 to AD 305) created his tetrarchy.

Achaia was also a Senatorial province but far different in character, featuring some of the greatest cities of the classical world, particularly Athens, which styled itself a leading centre of culture and arts. Many of the great intellectual figures of the empire studied, taught or sought an audience there. It was also a key place for Roman emperors to visit, for example the philhellene Hadrian, who built the fine Arch of Hadrian, still a key feature of the city to this day, linking the centre of Athens with its religious precinct. Here, Hadrian also completed the Temple of Olympian Zeus, 600 years after its construction had begun. Other examples of his imperial patronage in Athens included a gymnasium, the Panhellenion shrine of all the Greeks, and a huge library. At the time of their construction, such benefactions were the latest in a long history of Roman largess in the city, which had included the construction of the Roman *agora* market place and the Odeon of Agrippa. Meanwhile, the provincial capital of Corinth also prospered under Roman rule, it being re-founded in 44 BC after its destruction by Republican Rome in 146 BC after the Achaean War.

Epirus, also a Senatorial province, extended from the Acroceraunian Mountains and Gulf of Aulon on the Adriatic coast to the Acheloos River in the south.[7] This was a fairly unremarkable province in the Principate, with its provincial capital located at *Nicopolis* from where the Ionian islands were also administered.

To the east, Thracia had originally been the Odrysian kingdom of Thrace, famous for its rhomphaia-wielding peltasts who'd served as mercenaries across the eastern Mediterranean in the mid and later Republican period. This became a Roman client kingdom in 20 BC, and was fully annexed into the empire by Claudius after the death of its last king Rhoemetalces III in AD 46. Given that it sat well within the empire, far away from its borders, Thracia remained prosperous and peaceful until the 'Crisis of the Third Century', after which it frequently found itself a border zone during the regular Gothic incursions into the Balkans. At the time of Severus, it featured no permanent military units, though occasionally the *Classis Pontica* Black Sea regional fleet (normally based at Trapzon, Roman *Trebizond*, on the north coast of Anatolia) forward deployed to Byzantium when needed to guard the entrance to the Bosporus. This was a city that was to incur the severe wrath of Severus after his accession to power given its support for his eastern rival Pescennius Niger. This is fully detailed in Chapter 5.

Moving across this waterway into Asia, Anatolia was a thriving economic and cultural powerhouse in the Roman Empire. The imperial presence here had its origins in the kingdom of Pergamum, left as a legacy to Rome by its last king Attalus III on his death in 133 BC. Rome used this as a springboard for the various campaigns of conquest eastwards by later Republican warlords including Gaius Marius, Sulla, Gnaeus Pompey (styled here Pompey the Great) and Caesar. Sequentially, they targeted the various kingdoms of Anatolia, including Bithynia in the northwest, Pontus in the north (fighting no fewer than three wars against Mithridates VI) and the Galatians in the centre.

The most westerly province in Anatolia was that of Asia. Senatorial in nature, its geography centered on the lands of the old kingdom of Pergamum. This featured some of the empire's leading cities, including the provincial capital of Ephesus (its temple of Artemis one of the seven wonders of the ancient world), Pergamum itself, Priene, Miletus and Halicarnassus.

To its north was the smaller Senatorial province of Bithynia et Pontus, sitting on the Asian side of the Bosporus. Its provincial capital Izmit (Roman *Nicodemia*) was one of a number of major cities there. The province of Galatia to the south was far more agrarian, with its provincial capital at Ankara (Roman *Ankrya*), while the south coast featured two other small provinces. These were Lycia et Pamphylia to the west, and Cilicia in the east. The former was governed from Demre (Roman *Myra*), the latter *Tarsus*.

Roman Anatolia was far more militarised on its most easterly flank, where sat the province of Cappadocia. Aside from a short period from AD 114 to AD 118, when Armenia, Assyria and Mesopotamia were incorporated into the empire following Trajan's eastern campaigns, the province was the border territory facing some-time friend, some-time enemy Armenia, and further east the Arsacid Parthian Empire.

The latter were the nearest to a symmetrical enemy faced by the Principate military until their overthrow by the Sassanid Persians. Originating in northeastern Iran, from the third century BC they had expanded westwards at the expense of the various Hellenistic kingdoms in the region and soon encountered the eastward expansion of the Romans. The Parthian army featured a very effective combination of armoured noble lancers and a multitude of lightly armoured horse archers, the latter famous for their 'Parthian Shot' tactic of approaching enemy formations at speed and then losing arrows over the croup of their mount as they wheeled away. This mixture of shock cavalry and missile troops proved highly effective against the Romans time and again, almost wiping out the Republican army of the triumvir Crassus in 53 BC at the Battle of Carrhae, where he and his son lost their lives.

Cappadocia featured the key crossing points in the upper Tigris and Euphrates valleys and was often the launch point for Roman campaigns eastward against Parthia and later Sassanid Persia.[3] Its key industry was olive oil production. While the provincial capital was at Kayseri (Roman *Caesarea*), the most important settlements were the two legionary fortresses and their *canabaes* at Sadak (Roman *Satala*) in the northeast and Malatya (Roman *Melitene*) in the southeast. The former was home to *legio* XV *Apollinaris*, the latter to *legio* XII *Fulminata*. These were the key anchor points of the *limes Cappadocia*, with the Black Sea port of Trabzon the regular home to the *Classis Pontica*. The province's military component was completed by a large number of auxiliaries, including many locally recruited mounted bowmen.

Moving south to the eastern frontier proper, this featured the key barrier provinces of Syria and Arabia Petraea, Syria Palaestina on the Mediterranean coast and the island of Cyprus in the western Mediterranean. Syria was the major bulwark against the Parthians in the east for much of the Principate, and later the Sassanid Persians. It was also highly fertile, sitting as it did on the western arc of the Fertile Crescent. The province was governed from the huge 4.5km^2 metropolis of Antakya (Roman *Antioch on the Orontes*), which by the later second century AD had a population of 250,000 and was the third largest city in the Roman Empire.

In addition to the northern section of the *limes Arabicus*, the border territory also featured a system of defence-in-depth based on client and allied kingdoms that often formed a buffer between the empire and their eastern opponents. These included Palmyra, Osrhoene, Adiabene and Hatra, the latter three all to later feature in Severus' two eastern campaigns. The principal legionary fortresses in Syria were at Zeugma (originally the Hellenistic *Seleucia-on-the-Euphrates*) in the north, Raphanaea near the Mediterranean coast and Danaba to the south. These were home to some of the elite legions of the empire, sequentially *legio* IV *Scythica*, *legio* III *Gallica* and *legio* XVI *Flavia Firma*.[4] In addition to the usual auxiliary complement, the military presence in the province was completed by the *Classis Syriaca* regional fleet that operated out of the port of Seleucia Pierra. Severus was later to divide the province of Syria into two after defeating the eastern imperial contender Pescennius Niger in AD 194, with Coele-Syria in the north and Syro-Phoenicia in the south. The former retained two legions, the latter one. Shortly after he also added two new provinces there to the east after his second eastern campaign, Mesopotamia and Osrhoene. These are detailed in Chapter 6.

The province of Arabia Petraea was the opposite of abundant Syria, being largely a desert inhabited by nomadic and transhumant Bedouin Arabs. For commerce, it relied on desert caravans operating through trading centres such as Petra. This was annexed by Trajan during his eastern campaigns, initiating the creation of the province. One legion was based here, *legio* III *Cyrenaica* at Bosra (Roman *Bostra*), which was also the provincial capital. From here the legionaries and their supporting auxilia (including camel riding *equites Dromedarii*) had the unforgiving task of manning the southern *limes Arabicus*. Defence-in-depth is also evident here, with the Romans frequently making use of their Ghassanid Arab allies to repel the Lakhmid Arabs who were supporters of the Parthians and later the Sassanid Persians.

Heading west to Syria Palaestina, this was formerly the province of Judaea. It proved to be one of the most troublesome provinces of the Roman Empire, and like Britain had a disproportionately large military presence. The province incorporated the territories of the former Hasmonean and Herodian kingdoms of Judaea, including Judaea itself, Samaria and Idumaea. The major issue for the Romans here was the native Jewish inhabitants, who proved the most recalcitrant adherents to the ways of Rome following the formation of the province in the early AD 40s. Three desperate Jewish Revolts were put down by the Romans in the most brutal fashion, the first featuring the siege of Masada and destruction of the temple in Jerusalem and the last in effect triggering the Jewish diaspora. It was after Hadrian crushed the last revolt that the provincial name was changed, with Jerusalem renamed *Aelia Capitolina* (the provincial capital was actually at *Caesarea Maritima* on the coast). Despite the defeat of the last revolt, the province still featured two legions at the time of Severus, *legio* VI *Ferrata fidelis constans* based at Caparcotna near Megiddo and *legio* X *Fretensis* based in *Aelia Capitolina*. Given their proximity to Syria proper and Arabia, these were frequently used as a strategic reserve when the eastern frontier was threatened, and to campaign in the east during Roman incursions into Parthia (both participated in Severus' second eastern campaign there in AD 199) and later Sassanid Persia.

Finally in the region, the province of Cyprus was as far within the empire as it was possible to get. It was originally incorporated into the Republican province of Cilicia, becoming an independent Senatorial province in 22 BC under Augustus. There was little Roman military presence there, with the provincial capital at Paphos (Roman *Nea Pafos*) famous for its 'Tombs of the Kings' Hellenistic and Roman necropolis. Given its prime location in the eastern Mediterranean, Roman Cyprus was fabulously wealthy as it acted as a mercantile hub. Severus visited the island when campaigning in the east, and here today can be found one of the best surviving statues of the emperor in the Cyprus Museum in Nicosia. This larger-than-life bronze sculpture was found in 1928 by a farmer while he was ploughing his fields in Kythrea in the north of the island, near the ancient city of *Chytri*. Here, Severus is depicted heroically naked, in imitation of earlier sculptures of Hellenistic kings in the eastern Mediterranean and Levant.

Heading south once more, Aegyptus was one of the powerhouse provinces of the empire, established in 30 BC after the then Octavian and his general Marcus Agrippa defeated Mark Antony and Cleopatra VII Philopator at the Battle Actium. Given its economic might, the province was always a place of difference within the empire, this based on the abundantly fertile Nile Valley that provided much of the grain supply to Rome and elsewhere across the Mediterranean. Aegyptus was also unique among Roman provinces in being considered the emperor's own imperial domain where he was styled the successor to the preceding system of Pharaonic rule. Here the governor was titled *praefectus augustalis*. We have great insight into the life experiences of all levels of society in Roman Egypt thanks to the thousands of surviving papyrus documents that detail every aspect of life there, many found at the key Roman site of *Oxyrhynchus* near modern El-Bahnassa, 160km southeast of Cairo.

The capital of the province was Alexandria, located on the Mediterranean coast of the Nile Delta. This vast city had been founded in 332 BC by Alexander the Great. Given it was also the location of his *Soma* mausoleum, the city was a particular draw for Roman emperors when touring the east, with many stopping off here to view his body in its glass covered golden sarcophagus, including Severus. By his time as emperor, the city's population had reached around 600,000, making it the largest urban centre in the Roman world outside of Rome itself. Roman Alexandria was best known for its 130m tall Hellenistic *pharos* lighthouse (another of the seven wonders of the ancient world), and its great library was the largest in the ancient world. Further south, the Great Pyramid of Khufu at the Giza Pharaonic necropolis was another of the seven wonders.

By the end of the second century AD, Aegyptus had enjoyed a century of prosperity. This included Hadrian founding the city of Antinopolis to commemorate his lover who drowned in the Nile in AD 130. However, it was also a source of continuing trouble, with a full revolt breaking out when Antoninus Pius raised taxes in the

Middle Nile Valley in AD 139. This conflict, known as the Bucoli War, lasted several years during which Alexandria was besieged. The rebellion was eventually put down by the Syrian *legate* Gaius Avidius Cassius, who later usurped in AD 175 when mistakenly told that Marcus Aurelius had died. Initially successful, he was recognised by the regional legions, but then killed by a centurion when word reached the province that Marcus Aurelius was approaching with a huge army.

The province featured one legion, *legio* II *Traiana Fortis*, originally founded by Trajan in AD 105 for his Dacian campaigns. This performed with distinction during the Bucoli War, deploying from its legionary base at *Nicopolis* to defend Alexandria during the siege. The region also featured significant auxiliary forces. The provincial capital was home to the *Classis Alexandrina Augusta* regional fleet that patrolled the southeastern Mediterranean and River Nile. This was one of the first regional fleets created by Augustus, in this instance in the later 20s BC. It received its imperial title after supporting Vespasian in AD 69, the Year of the Four Emperors.

In addition to countering the frequent native insurgencies in the province, the military forces here also fought the nomadic Blemmye and Nobatae, who lived in the desert between the Nile and Red Sea. Though not a sophisticated opponent in terms of tactics and technology, they often raided Roman Egypt in such numbers that they presented a real danger. The Romans countered this threat with a series of fortifications and watchtowers to protect the rich agricultural land in the Nile Valley. Most Blemmye and Nobatae warriors were unarmoured bowmen, often mounted on mules and donkeys, though they occasionally used elephants trained for war. Severus was to spend significant time in Egypt, and it was here that the Severan tondo was created.

To the west of Aegyptus was the twin Senatorial province of Cyrenaica et Creta. The former was named after the Pentapolis of five cities that sat along the Mediterranean coast in a well-watered fertile region known as the Gebel el Akbar. These cities, all originally Greek colonies, were Cyrene itself (the provincial capital), Ptolemais, Barca, Berenice and Belagrae. They were joined by a separate major regional port called *Apollonia*.⁵ Elsewhere, Cyrenaica was unremarkable, the south mainly unpopulated desert. It featured no significant military establishment. The latter was also true of Roman Crete, though this island economically thrived during the Roman period given its imperious location for trade in the central eastern Mediterranean.

Continuing west one next comes to the vast and hugely wealthy Senatorial province of Africa Proconsularis, comprising modern western Libya, Tunisia and eastern Algeria. Together with western Algeria and Morocco, this is a region we today call the Maghreb. Given the importance of North Africa to the Severan story, here I briefly set out the history of Roman engagement in the region.

Roman interest in North Africa began in the context of the Punic Wars, the first lasting from 264 BC to 241 BC, the second 218 BC to 201 BC, and third 149 BC to 146 BC. Here, they first encountered the Berber indigenous populations in the region, including the Garamantes in the Libyan Desert, the Numidians in the central Maghreb and the Mauri in the west.

In the immediate aftermath of the Third Punic War, which ended in total Roman victory and the utter destruction of Carthaginian power, the Senate in Rome initially shunned the region given its association with their former Punic opponents. However, the opportunity to acquire vast riches there proved too strong a draw for many in the Senate, and soon Roman interest there was revived.

The spread of *Romanitas* in North Africa once Rome re-engaged differed region by region. For example, Tripolitania in the eastern Maghreb proved particularly resilient in retaining its original Punic cultural roots. Bordering Cyrenaica to the east, Tripolitania had originally been established by Phoenician settlers in the seventh century BC, its three key coastal cities giving the region its name. These were called *Leptis Magna* (the birthplace of Severus), *Oea* (modern Tripoli) and *Sabratha*, all later flourishing as part of the Carthaginian empire. All became spectacularly wealthy as important trading centres in key port locations on the Mediterranean coast. There, Rome initially found it difficult to reestablish a presence, perhaps because after the defeat of Carthage in the Second Punic War the region was left largely to its own devices. Therefore, by the time of Carthage's final downfall at the end of Third Punic War, the region had enjoyed over 50 years of effective independence, with the three cities able to gather vast swathes of territory under their control, in the case of Leptis Magna over 5,000km^2. Thus, by the time Rome turned its full attention to prosperous Tripolitania, its principal city was already one of the richest in the Mediterranean. Nevertheless, the Romans persevered, and by the beginning of the first century BC, Tripolitania had become an official Roman province. However, even then its independent outlook long continued, with the first major manifestation of Roman power the classification of Leptis Magna by Augustus as a *civitas libera et immunis* free community. This was a classic Roman conceit given it meant the regional governor had total control over the city. Vespasian later made it a *municipium* mercantile city as he cast around for new sources of revenue towards the end of his reign, with Trajan then conferring Leptis Magna with *colonia* status allowing military veterans to settle there as part of their retirement gratuity. Throughout this lengthy period, the city's Punic origins remained overtly visible, with the family names of the super-rich aristocracy in prominence there. Our best example is with Severus' family, as detailed in Chapter 3. This association with Tripolitania's Punic past is also evident in the built environment, as evidenced in the theatre and *macellum* market in Leptis Magna. There, inscriptions show their construction was partly financed by a local notable called Annobal Tapapius Rufus in the early first century AD. His *prenomen* clearly references his Phoenician heritage.

Roman North Africa was protected in the south by the *limes Tripolitanus* (also called the *Fossatum Africae* in contemporary literature), this a series of fortifications built to defend the region from raiding by the various Berber tribes resident on the Saharan fringe. In the case of Tripolitania, these were the Garamantes, who are fully detailed in Chapter 3. They were resident in a region now called the

Fezzān in the southwestern Libyan interior, and their raiding of the rich coastal zone prompted Augustus to initiate the building of the first phase *limes Tripolitanus*, this in the east on the southern borders of Tripolitania. Initially, for much of its length this was an east-west trunk road along the Saharan fringe featuring a south-facing ditch and bank, with fortifications built at key choke points where raiders from the Fezzān could access the coast to mount raids. In Tripolitania, this was a simple matter for both parties, the Garamantes probing for weaknesses along the frontier which the Romans would then fortify, especially if there were oases. The fort at Bu Njem (Roman *Gholaia*) on the Libyan Saharan fringe provides a fine example.

Another key feature of the *limes Tripolitanus* in the Fezzān was the use of *centenaria* fortified farmhouses where veteran troops were settled after leaving the army. Some 2,000 of these are known in the southern peripheries of Leptis Magna and Sabratha alone, with examples including those at modern Gherait esh-Shergia and Gasr Banat (Roman names unknown). Here, the settled veterans were both *gendarmes* and farmers.

After its founding by Augustus, this section of the *limes Tripolitanus* was first expanded by Tiberius after Garamantes warriors fought with the rebel Numidian king Tacfarinas in the early AD 20s. It was then significantly expanded on three later occasions, first by Hadrian, then Trajan, and finally Septimius Severus. The latter carried out the last major Roman campaign against the Garamantes in AD 201 while returning to Leptis Magna as part of a triumphal progress through North Africa after defeating the Parthians in the east. Notably, all the settlements he passed through in the region feature a significant Severan phase dating to this time, particularly Leptis Magna which he effectively rebuilt.

Further west, the Roman province of Africa grew out of the core Punic territories around Carthage after 146 BC, alongside the unified Numidian kingdom created by Rome at the end of the Second Punic War. It comprised much of the territory of modern Tunisia and north-eastern Algeria and was bordered to the west by Mauretania.

Here, the Romans, having obliterated Carthaginian culture (literally in the case of Carthage) at the end of the Third Punic War, installed a new administration under a proconsul which rapidly set about re-ordering the local economy to ensure the enormous wealth generated across the region quickly found its way to Rome. By the end of the second century BC, the supply of grain had been formalised under early iterations of the *cura annonae*.

Roman interest in North Africa then received a boost when Julius Caesar championed full re-engagement in a region which many members of the Roman aristocracy still viewed with suspicion in the aftermath of the three Punic Wars. In 46 BC, after defeating his Pompeian and Numidian opponents at Thapsus, he established a third Roman province in the Maghreb after Africa and Tripolitania which he called Africa Nova, with the original African province now called Africa Vetus. After his assassination in 44 BC, the Senate then swiftly moved to unify the two with the single name Africa again, this finally taking place in 35 BC under the Second Triumvirate. The eastern province of Tripolitania was then added in 27 BC, around the time the Senate acknowledged Augustus as the first emperor. Shortly after, this new super-sized province was renamed Africa Proconsularis.

In particular, the *cura annonae* grain dole from North Africa was a vital component of the regional economy. The Maghreb had long provided much of the free wheat given to the population in Rome, surpassing Egypt as the main supplier by the mid-first century AD. Given the imperial capital's huge population, its non-arrival usually resulted in widespread rioting in the city, causing major problems for the sitting emperor.

To bring more land in Africa Proconsularis under agricultural productivity, major construction and engineering projects were also carried out, largely by the Roman military. This included building dams, cisterns, aqueducts and tunnels to further irrigate the Maghreb. A prime example is the enormous aqueduct and tunnel system constructed near the Algerian port city of Béjaïa

(Roman *Saldae*) in the mid-second century AD. One of the tunnels here, built through the Atlas range, was over 500m long. Meanwhile, the various emporia of Roman North Africa were also major ports of transit for North African goods around the Mediterranean, including (in addition to the agricultural surplus) gold, slaves, horses, and wild animals destined for butchery in the arena. Examples of the latter included the now extinct Barbary Lion and North African bush elephant. Having travelled extensively in the region, I am always struck by how many mosaics on view feature wild animal hunting scenes, showing the industrial scale of this operation

Carthage remained the provincial capital of Africa Proconsularis at the time of Severus. By that time, it had a population of 100,000, the fourth largest in the empire, and was likely home to the *Classis nova Libyca* regional fleet. Some believe this was based in Cyrenaica, but this is unlikely considering the proximity of the *Classis Alexandrina Augusta* fleet in Aegyptus, and the need to patrol the central and western North African littoral along the coast. Nearby cities included *Thapsus*, Constantine and Annaba (Roman *Hippo Regius*), the latter later home to St Augustine.

The Numidian west of the province was effectively a separate entity after being placed under the control of an imperial *legatus* in AD 40 by Caligula, though nominally remained within Africa Proconsularis until the reign of Severus when he officially detached it as the new province of Numidia, in the same manner he had divided the provinces of Britannia and Syria. Its new capital was located at *Lambaesis*, the key legionary fortress and *canaba* near Timgad (Roman *Marciana Traiana Thamugadi*) north of the Aures Mountains in modern Algeria.

Africa Proconsularis was one of the most articulate of provinces, renowned for its literature and as a source of leading lawyers in the Empire. It was also home to some of its wealthiest Senatorial and equestrian families who ran huge agricultural estates there, many often owned by the emperor.

The Saharan fringe of Africa Proconsularis (and later Numidia) was protected by a western extension of the *limes Tripolitanus* far more sophisticated than that to the south of Tripolitania. Here, it featured a system of defence in depth using the Aures Mountains as its anchor immediately north of the Sahara. Along the range's northern fringe sat the key military bases in the region, for example *Lambaesis*. From these sites, the Romans built a road through each of the key north-south mountain gorges from the northern edge of the Aures to the Sahara.

Along the length of these routes, which converge to the south of the Aures at Biskra (Roman *Vescera*), another key feature of this system of defence in depth in Africa Proconsularis is also visible today, namely a string of stone built signal stations. While researching this book, I had the pleasure of eating lunch in a Berber restaurant near modern Ghoufi, part way through the Oued el-Abiod. I noticed large amounts of Roman *spolia* reused in modern buildings, so I asked the proprietor where this came from. He pointed across the gorge to a tumble of Roman building stone, describing it as a beacon. On investigating, it transpired he was correct. It was indeed a Roman signal station. These allowed rapid communications from the frontier through the Aures range, alerting the regional headquarters in *Lambaesis* of any Berber raid massing on the Saharan fringe.

There, on the edge of the desert, could be found the final stage of this system of defence in depth, the physical *limes Tripolitanus* itself. In the western Maghreb, this featured the same east-west roadway with its ditch and bank which marked the frontier south of Tripolitania to the east. However, some sections here also featured stone built wall sections in addition to the usual south-facing ditch and bank, and regularly spaced watch towers. The main feature, though, was the frontier forts along its length, for example those at *Gemellae* and modern Tehouda (Roman name unknown). The remains of both are still visible today, the latter particularly enigmatic given its later reuse as a defended settlement, with its fine Roman arches bricked up and plastered over, and only now revealed again by centuries of natural sand blasting. Here, units of auxiliary cavalry patrolled the frontier, in the second century AD, this the *Ala* I *Pannoniorum* based on inscriptions in the local forts. This was notably a long way from their Danubian home.

For much of the Principate and Dominate phases of empire the *limes Tripolitanus* across the entire Maghreb was manned by North Africa's only legion, *legio* III *Augusta*, and its supporting auxiliary units. The legion was originally based in the Numidian west at Haidra (Roman *Ammaedara*) but was later moved further south to nearby Tebessa (Roman *Thevestis*) where it remained until finally moving to its long-term home of *Lambaesis*. As already noted, this became the provincial capital of Severan Numidia. Meanwhile, the key auxiliary bases, aside from those actually on the *limes*, were at Carthage and Utique (Roman *Utica*). The size of the various military installations in the Roman Maghreb indicates an overall military presence of around 20,000 at the time of Severus, with most based in Africa Proconsularis (and later Numidia). D'Amato highlights the particularly regional nature of the equipment worn by the legionaries and auxilia here, including pseudo-Attic helmets of Hellenistic provenance, linen armour and the use of round plank body shields (the latter, certainly in the case of legionaries, adopted earlier than elsewhere in the empire[6]).

Moving further west, the final two Roman provinces at the time of Severus were Mauretania Caesariensis and Mauretania Tingitana. Both were created by Claudius when he divided the original single province there into two. The former occupied the territory of the modern Mahgreb in Algeria, with its provincial capital at Cherchell (Roman *Caesarea*). The latter then extended west to the Atlantic coast of modern Morocco, with its capital at Tangiers (Roman *Tingi*). The main threat to both provinces came from the Berber Mauri tribes in the southern desert, with the *limes Tripolitanus* extending west from Africa Proconsularis to protect the rich agricultural strip along the Mediterranean coast.

IMPERIAL RULE IN THE PRINCIPATE

Severus was meticulous, tenacious and single-minded in everything he did. This was no more evident than his control of the imperial administration. To fully appreciate this crucial part of his story, it is essential to understand how a Roman Principate emperor exercised his power.

From the time of Augustus through to the end of the 'Crisis of the Third Century' the emperor styled himself the *princeps*. This was designed to officially project him as the first among equals, in name if certainly not practice given he was a dictator. Augustus was also the first to style himself *imperator* as an official title. Aside from this, the canny first emperor largely avoided the trappings of authority, all the while quietly removing the Republican checks and balances on power by sleight of hand, especially any Senatorial oversight. Soon, he had collected all the levers of imperial supremacy, while still maintaining the fiction that he was saviour of the Republic. These levers included the power to regulate the Senate: convening its sessions and setting the agenda for all its meetings. From this time the emperor also had total control over who was appointed a senator, a prime and unusual example the adlection (promotion to the Senate later in life) of the later emperor Pertinax by Marcus Aurelius and Lucius Verus. The emperor also had control of the Roman calendar, and the authority to consecrate temples and oversee religious ceremonies as the *Pontifex Maximus* leader of the college of priests. He was also the supreme commander of the Roman military, and assumed the powers of *tribunicia postetas* (the power of coercion) and *sacrosanctity* (legal inviolability through sacred law). Finally, he exercised regional authority through the appointment of governors in imperial provinces, approving the appointment of proconsuls in Senatorial provinces, and appointing the procurator in all provinces. Governors exercised military and legal authority in their province, while procurators were charged with making the province pay and ensuring it was *pretium victoria* – worth the conquest.

Using these powers, Augustus created a system that exercised imperial authority using three main bodies. These remained in place throughout the Principate, the first being the *Consilium Principis* main council, created to be the central imperial advisory body. This was effectively always in session, providing the emperor with advice on military, legal and diplomatic matters. Once Emperor Severus ensured his *Consilium Principis* comprised mostly North Africans, given his mistrust of the Senate. Next came the *fiscus* imperial treasury, controlled by an *a rationibus* financial officer (later replaced by one styled an *a rationalis*). This was the magnet for the wealth generated by each province and was used to fund all the emperor's activities, including the use of the military. The word *fiscus* is very specific and refers to the personal treasury of the emperor, literally translating as 'basket' or 'purse'. Finally came the Praetorian Guard, founded by Augustus and later institutionalised by Tiberius. This played a key, and negative, role in Severus' rise to power, after which he completely reformed it with loyalists.

Power was devolved from the emperor into the provinces through their governors/proconsuls and procurators in these two separate chains of command, the system designed to prevent one or the other accruing too much power and challenging imperial authority. Appointment as a governor/proconsul was the most senior post on the *cursus honorum* aristocratic career path for a senator and usually followed a term serving as a consul in Rome. To exercise their authority in the province, each governor/proconsul headed an executive body called the *officium consularis*. In most provinces, this included an *iuridicus* legal expert, *legates* from any legions based there, senatorial-level military tribunes from any auxiliary units, and equestrian-rank officers. Meanwhile, the procurator, always an equestrian, had a personal staff of equestrian and freedmen administrators called *procutatores*, known collectively as his *caesariani*.[7] These personnel were registrars, finance officers and superintendents. The procurator's specific responsibilities included the collection of all taxes within the province, for example the land tax (*tributum soli*), duty on the carriage of goods on public highways (*portorium*) and the poll tax (*tributum capitis*). They were also responsible for the collection of rents from any imperial estates in the province owned by the emperor, the management of all major *metalla* mines and quarries (to run these the procurator appointed one of his staff as a *procurator metallorum*) and distributing pay to public officials and the military.

One might note here how small the executive teams of the governor/proconsul and procurator were, in total no more than 60 staff in a normal province. To give context, in Roman Britain this amounted to only 0.0017 per cent of the estimated population of 3.5 million (compared to around 25 per cent in public employ today). Clearly, this was an insufficient number of civilians to run the province, and therefore both teams were bolstered by the appointment of military personal assigned from the provincial military presence to assist with official duties. Those appointed to the *officium consularis* were known as *beneficiarii consularis*, and those to the procurator's staff *beneficiarii procuratoris*. A good example of an actual individual fulfilling one of these roles could until recently have been found in the Museum of London, where the funerary monument of centurion Vivius Marcianus from *legio* II *Augusta* was displayed. This man served as a *beneficiarii* based at the Cripplegate vexillation fort there in the early third century AD during Severus reign.

TRANSPORT IN THE ROMAN WORLD

The Roman Empire featured a highly developed imperial transport network based on sea borne and river borne maritime transport, and the use of an extensive network of imperial trunk roads. Speed of travel and the transference of news played a key role in the story of Severus, and so I detail this key aspect of his world here for future reference.

In the Roman world, the most cost-efficient and usually speediest way of transporting goods and people over long distances was by sea or river. Hard data for this transport price differential between water and land can be seen in the Edict of Diocletian. Here, the first emperor of the Dominate tried to curb the rampant inflation he had inherited at the end of the 'Crisis of the Third Century' by setting the maximum prices that could be charged for a vast array of services, finished goods and raw materials throughout the empire. This clearly shows sea travel as the cheapest means of transporting goods, followed by inland waterways and finally (by some distance) roads.

Moving on to road travel, this was a central feature of the Roman experience, both politically and economically. In the first instance, the building of a substantial, metalled road network across a newly conquered landscape was the ultimate stamping of Roman authority on a new territory. Such roads often tracked the primary routes of conquest into a new province, and were built early.

Barri Jones and David Mattingly use Roman legal codices to identify three types of Roman road, these being:[8]

- State-built roads, often principle trunk routes, implicitly associated with the military.
- Those built locally by regional Government, often associated with *civitas* capitals and *coloniae*.
- Roads built by industry or smaller settlements for local convenience.

All Roman state-built trunk roads, and often lesser types, too, were built by the Roman military which provided the empire with its principal engineering resource. Thus, in a British context, we see roads tracking the legionary lines of advance across the country, then further branching out as the economy of the new province grew.

Such good quality roadways enabled the rapid deployment of military personnel up to army group size across a province as required, also facilitating the rapid communications needed for the smooth running of the imperial administration. In that regard, the emperor and his officials were able to make use of the *cursus publicus* long-established high-speed means of transmitting news around the empire. Here, *mansio* (from the Latin *mansus*, meaning to remain or stay) waystations every 30km provided regular changes of mount and rider which allowed news to travel at 250km a day, unlike the 60km a day using horse or fast carriage lacking such state-managed infrastructure. For completeness, an ox-cart travelling by road could manage around 12km a day. These principal roadways were also used to a lesser extent for transporting goods, though maritime routeways were always the preferred option for bulky cargoes.

State trunk roads were maintained by the Roman military, under the auspices of highways superintendents called *curatores viarum*, who were initially based in Rome. As the empire expanded, they were increasingly deployed to the provinces where they served under the regional procurators.

ROMAN RELIGION

Spirituality in Severus' world revolved around the Classical pantheon, with worship largely transactional around temple altars located outside the place of worship, rather than within. In the Republic, citizens were encouraged to honour the Gods of the Roman pantheon, in particular the Capitoline Triad of Jupiter, Juno and Minerva. Later, with the onset of the Principate empire, worship of the imperial cult was added. This is still visible in the surviving Roman built environment today, where a *Capitolium* temple and a temple to the imperial cult (often dedicated to the sitting emperor) are two of the most common features surrounding *fora* across the Roman world. A prime example of the latter is the Temple of the Gens Septimia in Djemila (Roman *Cuicul*), a key Roman city linking the Mediterranean coast with the Saharan interior in the Atlas Mountains in modern Algeria. Built by Severus Alexander, the temple was dedicated to the dynasty's founder and featured a larger than life statue of Severus, its head now prominent in today's site museum. Other popular deities included

Mars, Venus, Vesta and Mercury. Additionally, worship of other Gods associated with a given location within the Roman world was also encouraged, these often local deities appropriated in some way into the Roman pantheon.

Meanwhile, as Rome expanded its territorial control eastwards, new eastern deities soon joined the Gods of the Classical pantheon to become popular cults. These were more congregational in nature than the old transactional style of worship associated with the Classical pantheon, the worshipper often playing a much greater role in the religious ceremony. Examples of such cults included the worship of Isis (note the fine temple in Pompeii), Mithras (with associated subterranean temples found across the empire, such as the fine example beneath the Basilica of St Clemente in central Rome) and Bacchus.

However, religious belief in the Roman world was not just focused on the 'above', but also the 'within', in this case at a more domestic level with *lares familiares* household Gods. These were domestic spirits of many kinds, who, again through transactional worship, took care of the prosperity and welfare of those within a household, including those of the Severans. In a standard Roman townhouse or rural villa, they were worshipped in the *lararium*, an alcove shrine often in a corner of the *atrium*. It is also within such a domestic setting that one can see another key facet of Classical world religious belief, specifically in the context of the 'evil eye'. In an age where there was little understanding of socially transmittable illness, it was commonly believed that one individual could curse or infect another with ill fortune or illness through the simple act of looking at them with harmful intent. This was called the 'evil eye'. To counter this, an individual would deploy their own spiritual countermeasures, often featuring other 'eyes' to deflect the harmful gaze. Prime examples were the peacock feathers that so frequently appear on painted wall plaster in Roman households, and medusa heads with their multitude of snake eyes. It is no coincidence that such medusas were also one of the most common decorations used on Roman amour and shields, especially on imperial busts and statuary. Severus himself is no exception here, with the gilded bust of the emperor currently on display in the Komotini Archaeological Museum in eastern Greece a particularly fine example. Found nearby in 1965 during excavations of the ancient city of *Plotinopolis*, this striking 28.4cm high gold figure features a well-defined medusa on the aegis of the emperor's cuirass.

One aspect of Classical worship that the Roman state specifically discouraged was prophets, defined by Hornblower and Spawforth as mortals who spoke in the name of a God, or interpreted his or her will.[9] Given these usually operated outside the context of state-sponsored religion, and certainly the imperial cult, prophets were thought very dangerous and were often referenced as wizards and witches in contemporary literature. Indeed, most Roman emperors from Augustus onwards issued edicts against such unauthorised contact with the divine.[10] One result was to set the Roman state on a collision course with the two eastern religions which specifically featured a plethora of prophets, namely Judaism and Christianity, and whose adherents were also the most belligerent when encouraged to worship the imperial cult. While Rome's conflicts with the Hebrew faith through three revolts was sanguineous in the extreme and played a key role in the political and military history of the Principate, here I concentrate on Christianity given Severus' clumsy interaction with its followers during his reign.

Of all the empire's eastern cults, Christianity proved the most resilient, even more so than Judaism. Its successful dispersal was helped by the empire's well-defined transport network detailed above, with Augustine's *pax romana* providing comparative safety when traversing from one region to another. Meanwhile, the nature of Roman society also provided a fertile setting for the new religion to thrive. This was particularly the case among the lower classes, with, for example, slaves and manumitted freedmen given the promise of salvation in the afterlife. However, certainly to the surprise of the Roman authorities, Christianity also proved increasingly attractive to freemen merchants, artisans and soldiers, and even with members the aristocracy, no doubt tapping into the more stoical leanings of Classical pantheon worship. Further, especially in the east, the common use of Greek as the language of government and commerce also enabled the easy transfer of ideas, including those of a religious nature.

Initially, early Christians worshipped alongside Jewish believers, but by the mid-first century AD a schism occurred (the first of many within the Christian Church) which saw Sunday recognised as the primary day of worship in Christianity. Things progressed rapidly from that point, and by the end of the century over 40 independent Christian communities had been established. These were located as far afield as Rome in the west, Cyrene in eastern Libya, and Edessa in upper Mesopotamia. This wider community was then first called the Catholic Church (*Ecclesia Catholica Romana*) around AD 110 by Saint Ignatius of Antioch in his Letter to the Smyrnaeans.

Persecution at the hands of the Roman state was a key aspect of early Christian worship, at its most extreme in the form of martyrdom. As detailed earlier, Christianity is a monotheistic religion, requiring its adherents to renounce the worship of any other Gods. Given that in the world of Rome this included the imperial cult, Christians were frequently viewed with suspicion when they refused to participate in the worship of the emperor, becoming a common scapegoat when the Roman authorities needed a culprit to blame for any negative occurrence, man-made or otherwise. Significant persecutions occurred in the reigns of Nero, Domitian, Trajan, Hadrian, from the time of Marcus Aurelius into the mid-third century AD, and then later under Valerian and Diocletian (the latter one of the most severe).

Here, Severus was no exception, though he was not noted for persecution on the scale of the above. Burdened with the need for imperial unity given the nature of his rise to power, and having experienced rebellion and civil war early in his reign, he decided an elegant way to achieve this was through religion. Thus, instead of imposing harsh strictures on religious practice, he opted for religious tolerance, though on his terms. The catch here was his decree that while all Gods were to be accepted as legitimate subjects for worship, within this pantheon the 'Unconquered Sun' was to be universally acknowledged as ruling over all the other deities throughout his wide empire. While in general terms a shrewd move, it grossly misjudged Christian theology and so began another clash between the Empire and Church. In AD 202, he went further, forbidding conversion to Christianity under the threat of dire penalties.

In addition to his devotion to the Classical pantheon (he took his post as *Pontifex Maximus* very seriously), Severus was also notably superstitious, with a variety of contemporary sources commenting on this. In particular, he was deeply interested in astrology, with Cassius Dio saying the emperor kept a false version of his own horoscope painted on the ceiling of his audience chamber in the imperial palace atop the Palatine Hill, while the true one adorned the ceiling of his bed chamber.[11]

3

Early Life and the Rise to Power

Septimius Severus was a proud North African whose early life was spent in Leptis Magna, his family's home city in Tripolitania. Here, I first detail the geography, climate and population of the region in the later Principate, before turning to his early life and upbringing. This includes a description of Roman education at the time. I then turn to his early career on the *cursus honorum* as he came of age, before setting out stage by stage how he rose through the ranks of the Roman imperial administration to a position where he was able to challenge for the throne in AD 193. To avoid confusion, given the profusion of Septimii and Severans mentioned, the later emperor is still referenced Severus while others are differentiated.

GEOGRAPHY, CLIMATE AND POPULATION IN ROMAN NORTH AFRICA

The physical geography of Roman North Africa comprised two distinct regions. These was modern Libya in the east, and Tunisia, Algeria and Morocco in the west. The latter region is a true north-south layer cake of different geological areas, these the coastal zone, the Atlas Mountains, the high plains, the Aures Mountains and the Sahara. Meanwhile, Libya has a far more limited layer cake, these the coastal zone and the Sahara. Today, both regions comprise the Maghreb.

Here, the climate in the Roman period was broadly similar to that today, though perhaps slightly wetter except in the Libyan desert. With the predominant easterly and north easterly weather systems, winters were usually mild and wet, with rainfall continuing into the spring and then picking up again in the autumn. Summers were warm and dry, with the climate getting dryer as one headed further inland, especially approaching the Sahara.

These weather patterns, together with the regional geology, dictated the agricultural land use set out in Chapter 2. Thus, in the west, the coastal zone and Atlas range were fertile all year round, the high plains and the gorges of the Aures fertile seasonally (all year round if irrigated as by the Romans), with the Saharan fringe fertile only for the hardiest crops. In the Libyan east, the transition from the fertile coastal zone to the arid Sahara was far more marked. It is only here we have evidence of classical world climate change in the Maghreb, with a centuries-long small but steady decline in rainfall leading to increased desertification.

North Africa has a rich history featuring a multitude of different peoples, some indigenous and some colonists, the latter including the Phoenicians/Carthaginians, Romans and, later, the Vandals and the all-conquering armies of the Arab Conquest. In that sense it features a chronological layer cake of a complexity to match that covering its geography.

In the historical record, the indigenous people of the Maghreb were the forebears of today's Berbers (also called the *Imazighen*). Then, as now, the Berbers were a diverse collection of ethnic groups linked by their usage (for the most part) of Berber languages, which are part of the Afroasiatic language family. They are first referenced in dynastic Egyptian texts, with some believing their original homelands were in the eastern Libyan desert. By 2000 BC, the archaeological record shows the spread of their distinct Berber material culture eastward towards the Nile Valley, and westwards through the Maghreb, ultimately to the Atlantic coast of modern Morocco and beyond to the Canary Islands. They are an important part of

Severus' story given they made up by far the largest component of the local population in North Africa as he knew it.

In our period of interest, the primary sources reference three specific Berber peoples. These were the Garamantes, who inhabited the Fezzān south of Tripolitania, the Numidians, who were resident in modern Tunisia and eastern Algeria, and the Mauri of Mauretania in western Algeria and Morocco. I detail each in turn here, using the term Berber when referencing more than one group.

The Garamantes were the dominant Berber culture in the Libyan interior from 1000 BC to the late seventh century AD. They are first mentioned by Herodotus in the mid-fifth century BC, when he referred to them as 'an exceedingly great nation' who farmed dates and herded cattle.[1] He adds their main regional competitors were an unknown aboriginal population he called Troglodytes (cave-dwellers in ancient Greek).[2]

The Garamantes were a significant civilisation. At the height of their power, the kingdom featured at least six known major settlements. The capital was located near modern Germa, 150km west of Sabha in south-western Libya. Archaeologists excavating the ancient site in the 1960s named it Garama, and that is the name by which it is still known today. At its largest extent, the city had a population of 10,000, and from here the king of the Garamantes ruled an aristocratic elite famous in the classical world for riding into battle in four-horse chariots, long after they fell out of use in Egypt. Garamantian warriors were also renowned for wearing ritual tattoos and bearing facial and body scars. Meanwhile, reflecting the origins of the Berber-speaking peoples in the eastern Libyan desert, their religion was heavily influenced by that of dynastic Egypt. The first century AD Roman writer Silius Italicus says their main deity was called Ammon, clearly a derivative of Amun-Ra, the principal God of the Egyptian pantheon.[3] He adds that instead of using traditional temples they worshipped in 'prophetic groves'.[4]

Unlike the Numidians to their west, the Garamantes remained a Saharan fringe culture, showing little interest in expanding their political reach north to the Tripolitanian coast, even after the first Phoenician settlements were established there. Matyszak says the Garamantes proved particularly adept at exploiting their relationship with their rich northern neighbours in Leptis Magna, Tripoli and Sabratha, saying:[5]

> 'The Garamantes quickly established themselves as the middlemen in goods passing between the trans Saharan region and the Mediterranean world, and traded with peoples to the south for gold, ivory and slaves.'

The Garamantes also established a thriving trade supplying wild animals to the cities of Tripolitania, and introduced the camel to the Sahara to assist their south-north trade from the Fezzān to the coast.

In extremis, the Garamantes also raided the coastal zone to their north, this reflected in the epithets used by the Romans to describe them which often focused on their martial nature. Examples include savage, fierce and indomitable. Intriguingly, recent paleo-osteological research on male and female Garamantian skeletons (these from several locations, and a wide date range) have shown little sign of sexual dimorphism in the upper limbs of the individuals examined. In her analysis of past populations in the region, Nikita says this best fits patterns of agricultural activity rather than warfare on the part of the male population.[6] The inference here is that the Garamantes, in normal circumstances, were perfectly happy to maintain their thriving trading relationship with Tripolitania, only risking conflict with their northern neighbours when absolutely necessary. They knew that, if they did, massive retribution would follow, for example the Roman expedition led by Lucius Cornelius Balbus in 20 BC. In Roman eyes, this was a remarkable success given he not only defeated the Garamantes but also 'conquered the desert', leading to a triumph in Rome, the last by a person outside the imperial family.

In terms of the Garamantes' warlike nature, there is an interesting debate to be had regarding the frequency of their raiding of the coast. Certainly, the longevity of their culture indicates for the most part theirs was a stable society, indicating infrequent conflict. However, their aggression north into Tripolitania was frequent enough to prompt Augustus to build the first phase of the *limes Tripolitanus* in the east on the southern borders of Tripolitania, this later upgraded by subsequent emperors including Severus who carried out the major expedition there detailed in Chapter 7. It is worth noting we are relying completely here on Roman or pro-Roman sources, with the Garamantes having no voice at all. Perhaps the answer lies somewhere in between, with the Garamantes raiding north when their own circumstances required it, but the Romans also knowing where to pick a fight when political kudos was required by an emperor, in much the same way a conflict could always be found in northern Britain and Parthia.

For the Garamantes' part, the most likely trigger of such high-risk raiding of the Mediterranean hinterland was climate change. Given the location of their kingdom on the Saharan fringe, the Garamantes were more susceptible to the vagaries of climate than the other Berber peoples of the Maghreb, who could always rely on precipitation caused by the Atlas and Aures ranges. In particular, the Garamantes faced the challenge of steadily declining rainfall, leading to the onset of desertification in the south of the kingdom. To counter this, they became expert hydraulic engineers, eventually building a spectacular network of subterranean tunnels extending for thousands of kilometres to sustain their settlements from the natural aquifers deep within the bedrock. Nevertheless, the archaeological record shows that by the beginning of the seventh century AD population levels had started to diminish as some locals turned to transhumance as a coping mechanism. The Garamantian civilisation was finally extinguished in AD 669 when the Arab Conquest swept through the region.

Moving west, the Numidians inhabited the region of modern Tunisia and eastern Algeria. Here was a Berber ancient-world civilisation fit to match any in the Hellenistic eastern Mediterranean or early Republican Roman world. Crucially, the Numidians were the first to make full use of the bountiful potential of the fertile western Maghreb, its rich agricultural return in stark contrast to the more arid landscape farmed by the Garamantes in the Fezzān.

The Numidians were originally a semi-nomadic people, arriving in the region as part of the second wave of Berber migrations after the first settled the Fezzān. They are first mentioned in contemporary literature by Polybius in the context of the First Punic War when he describes Numidian light cavalry in action.[7] These became famous in the ancient world for their skill with the javelin, and for the brutal hamstringing of foot opponents in the pursuit. This allowed them to continue the chase, and then later return to kill their immobilised prey. They were widely believed by contemporaries to be the most efficient light cavalry in the ancient Mediterranean, immortalised on Trajan's Column in Rome where Numidian horse auxiliaries are depicted chasing the emperor's Dacian opponents, resplendent with braided dreadlocks and clipped beards. Appian says the small horses they used were ideally suited for life on campaign given they were content to eat only grass, and rarely needed to drink.[8] The Numidians also made use of war elephants, training locally captured or captivity reared North African forest elephants for battle.

The Numidians were early traders with the Phoenician settlers establishing colonies along the Mediterranean coastline to their north and east, particular around the Gulf of Gabes. These new cities were direct contemporaries of those being founded at the same time in Tripolitania. In particular, the founding of Carthage had a big impact on the Numidian tribes in the region. This city developed rapidly from one of the earliest Canaanite Phoenician colonies in North Africa to become the capital of a Carthaginian empire that came to completely dominate the western Mediterranean. Close proximity to this economic powerhouse soon saw the various Numidian peoples in the region coalesce into two distinct

Numidian kingdoms by 250 BC. These were the Massylii in the east and the Masaesyli in the west.

As the Carthaginian Empire continued to grow, its relationship with the Numidians further blossomed, in effect becoming symbiotic. This can be seen in the later regional built environment, for example at Constantine in modern Algeria, the city in the clouds. Founded by the Carthaginians on a plateau 640m high in the Atlas Mountains, it later became a regional capital for the Numidians, and one of the most secure locations in the whole of North Africa.

Numidia continued to supply their famous light cavalry to fight in Carthaginian armies as the latter's conflicts with Rome progressed, particularly in the climactic Second Punic War which lasted from 218 BC to 201 BC. This no doubt seemed a shrewd move when Hannibal was victorious, winning his three famous Italian victories over the Romans at the Trebia, Lake Trasimene and Cannae. However, when the tide turned in favour of the Romans, it soon became evident to many Numidians they were backing the wrong side. The first leader to begin negotiations with the Romans was Syphax, king of the Masaesyli, though the Carthaginians quickly ensured his loyalty by granting him extensive territory around Constantine. However, it was Massinissa, the young king of the Massylii, who finally made a break with Carthage and sided with Rome. This led to a spectacular rise in power as, after the end of the Second Punic War, the Romans also made him king of the Masaesyli, for the first time uniting Numidia. The unfortunate Syphax was taken back to Italy a prisoner and later died in Tivoli (Roman *Tibur*), though his reign was monumentalised with the immense Mausoleum of El Khroub near Constantine. From that point, Numidia flourished as a key trading partner with Rome, with grain, olive oil and fruit its key exports to Italy, and the rest of the Roman world.

Things only soured for the Numidians after the ill-favoured Jugurtha, king from 118 BC, overreached his authority and fell out with Rome, the resulting Jugurthine War lasting until 105 BC. Despite initial Roman incompetence in the conflict, they eventually won, with Jugurtha dying an ignominious death, executed by strangulation after the Roman victor Marius' triumph in 104 BC. The Romans then punished Numidia severely, ceding much of its territory to its western neighbour, the Roman client state of Mauretania. From that time the diminished kingdom of Numidia increasingly fell under Roman control, often finding itself engaged with one side or another in the civil wars of the late Republic, and ultimately forming the core territory of the Roman province of Africa Nova.

Finally, Mauretania was the land of the Mauri, whose territory stretched across a vast region from western Algeria to the Atlantic Moroccan coast. Although there are references to Carthaginian kings seeking alliances with those inhabiting the region, including Hanno I who ruled from 340 BC to 337 BC, the name Mauri first appears in literature in Strabo's *The Geography* at the end of the first century BC as a Latinised version of the Greek *Μαῦροι*.[9] The first known historical king from the region was called Baga, who ruled during the Second Punic War, supplying light cavalry to the Carthaginians, these fighting in the same way as the Numidians.

Later, after the demise of Carthage with its destruction at the end of the Third Punic War in 146 BC, the Mauritanians initially forged close links with the Numidians. For example, King Bocchus made the mistake of supporting Jugurtha against Rome, though quickly changed sides and was handsomely rewarded with the Numidian territory previously detailed. From that point, Mauretania then maintained a close relationship with Rome, though was perhaps too successful in its self-promotion given that, after the death of Bocchus II in 33 BC, Rome began to establish administrative centres there. This soon led to indirect rule from Italy. Finally, Mauretania became a Roman client kingdom in 25 BC when Juba II of Numidia was installed as its king. His reign is monumentalised by the enormous rotundral Royal Mausoleum of Mauretania in Algeria, sitting high above the modern coastal route between Algiers (Roman *Icosium*) and Cherchell, the latter his capital. In this immense tomb, he was buried with his wife, Queen Cleopatra Selene II, daughter of the late Republican warlord Mark Antony and Cleopatra VII Philopator, last ruler of Ptolemaic Egypt. On Juba's death in AD 23, his Roman-educated son Ptolemy succeeded him, though was later executed on the orders of Caligula in AD 40, having been invited to Rome as a friend of the emperor. Caligula's motives here are unclear, though Cassius Dio suggests he was jealous of the Mauritanian king's fabulous wealth.[10] Mauretania was then directly annexed by Rome under Claudius in AD 44.

THE ANTECEDENTS OF SEPTIMIUS SEVERUS

The future emperor and imperial strongman Septimius Severus was born in the North African city of Leptis Magna, Tripolitania, on 11 April AD 145, seven years into the reign of Antoninus Pius. Thus, he was born into an unusually long period of imperial stability, which played a key role in his later world view.

Severus' father was called Publius Septimius Geta, while his mother was called Fulvia Pia. The Septimii were a wealthy and distinguished family of largely equestrian rank (although with some Senatorial pedigree), with some experience of the world of Rome from the mid-first century AD. Meanwhile, his mother was a member of the wealthy Italian Fulvia family, with extensive agricultural estates in Etruria in central Italy.

Geta was a minor provincial official who never seems to have held high public office, surprising given the growth of the Leptis Magna at this time when there would have been plenty of opportunity for advancement in the imperial administration there. By way of contrast, Severus' grandfather on Geta's side, Lucius Septimius Severus (called L. Severus from this point, and after whom the future emperor was named), had been a notable character in Rome as one of its leading equestrians when a young man, then becoming Leptis Magna's leading magistrate on his return to his home town.

Meanwhile, two of Geta's older first cousins, Publius Septimius Aper and Gaius Septimius Severus, had risen to Senatorial rank and served as *consuls* under Antoninus Pius. The picture we get here is of the Septimii family on the rise, making its breakthrough in the high politics of both the imperial capital Rome and in their home town Leptis Magna, though with his father perhaps a bit of an under-performer compared to others.

In terms of the aristocracy in Leptis Magna, the key transition of these elites from styling themselves as Punic to presenting as fully Roman took place towards the end of the first century AD after the city had become a *municipium*. This was a key development for Leptis Magna, given it automatically conferred Roman citizenship on those annually elected as magistrates, and prompted an outbreak of desire among the local elites to display their *Romanitas*. As an example, it was around this time that the nobility of the city began changing their family names from the original Punic to Roman.

One was the Septimii, who seem to have been early starters in that regard, with two family members the first to style themselves Roman through their names by taking the Roman *gentilicium* Septimius. The first is a senator from Tripolitania called Septimius, who is recorded taking a son called Septimius Severus to Italy, with the boy then being raised in Rome. It seems likely that the elder Septimius here is Septimius Macer (interestingly retaining the Punic Macer, the last generation to do so), Severus the emperor's great-grandfather, this then identifying the boy as Severus' grandfather L. Severus. The second candidate is Septimius Flaccus, recorded with the same *gentilicium* around the same time, who has been identified by some as the legionary *legate* Gnaeus Suellius Flaccus, who led *legio* III *Augusta*. He is also recorded in epigraphy adjudicating a boundary dispute along the Tripolitanian coast in the AD 80s.

In terms of the family wealth of the Septimii, its origins are unclear but certainly they possessed extensive North African grain and olive plantations. They were also most likely involved in trans Saharan trade, certainly in gold and perhaps slaves, though the latter is unclear. However, as they began to establish themselves in Italy in the mid to late first century AD, they then began to acquire land there too, and by the time L. Severus was being raised in Rome they owned property in three specific areas, these being:

- Near Veii to the north of Rome, along the *via Cassia* trunk road which traversed Etruria. Also perhaps at a place called *Baccanae* on the borders between Etruria and Latium.
- Slightly further to the northeast, near the *via Salaria*, the key east-west trunk road running from Rome to Porto d'Ascoli (Roman *Castrum Truentinum*) on the Adriatic coast. The specific location is thought to have been the ancient Sabine town of *Cures Sabini*, not far from Rome.
- To the southeast of Rome, possibly at *Anagnia*, an ancient Hernician town on the *via Latina* trunk road which ran southeast from Rome to Benevento (Roman *Benevuntum*) in Campania.

Once in Rome, L. Severus began his education, which would have been to the uppermost standards of the day alongside the offspring of the empire's highest ranking great and good. Any trace of his Punic accent would soon have been stamped out to ensure conformity, and his grasp of Latin and Greek tightened until the reading of literature in these languages became second nature to him. L. Severus did well in his schooling and seems to have been part of a golden generation as the Principate matured, completing his studies under the great master of Roman rhetoric Quintilian, originally a native of Calahora (Roman *Calagurris*) in Hispania Tarraconensis and the first holder of an imperially endowed chair of rhetoric. Meanwhile, his classmates included the future Senator Marcus Vitorius Marcellus, later the governor of Africa Proconsularis, and other notables, while Quintilian could count on Pliny the Younger as another former pupil. This was heady stuff indeed for the young boy from North Africa.

As he grew to manhood, L. Severus could have acquired the *toga laticlavius* 'broad stripe' of a senator (as with his father), although he instead settled on the *toga augusticlavius* 'narrow stripe' of an equestrian. He then trained for and practised law as a barrister in Rome, an achievement for a native North African at the time, also turning his hand to verse as a pastime. In that regard, he counted as a close friend the noted poet Publius Papinius Statius, author of the Thebaid, a Latin epic poem in twelve books written in dactylic hexameters covering the then famous Theban Cycle of stories about the assault of seven champions from Argos against Thebes. Most usefully for us given the insight it provides, Statius also wrote a poem in honour of L. Severus. Here, the ode of fifteen four-line stanzas emphasises that his 'sweet' friend Severus spoke like an Italian, not with a North African accent, and equally dressed like a Roman, with the expensive education clearly having done its job. Noteworthy here is the big age difference between the young man and the poet, Statius having been born in AD 45 and dying in AD 96. Thus, he may also have been a patron for the young man making his way in Roman aristocracy.

Another such patron seems to have been Rome's *praefectus urbi* city prefect Rutilius Gallicus, who had met Septimius Macer in Leptis Magna in the early AD 70s. This was a very powerful benefactor indeed for L. Severus to have in the imperial capital. The role of city prefect there had originated with its traditional founder Romulus, who allegedly established a post called the *custus urbis* to serve as the king's chief of staff. This role became an elective magistracy under the Republic, initially only open to former *consuls* until 450 BC when the post was retitled *praefectus urbi* as part of the wider reforms of Republican government at the time. From that point, any member of the Senatorial class was allowed to become the prefect, though over time his powers were reduced until it was only an honorary post. This, then, all changed under Augustus, with the holder again tasked with maintaining order in Rome and additionally its port Ostia. By the time of L. Severus, this geographic area of responsibility had increased to include a huge zone extending 160km around Rome. Further, as the Principate progressed, new responsibilities were added, including overseeing the city's artisan guilds and corporations, supervising the *praefectus annonae* magistrate in charge of Rome's grain supply, maintaining Rome's waste water system, having overall charge of Rome's *cohortes urbanae* urban cohorts and *vigiles urbanae* watchmen/firemen, publishing any laws enacted by the emperor, and finally having legal jurisdiction in certain cases, for example between masters and slaves, and patrons and freedmen. Thus, by the time of L. Severus, the city prefect was even more powerful than the old *custus Urbis*, with no appeal allowed to his rulings unless approved by the emperor himself. Given such illustrious connections, L. Severus was ideally placed in Roman society as new pathways opened for advancement in the highest Roman political circles for non-Italians for the first time, with *consuls* of non-Italian birth serving by the end of the Flavian period.

We next hear of L. Severus around the time of Domitian's assassination in AD 96, when he was appointed an *iudex selectus*, this a senior position as a judge able to adjudicate cases involving the Senatorial class. After a few years in this post, he then returned to Leptis Magna, and we next hear of him in the context of the high-profile trial of the governor of Africa Proconsularis and his most senior military officer, the *legate* of *legio* III *Augusta*, both unnamed. These were accused of bribery, with the city in some way involved, their trial a long-lasting event which concluded around the time Trajan became emperor in AD 98.

Now back in the family home, L. Severus continued to prosper and was soon on the rise there to become the city's leading man. He was already a *sufes* (the old Punic name for a high ranking civil administrator) of the *municipium* by the time Trajan made the city a *colonia*, when he automatically became one of the city's first two *duoviri* magistrates. These were the highest level judicial magistrates in Roman cities whose chief duties included the administration of justice. Additionally, at some stage in the previous decade, L. Severus had also become a Roman citizen, the first in the family.

L. Severus also married, although we do not know his wife's name, with some speculating he may have been married more than once. With this wife he had two children that we know of, his son Geta (Severus' father) and a daughter called Septimia Polla. Geta is an unusual name to choose given centuries earlier it had been a slave name, though it seems that L. Severus chose it because his old Italian school friend and now Senator Marcellus had so named his own son. In that context, L. Severus' naming of his own son Geta was a clear nod that his allegiance was now with Rome, not his family's Punic past.

We have little other detail of the lives of L. Severus and his less successful son Geta, also of equestrian rank, although other members of the Septimii seem to have been making their mark in Leptis Magna given one Gaius Claudius Septimius Aper (possibly the brother of L. Severus) dedicated a new statue of Cupid in the *Chalcidicum* there (this an annex of the *Basilica* law court). The next we then hear of the Septimii is with the birth of Geta's three children, an elder son called Publius Septimius Geta, a younger son who is our Severus, and a daughter called Septimia Octavilla.

THE EARLY LIFE OF SEPTIMIUS SEVERUS

Regarding Severus' early life we have few details. However, we do know the various stages of a free Roman child's upbringing broadly tracked those of a modern child, and can use this by way of analogy. At the age of five, the *infantia* infant stage ended. For the next two years, Severus would then have been given increasing responsibilities around the home. Tasks would have included looking after the household animals. At this age, children were also differentiated based on gender for the first time, with the social and educational pathways of boys and girls separating.

Only ten per cent of Roman society was literate. However, at elite level in Roman society it was very important, being compulsory for the children of the aristocracy and desirable for other citizens who could afford it. Primary schooling began at the age of seven, this in the home with a *pedagogus* private tutor for the children of the wealthy. At this stage, the focus was on the rudiments of literature, grammar and arithmetic, with a wax tablet and stylus used to learn written Latin and Greek and an abacus to help with mathematics. Another focus at this age was on the traditions and rituals of Rome, this particularly important for leading families in the provinces, for example the Septimii in Leptis Magna. Severus' favourite game at this age was 'judges', with him making his friends act as lictors carrying imitation rods of office before him. This is rather grand behaviour for the son of a relatively minor provincial official, although one should not forget the influence his grandfather had across the entire Septimii family.

After his primary education, Severus went to a more advanced school where he was educated as a *discipuli* student in his teacher's home. The tutor at this stage of a child's education was called a *grammarian*. Here, Severus continued to be taught Latin and Greek literature, with the primary sources saying that as he grew he excelled at Latin and Greek, although he was also fluent in the Punic language of his family. Children at this stage in their education were now also taught the 'seven liberal arts' of geometry, advanced mathematics, music, astronomy, more grammar, logic and rhetoric. The latter was thought particularly important for a young man who wanted to make his way in the Roman world. Physical training also played a key role in the education of boys, and they were taught martial skills, running and swimming. They were also taught how to ride a horse, initially bareback.

Schooling for Roman children was onerous, repetitious and prone to regular corporal punishment for even the smallest error. Because of this, it was common for families with slaves to send one with the child to school to ensure that no abuse took place. This was usually the slave who supervised the children in the home. Boys were also taught seven days a week with no weekend off, and no doubt the young Severus would have been delighted when, at the age of fifteen, he underwent an important ritual that transitioned him to manhood. This involved the removal of his *bulla* amulet, a locket given to him nine days after his birth (as with most free male Roman children), and his child's tunic. Then a year later he graduated and began his life among the adult population of the Roman world. At the age of seventeen, he is then recorded giving his first speech in public, a declamation against an allegation against him in which he was successful in clearing his name. Some contemporary commentators speculate this was a charge of youthful adultery, though there is no actual evidence of this.

In terms of the wider family, it is likely that by this time his elder brother Geta had already left the city to begin his own career in imperial service, for we know that shortly afterwards he became a Senatorial tribune (as the *tribunus laticlavius*) in *legio II Augusta*, the legion based at the legionary fortress of Caerleon in southeastern Wales. One can perhaps see here their grandfather's influence again, especially as the British governor at the time was Sextus Calpurnius Agricola, a native North African from Numidia. This was an individual later to appear in the context of Severus' own association with Britain, as we shall see in Chapter 8.

RISE TO POWER

Having finished his education, Severus now set out for Rome on his eighteenth birthday in April AD 163 to make his way in the world. We have no detail of his appearance as a young man, or indeed the nature of his character, though both Cassius Dio and Heriodian later describe him as an older man. From this we can get some sense of his younger self. Dio, who knew him personally, says he was short but physically powerful, and a man of few words but with an original and active mind.¹¹ Meanwhile, Herodian describes him as a physically tough, natural administrator, who was capable of living in rough conditions when on campaign, and who was quick to act on a problem and decide on a course of action to deal with it.¹² The *Historia Augusta* adds he chose to retain his North African accent as a means of setting himself apart from other more mainstream contemporaries, even after his fine classical education, though its description of him as 'huge' in size is clearly flawed for two reasons.¹³

First, Dio was a fellow Senator with Severus, who later lived through his reign as emperor and so is a far more reliable witness. Second, we have the life size images of Severus as emperor and Julia Domna as empress on the inner face of the 6.15m high white marble *Arcus Argentariorum* Arch of the Moneychangers in the *forum Boarium* Roman cattle market. This was built on a level piece of land alongside the River Tiber equidistant between the Capitoline, Palatine and Aventine hills. Some argue it was not an arch given its differing, squared form which more resembles an architrave. However, it was called an arch by contemporary historians, and so I stick with that.

The arch was specifically the monumental gate through which the *vicus Jugarius* street of the rope makers entered the *forum Boarium*. The images of Severus and Julia Domna feature on a panel on the eastern inside face of the 3.3m wide passage and show them carrying out a sacrifice. Meanwhile, on the opposite western face, a panel features Caracalla also carrying out a sacrifice. It originally included his wife Plautilla and Gaius Fulvius Plautianus, the Praeterorian prefect and father of the former. However, as with Geta, the latter two were also removed by Caracalla once sole emperor. The names of Geta, Plautilla and Plautianus in the dedicatory inscription have also been chiselled away, making this monument a very complete example of *damnatio memoriae*. The top of the arch was almost certainly adorned with statues of the imperial family, though these have long since been lost.

Given the *forum Boarium* was the site of the original docks in Rome, it was an intensely busy area, with this representation of the emperor and empress likely one of the most frequently viewed on a regular basis anywhere in the empire. It was completed in AD 203 after Severus returned to Rome from his eastern and North African travels and dedicated in AD 204, and shows him notably shorter than Julia Domna. Given the sculpture would have gone out of his way to show the emperor at his masculine best, this must indicate he was shorter than his wife, possibly even more so than depicted.

Meanwhile, in terms of Severus' facial features, he is well represented in sculpture across the empire when emperor, always sporting a forked, trimmed beard which became his defining sculpted feature. We have no detail to say if he wore the beard as a younger man.

Back in Rome, by the time Severus arrived the empire was being ruled by its first diarchy under Antoninus Pius' adopted sons Marcus Aurelius and Lucius Verus, the latter a year into leading imperial forces in the Roman-Parthian War on the eastern frontier. This had begun the year they became emperors after the Parthian King Volgases III took advantage of the imperial transition to invade Armenia. Birley describes the imperial capital in the AD 160s as having an atmosphere of urgency after the long years of calm under Pius came to an end.[14] It was in these circumstances that we see North African aristocrats rising to multiple positions of authority across the empire, with for example Geminius Marcianus from Constantine being given command of *legio* X *Gemina* when it transferred from the Danube to bolster the eastern frontier, Antistius Adventus from *Thibilis* in Numidia commanding *legio* II *Adiutrix* on the Danube and later *legio* VI *Ferrata fidelis constans* in Cappadocia, and with the governor in Britain Sextus Calpurnius Agricola as already detailed.

Once in Rome, Severus studied law under the leading jurist Quintus Cervidius Scaevola, an equestrian member of Marcus Aurelius and Lucius Verus' *Consilium Principis* main council. He was a prolific author of legal treaties, with his *Digesta, Quaestiones, Responsa, Quaestiones publice tractatae* and *Regulae* all preserved today as part of the *Codex Justinianus* created by Justinian I in the AD 520/30s.

Severus then went on to hold the post of *advocatus fisci* established under Hadrian, with the holder tasked with helping manage the imperial *fiscus* treasury.

Severus was clearly ambitious, and from an early age had set his eyes on the broad purple stripe of Senatorial rank as worn by his father's cousins Publius Septimius Aper and Gaius Septimius Severus, who as detailed had already served as *consuls* in AD 153 and AD 160 respectively, rather than the narrow equestrian stripe of his father and grandfather. Indeed, it was the latter second cousin who took Severus under his wing in Rome and petitioned Marcus Aurelius (with Lucius Verus away in the east) to admit the future emperor into the ranks of the Senate. This was quickly granted through adlection, the process of promoting a non-Senator into the Senatorial class. Severus now began his journey along the *cursus honorum*, in the first instance serving as a *vigintivir* (the college of 26 minor magistrates) before being allowed to enter the Senate itself. For completeness, some argue this adlection process to the Senate took place later in his career, but that interpretation does not fit his career path from this point.

Once wearing the broad stripe, Severus thrived, holding his first *quaestorship* in AD 169/170. This was the next level of magistrate up from *vigintivir* and could be a civil or military posting, the latter as a junior officer in a legion, auxiliary unit or fleet. For Severus, however, the future imperial military hardman, his first posting was civil in nature, though we have no exact detail of his responsibilities. Becoming a *quaestor* also meant he was now able to style himself *vir clarissimus*, translating today as the Right Honourable. He then gradually made his way through the various positions in the *cursus honorum*, though notably at this stage in his career they continued to be civil and not military. For example, we have no indication he followed his brother into the legions as a *tribunus laticlavius*. Michael

Kean and Oliver Frey argue this was because his network of connections in Rome by this time was good enough for him not to have had to go down the military route, this usually seen as a means building up such a network in the first place.[15]

We next hear of Severus returning to Leptis Magna for a short time, this coinciding with his brother Geta becoming the *quaestor* (a mid-ranking magistrate) to the proconsul in the province of Crete and Cyrenaica. He then spent some time in Carthage before returning to Rome. Geta and Severus continued to progress along their *cursus honorum* aristocratic career paths, the former next serving as the *curator* of the key Adriatic port town of Ancona (this also its Roman name) on the eastern coast of Italy in AD 170, a year after the death of Lucius Verus. In this post, he was responsible for the town's fresh water and grain supply, and wastewater provision. This was an important posting given events to the north, where the Marcommanic Wars were raging, and for the first time since the Cimbrian wars at the end of the second century BC, northern Italy was invaded by 'barbarians'.

In contrast to Geta's progress along the *cursus honorum*, where even his civilian postings put him near a war zone, Severus continued happily along a civilian career path. With Geta otherwise engaged in Ancona, it then fell to Severus to return to Lepcis Magna in the early AD 170s to settle family affairs there after the death of their father. This move prevented Severus from taking up his first foreign *quaestorship* in Hispania Baetica (the province of southern Spain centred on modern Cordoba, Roman *Corduba*). It presented him with his first challenge; when he was at last free to take up the post, Mauri pirates from Mauretania had started raiding the province. It seems the Senate decided his lack of military experience counted against him here as, instead, he was appointed to the more peaceful province of Corsica et Sardinia. There, in this comparative backwater, he stayed for a year, perhaps appointed to the island because of its Carthaginian roots given Punic was still being spoken there.

With North Africans prospering in Marcus Aurelius' court, Severus' family connections now offered him the chance of a rapid boost along the *cursus honorum* to make up for lost time. This was because his second cousin and earlier champion Gaius Septimius Severus became the proconsul of Africa Proconsularis in AD 173. He chose Severus to be one of his civilian *legati pro praetore*, the young man returning once more to North Africa, this time to Carthage. While in post he deputised for the proconsul, for example in the settling of legal disputes given his extensive legal experience. He also travelled to his home town of Leptis Magna again, and one story of his time there during this visit is clearly meant to show that he had outgrown his native roots and was now a man of authority. This tale says that when he was travelling through his home town, attended by his *lictors* with their *fasces* symbols of office (an interesting image given the 'judges' games he used to play as a boy), he had an old *plebeian* acquaintance flogged after the man hugged him in a public greeting.

Now clearly styling himself a leading public figure as he approached his thirtieth birthday, we begin to see the serious upturn in Severus' career that was to eventually open the pathway for ultimate greatness and glory. In early AD 174, Severus returned to Rome, likely relieved once more to be at the centre of political life, this a marked contrast to his later negative view of life in the imperial capital once emperor. He then quickly took his next step along the *cursus honorum*, and a big one, too, being appointed *tribune* of plebs which indicates he'd once again attracted the attention of the emperor Marcus Aurelius, beginning his term on 10 December AD 174.

Next, no doubt with the encouragement of his family given his rising prominence in the imperial administration, Severus decided to marry. He chose a local girl from Leptis Magna called Paccia Marciana, whose family name indicates Punic (as with the Septimii) rather than Italian heritage, her ancestors gaining Roman citizenship through association with first century AD proconsuls in Africa

Proconsularis. They married in Rome in early AD 175, she having travelled back to the imperial capital with him when he had returned from North Africa.

Very little is known of her background, or even their life together, it being unclear if they had any children. Meanwhile, others have suggested that Paccia Marciana is the mother of Caracalla, this to explain Severus' elder son's hostility to his younger brother Geta. However, there is no evidence for this at all. Certainly, Birley believes Severus and his first wife had no offspring.[16] They were to remain together until her death a decade later, and given Severus later had statues erected in her memory it seems the future emperor was at least fond of his first wife. Meanwhile, Severus performed his tribunate duties well, for example helping preserve public order in Rome when the Syrian *legate* Gaius Avidius Cassius usurped in the east in AD 175.

As the Marcomannic Wars progressed, the Septimii continued to prosper, this time regarding Geta again. This was because in late AD 175, Pertinax followed a posting as *consul* by being appointed first the governor of Upper and then also Lower Moesia, with Geta serving under him as the legate of *legio I Italica*. This was the first time Pertinax, later the first emperor in the 'Year of the Five Emperors', was to engage with the Septimii, and as we will see certainly not the last.

Meanwhile, now married, Severus continued his public service career in Rome. He was designated *praetor*, a senior elected magistrate, at the beginning of AD 176, joining in the festivities when Commodus accompanied his father in celebrating a joint triumph on the 23 December that year. This followed Marcus Aurelius' defeat of the Iazyges king Zanticus, which, from a Roman perspective, brought the First Marcommanic War to a satisfactory end, with the emperor taking the title *'Sarmaticus'* and minting coins to celebrate victory.

By this time, the emperor's son had been granted the title *imperator destinatus* (heir apparent) in a move designed to smooth his accession to power given his father's ill health. Commodus was then made a full Augustus in January AD 177, just one step away from being sole emperor. Imperial favour continued to follow Severus, and before his *praetorship* was over he was posted to his first top-level position in the provinces as the *iuridicus* legal expert on the staff of the governor of Hispania Tarraconensis (northern and eastern Spain). This was the most senior position in a governor's *officium consularis*, the post holder being the key legal advisor to the governor. Meanwhile, Marcus Aurelius finally passed away on 17 March AD 180, beginning the troubled reign of Commodus that was to ultimately lead to Severus claiming the throne thirteen years later.

Severus' next posting, shortly after Marcus Aurelius' death, gave him his first real taste of direct engagement with the military, a relationship that was to define the rest of his professional and indeed personal life, to the extent that his dying words referenced keeping the troops happy above all else except family. Intriguingly, up to this point, the reader will have noticed that his career path along the *cursus honorum* had been distinctly lacking in front line military experience. In fact, given he hadn't chosen to go down the legionary legate route early on as had his elder brother, and then hadn't taken up his post in Hispania Baetica when this was under attack by Moorish pirates, a harsh interpretation would be that he had dodged the opportunity for conflict. Whether true or not, all that was now about to change, and from this point he never looked back from immersing himself in all matters military.

The posting that began this relationship with the military was a case of being dropped in at the deep end when he was sent from the far west of the empire to the far east, becoming the legionary legate of *legio* IV *Scythica* in Syria. This famous legion, based at Zeugma in the upper Euphrates valley, had been founded by Marc Antony in 42 BC to campaign against the Parthians, and had remained a bulwark against the enemies of Rome in the east ever since. It was also the most senior of the three regional legions in Syria, being based closest to the provincial capital *Antioch-on-the-Orontes*, and it seems highly probable that Severus experienced his first taste of combat while here, likely against the Parthians or their regional proxies. His journey east to take up his post would have been an experience, too, taking him through some of the richest parts of the empire, cultural and otherwise, including Greece and Anatolia. Then, once in post, he found himself following in his brother's footsteps by serving under Pertinax, who by this time was the governor of Syria. So began a relationship which was to define both men, the older man the mentor, the younger the mentee, their relationship climaxing in the Year of Five Emperors in AD 193.

Here, as a legionary *legate*, Severus served on Pertinax's *officium consularis*, and it was no doubt from the governor that Severus learned first-hand of military command in the far off province of Britannia for the first time. This was because Pertinax had previously served as one of the five equestrian *tribunes* of the *legio* VI *Victrix* in York, then later serving on Hadrian's Wall in command of an auxiliary unit at Housesteads, the auxiliary fort built around AD 124. This was likely *cohors I Tungrorum*. Birley speculates that during Severus' time as *legate* at Zeugma, where his legion controlled the most direct access routes from the east to *Antioch*, he would have frequently inspected his main garrisons along the frontier, including Dura-Europus which since its capture in AD 162 was Rome's furthest outpost on the Parthian frontier.[17]

When Severus left this command is unclear, though it may have been associated with the recall of Pertinax to Rome in AD 182 after a fall from grace with Commodus which lasted three years. We do not know the reason for this, but by AD 185 Pertinax was back in imperial favour again, becoming governor of Britannia after a rebellion by the three legions there. Shortly after Severus followed his mentor west, becoming the governor of Gallia Lugdunensis in central modern France, this huge province running from the Channel Islands to the Alps. This was his first governorship and a mighty elevation in rank along his *cursus honorum*, with Severus acquitting himself admirably and proving an efficient

EARLY LIFE AND THE RISE TO POWER

administrator of this important, if not front line, province. His capital there was Lyon, which was also the key transport hub in Gaul, featuring the confluence of the Rhône and Saône rivers giving access from the Mediterranean to the continental interior, and where most traffic passing by road over the Alps from Italy transited to the north and west. There, he ruled his province from the governor's palace atop the Fourvière, a region of today's city built on a steep sided hill now usually accessed by funicular railway given its precipitous slopes. The Fourvière was also site of the original Roman city there. Today, Lyon's Roman heritage is set out in fine form in the modern Musée Gallo-Romain de Fourvière which sits next to the original Roman theatre and odeon. The Roman city also featured an imperial mint, this the reason it had a cavalry squadron based there unusually deep within the empire, the auxiliary cavalry *ala Asturum* unit. The mint was also the reason Lyon had a *cohortes urbanae* urban cohort based there, called *cohors I Flavia urbana*.

It seems likely Severus had his first personal experience of Britannia at this time, given this most northwesterly province of the empire lay to the direct north of his own. Indeed, his principal interaction with the military in the region outside of Lyon would have been with the *Classis Britannica*, the British regional fleet headquartered in Boulogne-sur-Mer (Roman *Gesoriacum* in Gallic Belgica). This was because one of its tasks was keeping the English Channel clear of Germanic piracy. Given their proximity, he would also, almost certainly, have renewed his acquaintance with Pertinax. Sadly for the latter, his tenure in Britain proved almost fatal, given one of the three British legions there refused his orders to return to barracks after the insurrection that had seen him appointed there in the first place. When he tried to enforce his authority, the troops from the legion then ambushed the governor and his mounted bodyguard, slaying many of the latter and leaving him for dead. Pertinax recovered, dealing with the rebels very severely, this leading to his growing reputation as a strict disciplinarian. However, he was forced to resign in AD 187 given the continuing hostility of the legions in Britain, a lesson not lost on Severus who later as emperor viewed Britain with deep suspicion, especially after the usurpation attempt against him by the later British governor Decimus Clodius Albinus.

Despite the tribulations of Pertinax, Severus continued to prosper in Gallia Lugdunensis. However, while there his wife Paccia Marciana passed away, likely in mid-AD 196. Severus spent little time mourning, no matter how close they were, quickly turning his attention to finding a new wife. This may seem a little callous to modern sensibilities, but as a by-now leading Senator with a prominent imperial posting, Severus was likely being encouraged by his family to settle down with a family, they no doubt reminding him he was over 40 and apparently childless.

Severus' obsession with superstition and astrology now comes to the fore; he apparently heard at this time of a noblewoman in Syria whose horoscope had predicted she would marry a king. The primary sources say he therefore sought her out, this the first reference to him having imperial ambitions. The woman proved to be his second wife, Julia Domna, the youngest daughter of Gaius Julius Bassianus, the High Priest of the cult of the sun God Heliogabalus in the Syrian city of Homs (Roman *Emesa*, by which I will refer to the city from this point). This was an Arabian-Roman deity, his name a Latinised form of the Arabic 'Ilah al-Jabal', meaning 'God of the Mountain'. Heliogabalus had associations with Ba'al who, in a number of Levantine religions, was the senior deity. He was certainly such in Emessa where, before Roman annexation in the AD 70s, worship of his cult was led by the ruling dynasty of whom Bassianus was a descendent.

Julia Domna's family had enormous wealth, not surprising given her family heritage, and had earlier been promoted into the Roman Senatorial aristocracy. She herself owned substantial wealth in her own right, having inherited the estate of her paternal great-uncle Julius Agrippa, a leading Syrian noblemen.

EARLY LIFE AND THE RISE TO POWER

This story, with its astrology references, clearly sounds fanciful, especially given Severus had been based in Syria as the senior legionary *legate* at Zeugma and would certainly have visited *Emesa* which was only five days away by horse using the imperial trunk roads there. Both Severus and Julia Domna would also have frequently visited the regional capital *Antioch-on-the-Orontes*, no doubt for official functions in the governor's palace. It therefore seems highly likely Severus had already met Julia Domna, and perhaps even developed some sort of relationship with her. Barbara Levick says Severus came to know a variety of oriental cults during his time as a *legate* in Syria, and such a meeting might also have taken place in that context.[18] Whatever the truth, a proposal of marriage was quickly on its way from the Rhône Valley to Syria (a journey of twenty days using imperial horse relays), with events developing rapidly from there. Bassianus accepted Severus' marriage proposal, with Julia Domna then travelling to the far west of the empire to join Severus, her journey a more sedate 30 days by water and fast carriage. The couple then married in early AD 197.

Julia Domna was considered a great catch for Severus by contemporaries given she was not only wealthy but is also described by the primary sources as very attractive, too. The marriage took place in the summer of AD 187 in Lyon, the proximity to the death of Paccia Marciana again noteworthy, and proved to be a very happy one, with Severus clearly cherishing his wife and valuing her political counsel. Given her family background, she was very well read and a patron of philosophy, and when empress was a renowned champion of the arts, also helping the social sciences to flourish in Rome. The couple had two sons, Caracalla born on 4 April AD 188 and Lucius Publius Septimius Geta born on 27 May AD 189, the former in Lyon, the latter Milan. This was not Caracalla's birthname, he originally being called Lucius Publius Septimius Bassianus for the first eight years of his life, the latter name commemorating his mother's Syrian family. Severus later renamed him Marcus Aurelius Antoninus during his first eastern campaign, a clear and illuminating attempt by Severus to attach himself to the Antonine dynasty once secured as emperor. Antoninus is often the way he is referenced in contemporary epigraphy, much detailed in later chapters. However, he is best known by his nickname Caracalla, this referencing a type of Gallic hooded tunic which he was prone to wear as an adult, and which he made fashionable. This name stayed with him both in life and posterity. Meanwhile, Geta's full appellation appears to have been his original birth name. Also worthy of a final note here is how well the wider family of Julia Domna flourished from this point, with her elder sister Julia Maesa being grandmother to two later Severan emperors, Elagabalus and Severus Alexander.

In modern historical commentary and popular fiction, Julia Domna is universally well received, often portrayed as an equal imperial partner to Severus helping balance out his more aggressive, masculine qualities. However, that was not universally the case in contemporary literature, with Dio (who, as with Severus, knew her well) portraying Julia Domna as foreign and power-hungry.[19] However, in his recent analysis of her character development and function as portrayed by the primary sources, Andrew Scott provides balance, suggesting Dio's view in particular was coloured by her bridging two halves of the dynasty.[20] In this context, he argues the later Severans, who Dio viewed as foreign and dominated by powerful female figures, informed his representation of Julia Domna in her earlier life, too. Therefore, relying purely on contemporary writings when considering Julia Domna comes with a note of caution. One should further note the usual casual misogyny here of classical historians when portraying female figures, particularly in positions of power.

As a final note on Julia Domna here, her depiction in contemporary sculpture and art almost always features a very specific hairstyle, which, once empress, she made popular across the empire. While not important when taken at face value, it, from an archaeological and historical perspective, given its uniqueness, helps date imagery from the period. The coiffure in question features a wig-like structure of solid waved hair with a coiled disc behind the head.

Severus' last act as governor of Gallia Lugdunensis was helping suppress the *bellum desertorum* rebellion of Maternus. Here, this former soldier (we have no idea of his other names, or rank when serving) deserted the army on the Rhine frontier in the aftermath of the Marcommanic Wars and, followed by other disgruntled colleagues, fled into central Gaul to become a *bagaudae* brigand leader. Soon, he and his followers were successfully raiding the rich villa estates there, their exploits attracting others to their cause including runaway slaves, criminals and prisoners. Herodian says Maternus' band gradually grew until it became an 'an enemy troop'.[21] He then adds they ravaged the 'Gallic and Iberian territories'.[22] At this point, Commodus intervened, ordering Severus to deal with the *bagaudae*, the governor being typically thorough once in action, quickly capturing and executing Maternus and wiping out his men.[23] This was a rare example of imperial lucidity for the increasingly deluded emperor, who, by this point, was behaving very erratically.

Severus left Gaul in AD 189 after Caracalla was born, moving first to Milan where Geta was born eleven months later, and then finally back to Rome where imperial favour led to his appointment as proconsul of Sicily. Birley indicates that his brother Geta may have preceded him in this post.[24] Here, Severus then made a rare error of judgment, courting controversy through his obsession with superstition when he apparently consulted 'magicians' over his future. This left him exposed to an impeachment by an unnamed imperial rival, indicating the heady heights to which he had now risen along the *cursus honorum*. However, this was quickly quashed by Commodus and the accuser crucified, again testament to Severus' growing power and ongoing favour with the emperor.

While still in Sicily, Severus then received another major promotion in-absentia, becoming a *consul* for the first time on 1 April AD 190. This was a suffected appointment, the term referencing that he was appointed to complete the consular year of an appointee who had stepped down early, in this case Commodus who was more interested in participating in gladiatorial combat in the arena, an obsession dating to the mid AD 180s. Here, not only the emperor had a hand in his advancement, but also his mentor Pertinax again given that by this time the veteran soldier had followed a term as proconsul in Africa Proconsularis to become the *praefectus urbi* city prefect in Rome.

Severus served as *consul* alongside a fellow senator called Apuleius Rufinus, though only for only a short time, as he next received yet another promotion, and one that really set the wheels of fate turning in his favour. This was because late in the year he was appointed governor of Pannonia Superior, the key province anchoring the Roman defences on the upper Danube. Here, the provincial capital was the vital legionary fortress and *canaba* at *Carnuntum*, where in AD 170 the Marcomannic overking Ballomar had savaged *legio* XIV *Gemina Martia Victrix*. However, the legion had cleary been fully re-constituted after the event given twenty years later it was one of the three legions Severus inherited there, the other two *legio X Gemina* and *legio I Adiutrix pia fidelis*. This appointment was as much political as a reflection on his undoubted administrative (and emerging military) capabilities given it was once more at the suggestion of Pertinax, and this time the Praetorian Prefect Quintus Aemilius Laetus, a fellow North African. The post placed him at the heart of the imperial defensive network, with his three legions and an equivalent number of auxiliaries the closest large army to Italy. Further, at the same time his brother Geta was posted to the governorship of Lower Moesia on the lower Danube, a lesser posting showing Severus was now ahead of his brother on the *cursus honorum*. Meanwhile, another North African Decimus Clodius was appointed governor of Britain, a post from which he was to challenge Severus for the throne three years later. This meant eight of the legions on the northern frontier were now under the control of North Africans.

EARLY LIFE AND THE RISE TO POWER

Before leaving for the north, Severus set his financial affairs in order in Rome to ensure the future security of his family, this including buying extensive agricultural land in Latium and also elaborate *horti* landscaped gardens in *Veii* in southern Etruria. This important city, 16km northwest of Rome, was near one of the areas where his family had acquired land from the mid/late first century AD, and where by the time of Severus he owned a fine town house there, too. To this he now added his new *horti*. He then headed to the northern frontier to take command of his new province in *Carnuntum*, from where three years later destiny called.

4

AD 193: 'The Year of the Five Emperors'

Severus rose to power at the point of a very sharp sword as the last man standing in the sanguineous 'Year of the Five Emperors' in AD 193. Here, five protagonists fought for the imperial throne in a brutal death struggle. First, Pertinax, the son of a slave who became Roman emperor. Second, ambitious patrician Didius Julianus, also briefly emperor. Next, hardman British governor Decimus Clodius Albinus. Then, aloof Syrian governor Pescennius Niger. Finally, Severus himself, governor of the key Danubian province of Pannonia Superior and ultimate victor. All were veteran generals, a band of brothers who had played leading roles in the Marcomannic Wars under Marcus Aurelius, and later his mad and bad son, Commodus. Now, with the imperial throne the prize, they turned on each other with savage fury.

Commodus' assassination on New Year's Eve AD 192 began a year of mayhem in Rome more outlandish than anything in modern popular fiction. Within three months, the worthy Pertinax was dead, killed in cold blood by the unruly Praetorian Guard in his own palace on the Palatine Hill. Julianus then outbid Rome's city prefect Flavius Sulpicianus (Pertinax's father-in-law) for the purple in an unruly auction at the *Castra Praetoria* Praetorian camp on the Quirinal Hill. This was an event first-hand observer Cassius Dio described as 'the most disgraceful business' in all Roman history.[1]

News of these shocking events was soon on its way to Severus, Niger and Albinus, reaching the former first, five days later at his legionary headquarters at *Carnuntum* on the Danube. The great soldier was enraged at the murder of his mentor and friend Pertinax, and soon the veterans in *legio* XIV *Gemina Martia Victrix* declared him emperor. He then descended on Rome at lightning speed with his troops, an avenging angel intent on brutal retribution. On the way he gathered *legio* I *Adiutrix pia fidelis*, giving him 11,000 battle-hardened legionaries. The terrified Senators panicked, with Julianus quickly assassinated. On arrival Severus then entered the Senate *curia* with sword drawn. The patricians there swiftly acknowledged him emperor, their choice that or a cruel end in the arena.

However, that was not the end of matters. Six days after Severus, both Niger in Syria and Albinus in Britain also heard of Pertinax's death. Both were also declared emperor by their own troops. Civil war followed, with Severus finally unchallenged after beating Albinus in the titanic Battle of Lugdunum in AD 197, the largest civil war engagement in Roman history.

COMMODUS: MAD AND BAD

Commodus, the eldest surviving son of Marcus Aurelius, became sole emperor at the age of eighteen when his father died in March AD 180. Sadly, however, he proved a huge failure, universally condemned by all contemporary sources and completely failing to live up to his father's high standards. Dio neatly sums up his character:[2]

> 'This man was not naturally wicked, but, on the contrary, as guileless as any man that ever lived. His great simplicity, however, together with his cowardice, made him the salve of his companions, and it was through them that he at first, out of ignorance, missed the better life and then was led on into lustful and cruel habits, which soon became his second nature.'

AD 193: 'THE YEAR OF THE FIVE EMPERORS'

The fact Marcus Aurelius set in place 40 patrician-level guardians to guide Commodus once emperor shows he was well aware of his son's shortcomings. These soon came to the fore as it became apparent Commodus had little interest in running the empire, instead relying more and more on powerful advisors to control his administration while enjoying a lavish lifestyle in Rome.

His first favourite was Saoterus, a freedman who became Commodus' *a cubicolo* court chamberlain. Such was their closeness that when Commodus first arrived in Rome as emperor in AD 180, Saoterus accompanied him in his chariot. This was to a hero's welcome after the new emperor had swiftly concluded the final phase of the Marcomannic Wars after his father's death. Such adulation was not to last.

One of Commodus' first acts, no doubt under advisement from Saoterus, was to devalue the Roman currency. Here, his aim was to free up silver to increase the amount of coinage in circulation given the cost of the larger than usual military complement along the Danube after the hard-won peace there. This proved the largest devaluation of the *denarius* since the reign of Nero and was Commodus' first unpopular act given the confusion it caused. Saoterus quickly fell from favour, implicated in a failed attempt to assassinate Commodus led by the emperor's elder sister Lucilla in AD 182. The chamberlain was accused by the *praefectus praetorio* (Praetorian Prefect) Sextus Tigidius Perennis of being a ringleader in the plot. He was murdered shortly afterwards by Marcus Aurelius Cleander, another senior imperial freedman, whose star had also risen impressively. A former Phrygian slave, Cleander then succeeded Saoterus as court chamberlain. Perennis next eliminated his fellow *praefectus praetorio* Publius Tarrutenius Paternus (there usually being two) and so became the new power behind the throne. Indeed, for months after the assassination attempt when Commodus refused to appear in public, Perennis physically became the public face of Roman government.

This suited Commodus, who was only interested in pursuing his own pleasures. The Antonine Dynasty was traditionally associated with the cult of Hercules, and the emperor now started dressing as the demigod, wearing a lion skin and carrying a large club. This is the image most associated with him to this day given his depiction as such in contemporary sculpture and on his coinage. It was also the first public sign of the madness that was to follow.

Commodus was a fan of the games in the arena, and now decided to become a participant, wearing specially designed equipment given he was left-handed. He started to appear frequently in the Colosseum and other amphitheatres, physically taking part in gladiatorial combat and wild beast fights. The latter included fighting or shooting lions, leopards, elephants and bears. A particular favourite was shooting the heads off ostriches using crescent-shaped arrows, sometimes hundreds at a time. However, word soon spread that his gladiator opponents were using wooden swords, and the more dangerous animals were drugged. Commodus quickly became the subject of public derision.

Perennis' time as the imperial favourite was short, coming to an end in AD 185 when Commodus was forced to deal with accusations of treachery against the *praefectus praetorio* by a military delegation, unusually from Britain. Soon he was dead, along with his sons, with Cleander now stepping forward to replace him as the emperor's favourite. Perennis was a paragon of virtue compared to his replacement, with Cleander soon abusing his position for personal gain. In particular, he amassed a vast fortune selling public offices to the highest bidders. As an extreme example, in AD 190 he sold no fewer than 25 consulships. To secure his position amid the increasingly insecure reign of Commodus he also started to gather other official titles, including appointing himself an unheard of third *praefectus praetorio* (two had been appointed to replace Perennis). However, his luck ran out when his competitors at court began to disappear in mysterious circumstances, the final straw being the sudden execution of a popular official called Arrius Antoninus in AD 189. Even Commodus realised Cleander would soon have to be sacrificed if he wanted to remain emperor.

AD 193: 'THE YEAR OF THE FIVE EMPERORS'

The opportunity came in AD 190 when the *annona* grain supply to Rome partially failed, leading to a famine. The *praefectus annonae* Papyrius Dionysius spread word that the shortage had been caused by Cleander, accusing him of selling grain for personal profit. Rioting then broke out, with Cleander overreacting by deploying the *equites singulares Augusti* imperial guard cavalry. Hundreds were slaughtered, though the crowd's resolve was bolstered when members of the Praetorian Guard arrived to side with them against Cleander. Herodian then has Commodus' eldest sister Fadilla rushing to him in panic, saying his life was in danger. The emperor reacted predictably, with Herodian saying:[3]

> 'He was terrified by this pressing danger, which did not merely threaten but was already upon him. In his panic he sent for Cleander, who knew nothing of what had been reported to the emperor, but had his suspicions. When he appeared, Commodus ordered him seized and beheaded, and, impaling his head on a long spear, sent it out to the mob, to whom it was a welcome and long-desired sight.'

A series of short-lived court chamberlains and *praefecti praetorio* followed, all vying for influence over the increasingly deranged Commodus, who was now demanding to be called Hercules only. For most candidates, such imperial attention proved fatal, for example the *praefecti praetorio* Gratus Julianus and Regillus executed on trumped up charges in AD 189 soon after taking office. They were replaced by a single incumbent, Quintus Aemilius Laetus.

Then, later in AD 191, disaster struck. Rome was extensively damaged by a fire that raged for days, with many public buildings destroyed including the Temple of Pax and Temple of Vesta in the *forum Romanum*, and some areas of the imperial palace on the Palatine Hill, too. Dio adds that many state records were also burned, indicating the *tabularium* public records office may have also caught fire. He also says many warehouses full of luxury Egyptian and Arabian goods were also burned.[4] He goes on to describe the large scale of the blaze in detail, saying:[5]

> '... the conflagration could not be extinguished by human power, though vast numbers both of civilians and soldiers carried water, and Commodus himself came in from the suburb and encouraged them. Only when it had destroyed everything on which it had laid hold did it spend its force and die out.'

In true Neronian fashion, Commodus sensed an opportunity and declared himself a newly reborn version of Romulus, his psychosis now reaching new heights. Ritually re-founding Rome, he renamed the city *Colonia Lucia Annia Commodiana*. Further, the months of the year were renamed to ensure they corresponded with his now twelve names, these being *Lucius Aelius Aurelius Commodus Augustus Herculeus Romanus Exsuperatorius Amazonius Invictus Felix Pius*. Next, the legions were renamed *Commodianae*, the fleet which transported the grain supply to Rome the *Alexandria Commodiana Togata*, and the now repaired imperial palace and Roman people themselves the *Commodianus*. The specific days on which the reforms were decreed were then named *Dies Commodianus* as new religious festivals. Commodus also replaced the head of the Colossus of Nero/*Sol* next to the Colosseum at the foot of the *forum Romanum* with a likeness of himself, adding a large club and a bronze lion at its feet to reference Hercules. This was megalomania writ large, and by AD 192 the elites in the imperial capital were ready to begin a final move against the clearly deranged emperor.

Dio is typically dramatic when describing events in the last year of Commodus' life as the emperor spiralled out of control, the Senator a direct witness. Describing a typically bizarre event, he says:[6]

> '... fear was shared by all, by us senators as well as by the rest. And here is another thing that he did to us senators which gave us every reason to look for our death. Having killed an ostrich and cut off his head, he came up to where we were sitting, holding the head in his left hand and

in his right hand raising aloft his bloody sword; and though he spoke not a word, yet he wagged his head with a grin, indicating that he would treat us in the same way. And many would indeed have perished by the sword on the spot, for laughing at him (for it was laughter rather than indignation that overcame us), if I had not chewed some laurel leaves, which I got from my garland, myself, and persuaded the others who were sitting near me to do the same, so that in the steady movement of our mouths we might conceal the fact that we were laughing.'

Commodus continued to behave bizarrely. On another occasion in the arena, he had the Senators arrive wearing dark woollen cloaks. This type of garb was normally associated with an imperial funeral. Further, after performing in the games, Commodus had his helmet carried out through the gate normally used to carry out dead gladiators. His motives here are unfathomable but proved prophetic given things now moved rapidly against the emperor. The key protagonists were the *praefectus praetorio* Laetus and the new court chamberlain Eclectus, a former freedman of Lucius Verus. As AD 192 progressed they decided to act, first trying to reason with the emperor that his actions were not becoming of his post. Predictably, things went badly for them, the emperor threatening to have them executed. Inspired by fear for their own lives, the two now began to plot Commodus' assassination in earnest, alongside Commodus' mistress Marcia who now became a key player in their emerging plan.

The final catalyst for the plotters was word reaching them that Commodus planned to murder the new consuls due to take up their posts on 1 January AD 193. These were Pompeius Sosius Falco and Julius Erucius Clarus Vibianus, with the emperor then planning to replace them with himself alone. The event would happen in the context of the games being planned for the beginning of the New Year to celebrate his earlier renaming of Rome. Dio says that he planned to announce the deed to Roman people by emerging dressed in his favourite gladiatorial garb from his personal cell in the *Lupus Magnas* gladiator school next to the Colosseum in Rome.[7] The historian adds dramatically 'let no one doubt this statement', though Herodian's account diverges at this point. He says Commodus had drawn up a list of those to be executed on New Year's Eve following the various attempts to contain his wild lifestyle.[8] This fell into the hands of a young imperial favourite called Philocommodus (Herodian's narrative indicates a pederastic relationship with the emperor), who handed the tablet to Marcia in a chance encounter in the palace.

Seeing her own name on it, and those of Laetus and Eclectus, she panicked and told them immediately. The plotters now set their plot in motion.

The cabal planned their move well. First they chose a time of year they knew many Praetorians, loyal to their emperor even if their prefect wasn't, would be unprepared and unarmed. This was New Year's Eve AD 192. Dio says they waited for nightfall.[9] Then Marcia tried to kill Commodus by feeding him poisoned beef delicacies in his private rooms in the palace. However, that night the emperor had been drinking heavily, and had also decided to take a hot bath. The combination of wine and the heat of the water slowed the effect of the poison and instead of dying he began to vomit copiously on the bathroom floor. Steadying himself, he quickly realised what was happening and began to make threats against those he suspected of trying to kill him. However, he next made a fatal mistake, deciding to return to his bath. This gave the plotters time to set their back-up plan into action. They knew the poison might fail and had on hand one of Commodus' wrestling partners, a man called Narcissus with a grudge against the emperor. He now rushed into the bathroom and finished the deed, overpowering Commodus and strangling him to death. At last, the 31-year-old Commodus was dead, his chaotic twelve-year reign over. Thus began the 'Year of the Five Emperors'.

THE RISE AND FALL OF PERTINAX

Pertinax was the imperial trouble shooter *par excellence* of his age, yet his rise to take the throne was the most improbable of any emperor. Despite being the son of a manumitted slave, he had a good education thanks to his freedman father Helvius Successus' desire to ensure the next generation of his family prospered. This made such an impression on Pertinax that he spent the first half of his adult life as a *grammarian* teacher of Latin and Greek literature. Then, in AD 161, while in his mid-thirties, he changed career dramatically and joined the military. Here, Pertinax's timing was propitious given the accession that year of the diarchs Marcus Aurelius and Lucius Verus. He was soon in action, leading squadrons of Gallic auxiliary cavalry on the eastern frontier in the Roman-Parthian War. Next, he served in Britain as a junior officer in *legio* VI *Victrix* in York, before moving on to command an auxiliary foot unit at Housesteads fort on Hadrian's Wall. Then, when the Marcomannic Wars began in AD 166, his career really took off. Soon, he was the admiral commanding the *Classis Germanica* regional fleet on the Rhine, and later a *legate* commanding legions on campaign north of the Danube. Pertinax served with distinction and was soon promoted to govern his first Roman provinces by Marcus Aurelius, unusually two at the same time, these Moesia Superior and Moesia Inferior on the lower Danube.

Later, under Commodus (Pertinax was one of the 40 guardians appointed for the new emperor by his father), he sequentially governed four other crucial border provinces, these Dacia, Syria, Britain, and finally Africa Pronconsularis. In Syria, he first met Severus who was *legate* of *legio* XIII *Scythica* at the time. The two formed a close bond, the elder Pertinax from that point always keeping an eye on Severus' career progress, particularly when Severus received his first governorship in Gallia Lugdunum (central Gaul) while Pertinax governed across the English Channel in Britain. Finally, in AD 190, he was promoted to become the city prefect in Rome as Commodus' chaotic reign reached its dramatic conclusion, this akin to the role of a modern metropolitan mayor. At the same time, Severus was promoted to become one of Rome's two *consuls*, the two men continuing their almost synchronous progress along the senatorial *cursus honorum* career path, the older Pertinax always one step ahead given he had previously been consul in AD 175.

Pertinax was a great success as prefect in Rome. His predecessor, Publius Seius Fuscianus, an old school friend of Marcus Aurelius, had acquired a reputation as a strict disciplinarian and proved unpopular. The *Historia Augusta* says that in contrast Pertinax was 'exceedingly gentle and considerate, and he proved very pleasing to Commodus himself', this no mean feat given the emperor's volatility.[10] Indeed, writing later, Herodian adds that Pertinax was:[11]

> '... the only survivor of the revered guardians appointed for Commodus by his father. Commodus had not had him put to death, this most distinguished of Marcus' companions and generals, either out of respect for his noble qualities or indifference to him as a pauper. And yet his poverty had contributed in no small measure to the universal praise Pertinax enjoyed: for despite responsibilities which far outweighed those of his colleagues, he was less wealthy than any of them.'

The reference to Pertinax here as a pauper is interesting given we know his father, the former slave, had as detailed become very wealthy running the family logging business he had established in the decades after his manumission. Further, Pertinax himself had accrued great personal wealth when a governor, particularly in Syria and Africa Pronsularis. The negative angle taken by contemporary sources about his financial circumstances therefore shows how fabulously rich some of his Senatorial colleagues were, including Severus. This casts an interesting new light on their relationship, the elder mentor more senior but less wealthy, and the younger mentee more junior but from a super-rich family.

Patrician-level Roman society was visibly pretentious and conceited and it would not have suited either for the 'new money' Pertinax to be seen to be a patron of the 'old money' Severus. Rather, I determine the former was the latter's mentor based on hard-earned graft, experience and expertise across the full spectrum of Roman governance, and the fact they both clearly liked each other's company. One can see this in Severus' fiery response to the news of Pertinax's death, the singular event that set him on the path to founding the Severan dynasty.

Additionally, this disparity in wealth between Pertinax and his peers might also help explain a key reason why he reached such heady heights in Roman society in such fatally turbulent times. To use modern parlance, he'd flown beneath the radar.

Pertinax's influence continued to play a key role in Severus' rise given it was he who, alongside Laetus, persuaded Commodus to promote the North African to the post of governor in Pannonia Superior in early AD 191. This was the key Danubian province guarding the northeastern approaches to Italy, and proved a fateful career move given it ideally positioned Severus for his attempt on the throne in AD 193.

That Pertinax was an imperial favourite of Commodus is not in doubt. To prosper so perilously close to this most highly unpredictable of emperors needed true nerves of steel and Roman grit, and soon the canny operator's hard work paid off. This was because while city prefect he was elevated even higher, to become a consul for the second time on 1 January AD 192, alongside Commodus himself.

Thus, as both city prefect and consul, he was the most senior individual in the empire when Commodus was assassinated. This begs the question as to whether Pertinax was aware of the plot against the emperor. Here the *Historia Augusta* directly implicates Pertinax, saying:[12]

'... while in this position, Pertinax did not avoid complicity in the murder of Commodus, when a share in the plot was offered him by other conspirators.'

However, for the record neither Dio (who knew him) nor Herodian implicate Pertinax.

All the primary sources are broadly aligned with what happened next, with Pertinax offered the throne in the middle of the night.

The *Historia Augusta* says Laetus and Eclectus immediately 'came to Pertinax',[13] while Dio provides a little more detail, saying:[14]

> 'While the fate of Commodus still remained a secret, Laetus and Eclectus came to him and informed him what had been done: for because of his excellence and his rank, they were glad to choose him as emperor.'

However, when they both arrived in the early hours at Pertinax's house on the Capitoline Hill above the *forum Romanum*, he feared his days were over. Herodian is the only source to report what happened next, here quoting Pertinax directly for the first time in any primary source:[15]

> 'For a long time now … I have been waiting for my life to end in this fashion, and I was surprised that Commodus was so slow to act against me, the sole survivor of the advisors his father appointed for him. Why do you delay? You will be carrying out your orders, and I will be relieved from degrading hope and constant fear.'

These last words give real insight into the desperate nature of the lives of those at the top of Roman society under Commodus. Herodian then has Laetus reply:[16]

> 'Please stop saying things unworthy of you and your past conduct. Our visit does not concern your death but our safety and the safety of the Roman Empire. The tyrant is dead, victim of a fate he richly deserved. What he planned to do to us, we have done to him. We have come to place the Empire in your hands, aware that you are not only the most distinguished Senator, because of your moderate life, and have won reverence for your greatness and the dignity of your years, but also enjoy the love and esteem of the people. All these reasons lead us to believe that what we are doing will please the people and save our lives.'

AD 193: 'THE YEAR OF THE FIVE EMPERORS'

To prove their trustworthiness, Eclectus then produced Commodus' proscription list, showing who was next for execution at the top of Roman society.

However, the wily Pertinax still needed convincing this wasn't a trap and sent a bailiff to view Commodus' body in person. When he reported back that Laetus and Eclectus were telling the truth, Pertinax quickly swung into action, despite the hour. He went straight to the Praetorian camp, knowing he would first need the support of the imperial guard. On arrival, Pertinax initially caused concern among the few guardsmen on duty, the consul an unlikely visitor there in the middle of the night. Laetus himself soon arrived though and allayed any concerns. Then, as more guardsmen gathered, some no doubt the worse for wear with the evening's celebrations, Pertinax addressed them. To buy their loyalty he then offered to pay each of them a donative of 12,000 *sesterces*, a huge amount. This seemed to win them over. However, in the first of several missteps in his dealings with the Praetorians that would eventually prove fatal, his closing words then almost lost their fragile trust, with Dio having him say:[7]

> 'There are many distressing circumstances, fellow-soldiers, in the present situation; but the rest with your help shall be set right again.'

Many guardsmen interpreted this as a threat to remove the many privileges they had enjoyed under Commodus, when most of the guard had enjoyed the high life in Rome. Soon a debate was taking place in the ranks about whether to continue supporting Pertinax or not. However, Laetus again came to the rescue, urging some guardsmen loyal to him to start shouting their support for Pertinax. Soon all joined in and the guard finally declared him emperor.

In was still not yet dawn, and Pertinax now needed to secure political support. He therefore headed back to the *curia* in the *forum Romanum*. However, when he arrived, he found it locked, with the attendant nowhere to be seen, no doubt celebrating the New Year. As bailiffs were sent to find the keys, Pertinax settled down on the steps of the nearby Temple of Concord to wait, alone with his thoughts after a tumultuous night.

As dawn broke, the keys duly arrived, and the *curia* doors were opened. Word now went out to summon the senators. Soon, they began to arrive in numbers. Pertinax tried to greet them individually but the gathering throng was too great. As they took their seats he now addressed them, though again his usually strong oratory skills seem to have failed him, with Dio describing his initial delivery as off-hand.[18] However, the genuine relief among many senators that the murderous Commodus was dead carried him through proceedings, with the two new consuls Clarus and Falco then making speeches in Pertinax's honour. Finally, the senior Senator Marius Maximus gave the official acclamation of Pertinax, making this son of a former slave the emperor of the Roman Empire. By way of celebration, the senators shouted their support for their new ruler, and then gave a huge, chanted execration of the dead Commodus.

Herodian says the Senate now turned its attention to the fate of Commodus' body. Pertinax reported that once confirmed dead by his bailiff, the conspirators had wrapped the corpse in bed linen, which they tied securely.[19] They then gave the disguised body to two loyal slaves and sent it out of the palace 'as if it were no more than laundry, somewhat bulkier than usual'.[20] The *Historia Augusta* then says it was taken to the procurator of the imperial estate, Livius Laurensis.[21] He handed it to a man the *Historia Augusta* calls the consul elect Fabius, though it is unclear who this actually was. Fabius then placed the body in a tomb in the Mausoleum of Hadrian, where it would later receive a headstone that simply detailed the dead emperor's name.

Despite his age and a sleepless night, Pertinax still had one final task to complete. This was to secure the backing of Rome's religious elite who managed the huge temple complex atop Capitoline Hill. There, he now entered the various sacred precincts where he found the priests as relieved at Commodus' demise as the senators. They quickly acclaimed their support for him. Mission accomplished,

AD 193: 'THE YEAR OF THE FIVE EMPERORS'

Pertinax now finally headed for the imperial palace atop the Palatine Hill. On the way he encountered the massed citizens of Rome, gathered in the *forum Romanum* to condemn Commodus and hail the new emperor. Dio paints a typically dramatic picture of the occasion, saying:[22]

> 'the populace ... joined in shouting many bitter words against Commodus. They wanted to drag off his body and tear it limb from limb, as they did do, in fact, with his statues; but when Pertinax informed them that the corpse had already been interred, they spared his remains, but glutted their rage against him in other ways, calling him all sorts of names. For no one called him Commodus or emperor; instead they referred to him as an accursed wretch and a tyrant, adding in jest such terms as "the gladiator", "the charioteer", "the left-handed", "the ruptured". To those Senators on whom the fear of Commodus had rested most heavily, the crowd called out: "Huzza! Huzza! You are saved; you have won." Indeed, all the shouts that they had been accustomed to utter with a kind of rhythmic swing in the amphitheatre, by way of paying court to Commodus, they now chanted with certain changes that made them utterly ridiculous.'

Pertinax then settled into his new suit of rooms in the palace, that evening hosting a banquet for the city's key magistrates and leading men. This was a practice that Commodus had discontinued, indicating Pertinax's desire to return to some kind of normality. Thus ended his first tumultuous night and day as emperor.

By that time, news of his elevation was already speeding along the *cursus publicus* state postal service using its horse relays on major imperial trunk roads and fast maritime transport. As detailed earlier, this high-speed means of communicating news around the empire allowed key intelligence to travel at 250km a day, compared to 60km a day by horse or fast carriage lacking the support of state-operated infrastructure. Thus, Severus on the Danube heard five days later his friend was the new emperor, and was no doubt delighted. Meanwhile, Pertinax's old colleagues Niger and Albinus in Syria and Britain got the news six days after that. Herodian says Severus later referenced their close relationship by recounting a dream he had the night he heard his mentor had become the emperor. Here, he saw Pertinax riding down the *via Sacra* in the *forum Romanum* on a large white horse.[23] In the dream, as Pertinax reached the *comitia* people's assembly, he was thrown off the horse which then gathered up Severus and paraded him to the acclamation of all present. The dream, clearly a device later used by Severus to endorse his own bid for power, proved prophetic.

However, back in Rome, all was not well. Only one day later the first attempt was made to remove Pertinax from power. Here, some rogue Praetorians, perhaps still unsure of their new emperor after the previous night's events at their camp, dragged a distinguished elder Senator called Triarius Maternus Lascivius there. They then tried to convince him to accept the throne but he fled, later presenting himself naked to Pertinax to absolve himself of any guilt.

The new emperor now moved quickly to bring the wider military onside with a raft of donatives and awards, aiming to counterbalance the power of the Praetorians. He then introduced a series of placating proposals in the Senate that were quickly endorsed given all wanted this newfound stability to continue. He also restored the names and reputation of those unjustly executed under Commodus. Dio describes the latter in gruesome detail, with many relatives exhuming their bodies, 'some of which were found intact and some in fragments depending on the manner of their death [some had been executed through *damnatio ad bestias* in the arena] or lapse of time in each case'. The bodies were then reburied reverentially, as appropriate to their faith.[24]

Pertinax strove hard to be a good emperor, initiating a new age of discipline and order after the chaos of Commodus. His role model was Marcus Aurelius, the emperor under whom he'd prospered to such a great extent, with Herodian saying:[25]

AD 193: 'THE YEAR OF THE FIVE EMPERORS'

'He tried to manage everything with decency and discipline, and in his judicial duties he was mild and moderate. By his consistent and deliberate imitation of Marcus' reign, he delighted the older people, and won the good will of the others without difficulty, released as they were from savage and oppressive tyranny to lead a well-ordered life, free from care. When the mildness of his rule became known everywhere, all nations subject to Roman rule or friendly to the Romans, and all the armies in the field as well, came to regard his reign as that of a God.'

The downside to this measured approach was that his relationship with the Praetorians continued to deteriorate, with Herodian later adding:[26]

'what pleased all the rest only galled the soldiers of the imperial bodyguard stationed in Rome. Now forbidden to loot and act with insolence, the Praetorians were directed to return to an orderly and disciplined way of life.'

Herodian adds that Pertinax also refused to allow his name to be stamped on imperial property, the new emperor saying these were not his personal property but those of the empire.[27] In one final populist flourish, he also removed tolls levied by Commodus at river crossings, harbours and crossroads.

By mid-January, Pertinax turned his attention to the biggest issue facing his new administration. This was the huge economic crisis created by the excesses of Commodus and his own donative to buy the loyalty of the guard. This left the imperial *fiscus* treasury, used to fund everything from the military to state construction projects, almost empty. At this point there was only one million sesterces available, set against the 50 to 70 million the treasury usually contained.

Ever the pragmatist, Pertinax decided to tackle the issue by selling off all of Commodus' luxurious possessions. These included a series of vastly expensive imperial carriages featuring seats that could be moved around to take in the breeze or shade, other carriages used for scientific purposes including measuring time and distance, masterpieces of art, and an enormous selection of sumptuous costumes from the dead emperor's wardrobe. The *Historia Augusta* describes the latter in detail, saying:[28]

> '... the following articles were especially noteworthy: robes of silk foundation with gold embroidery or remarkable workmanship; tunics, mantles and coats; tunics made with long sleeves in the manner of the Dalmations and fringed military cloaks; purple cloaks made for service in the camp. Also Bardaean hooded cloaks, and a gladiators toga and harness finished in gold and jewels'

Also sold were Commodus' personal effects, which the *Historia Augusta* (8.4) says included:[29]

> '... swords, such as those with which Hercules is represented, and the necklaces worn by gladiators, and vessels, some of pottery, some of gold, some of ivory, some of silver, and some of citrus wood. Also cups in the shape of the phallus [a potent good luck symbol in the Roman world], made of these materials; and Samnite pots for heating the resin and pitch used for depilating men and making their skins smooth'

Pertinax's imperial 'fire sale' even extended to Commodus' household, with many of the dead emperor's slaves also sold off. This included numerous 'youths and concubines',[30] and others who Birley describes as 'buffoons and other non-essential personnel'.[31] Pertinax next turned his attention to the various freedmen of Commodus' household who had become wealthy under the old emperor's regime, demanding they pay back any ill-gotten gains too. The amount made in these various fund-raising activities was immense according to the *Historia Augusta*.[32]

    With money now in the treasury, Pertinax next moved to bolster the imperial finances by initiating a census to benchmark the empire's taxable revenue. This determined who was due to pay taxes into the imperial *fiscus*, and how much. The complex process involved appointing census-taking officials in Rome, who were then dispatched to every corner of the empire where they worked with each provincial procurator to tabulate the taxable population. The results were then sent back to Rome for centralised recording in the *tabularium*. Pertinax also moved to improve the silver content in the coinage following Commodus' drastic debasement, the aim being to restore confidence in the economy. Ever the populist, he also initiated a series of land reforms to boost agricultural output. Additionally, the new emperor also drastically cut back expenditure in the imperial household, insisting his family and retainers lived a simple lifestyle. For example, the *Historia Augusta* says he 'reduced banquets from something absolutely unlimited to a fixed standard'.[33] The overall effect was to reduce the cost of running the court by half.

Next, he promoted his father-in-law Sulpicianus to be the new city prefect, a vital post in ensuring stability in the imperial capital. This gave his family control of the *cohortes urbanae* city gendarmes and *vigiles urbanae* city watchmen/firefighters. Pertinax hoped, wrongly as it turned out, that this would also help balance the power of the Praetorian Guard. The only other imperial appointment we specifically know of at this time was one made as a favour to Severus. This was regarding his relative Gaius Fulvius Plautianus, a fellow native of Leptis Magna, one of his maternal cousins and a long-term friend, and who was now made the *praefectus vehiculorum* in charge of the *cursus publicus* (and later became Severus' problematic *praefectus praetorio*). This post was a key role in such a time of imperial change and uncertainty, showing how close Pertinax and Severus were. It also gave the latter a serious advantage later when competing with Niger and Albinus for the throne.

Aside from his on-going rancour with the Praetorian Guard, Pertinax's reign now appeared to be settling down into a new routine much different from the near anarchy under Commodus. The *Historia Augusta* says that he always attended meetings of the Senate and when there made regular proposals, as opposed to being a disinterested onlooker like his predecessor.[34]

In terms of foreign policy, Pertinax also seems to have differed from his predecessor, taking a harder line with the Germans north of the Danube. As an example, he ordered couriers to intercept a delegation on their way back to their homeland who were carrying a gold subsidy handed to them by Commodus. The Romans demanded the money back, with the Germans being told to tell their leaders to beware now that Pertinax, nemesis of the Marcomanni and Quadi, was emperor.

As the new emperor's reign entered its second month, all seemed well except for his relationship with the guard. Here, the *Historia Augusta* says an ongoing issue was the fact only half the donative promised them on his accession had been paid, with the other half still due.[35] Further, though Pertinax still nominally had the support of their prefect Laetus, his new policy of strict discipline continued to sit badly with the Praetorians. Herodian ominously provides detail here, saying:[36]

> 'In a way of life so prosperous and well ordered, only the Praetorians complained of their lot. Longing for a return to the violence and looting of the preceding tyranny and to their extravagant and dissolute pursuits, they plotted to remove Pertinax on the grounds that he was a burden and a nuisance to them, and to choose an emperor who would restore to them their unbridled and uncontrolled power.'

Matters finally came to a head at the beginning of March when Pertinax was visiting Ostia, the port of Rome, where he was keeping a close eye on the grain supply to the imperial capital. While there, he met the *praefectus annonae* in charge, a Syrian equestrian called Gaius Julius Avitus Alexianus who was the brother-in-law of Severus' wife Julia Domna, again showing the close links between the two men. However, the *Historia Augusta* says word soon reached Pertinax that the Praetorians were attempting to make Falco emperor after the consul had made a complaint about Pertinax to the Senate.[37] Dio provides more detail, saying the guard chose Falco because of his distinguished family and wealth, this a clear reference to Pertinax's humble origins.[38]

Fortunately for Pertinax, the usurpation was half-hearted at best. Indeed, when he arrived back in Rome he gained easy access to the Senate where he berated any there who had supported Falco, and the Praetorians for being ungrateful given the donative (or part thereof) gifted them on his accession. The plot quickly fizzled out, with Falco allowed to quietly retire.

Whether Laetus was directly involved or even aware of the Falco plot is debatable. However, from this point his relationship with Pertinax began to deteriorate. The *Historia Augusta* says the emperor had already started rebuking him for 'babbling secrets', which caused great resentment with the prefect.[39] Pertinax was also planning to restore the traditional command structure of the guard by appointing a second prefect, which again sat badly with Laetus.

Pertinax now overplayed his hand with the guard, thinking he had the ascendancy after the failure of the Falco plot. The *Historia Augusta* says that in its aftermath several of the plotting guards were arrested and condemned on the testimony of a single slave.[40] They were then quickly executed, with Pertinax forcing Laetus to order the punishment himself. Dio says that after the event the *praefectus praetorio* ensured all knew he was only following orders.[41] Other guardsmen now started to worry about their own futures, with the Praetorians sensing more radical change on the way. They now decided to act decisively, this time under the direct guidance of the disgruntled Laetus who the *Historia Augusta* says began organising a full coup against Pertinax.[42]

The primary sources now speak of bad omens, with the *Historia Augusta* saying that on 25 March Pertinax looked into a pool and beheld a man attacking him with a sword.[43] Then, on 28 March, when Pertinax was carrying out his usual early morning sacrifice on the Capitoline Hill ahead of the day's business, the *Historia Augusta* ominously adds:[44]

> '... no heart was found in the victim, and when Pertinax tried to avert this evil omen by finding the upper portion of the liver, he was unable to find this also.'

From a religious perspective, this was double trouble. Pertinax had planned to go to the nearby *athenaeum* after his sacrifice to listen to a poetry recital, this the *iudus* school set up by Hadrian as Rome's centre of literary and scientific learning. However, given the inauspicious start to the day, he cancelled the visit and sent the Praetorians due to escort him back to the *Castra Praetoria* where the rest of the guard was at breakfast. When the dismissed troopers arrived back, a disturbance broke out. We have no other detail about what or how. Dio says that when word of this reached Pertinax, now on his way back to the imperial palace on the Palatine Hill, he immediately sent Sulpicianus there to quell the trouble.[45] The city prefect had orders to call out the *cohortes urbanae* and *vigilies urbanae* if he determined another usurpation was underway. Clearly worried after the Falco plot, Pertinax then called a special session of the Senate, which indicates he thought he had time on his side even if the issue with the guard proved a real threat.

However, in this he was drastically wrong. Sulpicianus arrival sparked a full real revolt among the guard. Events now moved quickly. The *Historia Augusta* says 300 Praetorians were soon on their way to the palace,[46] though Dio reports the number was 200.[47] It is unclear if this was part of Laetus' conspiracy earlier detailed by the *Historia Augusta*, or a spontaneous act of mutiny.

Whatever the cause, and however many guardsmen were involved, it is worth noting this was only a small proportion of the troopers in camp, given at this stage the Praetorians Guard usually numbered 5,000 men. However, the *Historia Augusta's* description of them warrants some careful consideration given it is very descriptive of their serious level of intent. It says that they were 'formed into a wedge' and 'under arms'.[48] The latter is self-explanatory, indicating they had donned their *lorica segmentata* and *lorica squamata* armour (instead of the usual tunics when on official duty in the imperial capital), helmets with their brilliant white plumes and large *scutum* body shields. In addition, they were carrying their *pila* javelins or *lancea* spears and *gladius hispaniensis* swords. However, the former phrase is most interesting, given the wedge described was a very specific Roman infantry formation known as the *cuneus* swine head. This was designed to punch through an opposing enemy battle line, with a senior centurion deployed at the apex, and may indicate the guards had trouble forcing their way through crowds angry at their appearance in full kit. It may also be a literary device used to indicate they meant business.

The time was now noon. Dio says Pertinax had no warning hundreds of Praetorians were approaching until they were marching up the Palatine Hill from the foot of the *forum Romanum*, literally on his doorstep.[49] Specifically, at that moment the emperor was in the portico of the palace inspecting his own household slaves. Dio says that suddenly his wife Flavia Titiana appeared to tell him the appalling news that fully armed Praetorians were already inside the palace,[50] though Herodian says it was palace attendants who bore the grim news.[51]

Their ease of access may seem odd given this was the most powerful man in his known world. However, here a new factor came into play. This was Pertinax's unpopularity with many of his own palace staff, most likely because they, like the Praetorian Guard, had been feted during the reign of Commodus, and left to get on with their own nefarious activities. Most of those serving Pertinax were Commodus' freedmen, with many of the latter's slaves already sold off in the earlier grand auction. Certainly, many senior figures in the imperial household feared their wrongdoing under the old regime would eventually be discovered by the new emperor, as later happened under Severus when many were condemned to the arena.

Dio provides real-time insight here into how exposed the unwitting Pertinax was, saying that the porters and other freedmen in the palace had actually opened all of the entrances to let the Praetorians in,[52] while the *Historia Augusta* goes even further, saying:[53]

> 'In fact, the palace-attendants hated Pertinax with so bitter a hatred that they even urged on the soldiers to do the deed.'

However, by way of counterpoint, Herodian is kinder to the palace staff:[54]

> 'The imperial attendants on duty in the palace were astounded at this unbelievable and unexpected assault. Since they were only a handful of unarmed men against a horde of armed soldiers, the attendants deserted their assigned posts and fled into the palace grounds or the nearby passageways.'

Whatever the truth, Pertinax was now faced with a truly life-threatening dilemma. A new usurpation was clearly underway, but he had no idea how serious it was. He immediately sent Laetus to confront the men. However, the *Historia Augusta* says that as soon as the the *praefectus praetorio* was out of the emperor's sight he avoided the troopers and, hood drawn to cover his face, left the palace for his home.[55] There he awaited the outcome of the events about to play out. Dio does say that Pertinax had nearby some of his *equites singulares Augusti* guard cavalry and his *'night guard'*, presumably a personal bodyguard loyal to him.[56] He therefore had the means to protect himself if he chose to call on them.

By now the Praetorians had passed through a room in the palace called the *Sicilia*, and then the Banqueting Hall of Jupiter, and were heading directly for the emperor's own private suit of rooms. Pertinax now made a fatal error, deciding to confront the angry guardsman with only Eclectus the court chamberlain by his side, and a few attendants. All three primary sources are worth considering in full here given the importance of what unfolded next. Dio says:[57]

AD 193: 'THE YEAR OF THE FIVE EMPERORS'

'... he behaved in a manner that one can call noble, or senseless, or whatever one pleases. For, even though he could in all probability have killed his assailants [given he had the cavalry and his own guards nearby], or might at least have concealed himself and made his escape to some place or other, by closing the gates of the palace and the other intervening doors, he nevertheless adopted neither of these courses. Instead, hoping to overawe them by his appearance and to win them over by his words, he went to meet the approaching band. The soldiers on seeing him were at first abashed, all save one, and kept their eyes on the ground, and they thrust their swords back into their scabbards; but that one man leaped forward, exclaiming 'The soldiers have sent you this sword,' and then fell on him and wounded him. Then his comrades no longer held back, but struck down their emperor together with Eclectus. The latter alone had not deserted him, but defended him as best he could, even wounding several of the assailants.'

Meanwhile, Herodian says:[58]

'The emperor did not follow the advice of those who suggested he flee. He considered this solution undignified and servile, unworthy of an emperor and unworthy of his previous way of life and his achievements. He preferred to face the issue squarely and came out to talk to the Praetorians, hoping to win them over and put an end to their insane anger. And so he left his rooms and approached them in an effort to discover the reason for their anger, and tried to persuade them not to act like madmen. Remaining cool and calm in this crisis and displaying the dignity of an emperor, he showed no evidence of fear or cowardice or servility. "For me," he said, "to be murdered by you is neither important nor grievous to an old man who has received so many honours in the course of a long life. It is inevitable that every man must die someday. But for you who are supposed to be the emperor's guardians and defenders to be his murderers, and for you to stain your hands with the blood of an emperor and, what is worse, that of a fellow

Roman, be sure that this is not only an act of pollution at the present but also represents a danger for you in the future. I know in my heart that I have wronged you in no way. If you are still grieved at the death of Commodus, remember that it is hardly surprising that death caught up with him. He was mortal. But if you think his death was the result of treachery, the blame does not lie with me. For you know that I am free of all suspicion on that score, and I know no more about what happened then than you do. So, if you suspect anything, bring charges against someone else. But even though Commodus is dead, you will not lack anything which can be supplied you fairly and deservedly, so long as it can be done without recourse to violence and confiscation of property." So persuasive were his words that he had now convinced some of them; indeed, quite a few of them began to withdraw, respecting the age of their revered emperor. But while he was still talking, the bolder praetorians attacked and killed him.'

Finally, the *Historia Augusta* details that:[59]

'... after the Praetorians had burst into the inner portion of the palace ... Pertinax advanced to meet them and sought to appease them with a long and serious speech. In spite of this, one Tausius, a Tungrian [so from the region of modern Belgian, then known for its fierce warrior recruits into the Roman military], after haranguing the soldiers into a state of fury and fear, hurled his spear at Pertinax breast. And he, after a prayer to Jupiter the Avenger, veiled his head with his toga and was stabbed by the rest. Eclectus also, after stabbing two of his assailants, died with him, and the other court chamberlains then fled away in all directions.'

Here a broad pattern is evident in all the sources, with Pertinax clearly not realising the scale of the imminent danger. First, he could have deployed his cavalry and guards to protect himself but didn't. Second, he could have fled, but didn't. Instead, he clearly felt able to avert the crisis through strength of personality and oratory, almost succeeding except for the one individual Dio and the *Historia Augusta* say was determined to kill him whatever happened. It seems likely he was personally tasked with assassinating Pertinax if all else failed, certainly if the assassination was part of Laetus' plot. Once this Praetorian had struck the first blow, the other guardsmen then joined in, with the veiling of Pertinax's head with his toga a clear analogous reference to the murder of Caesar in 44 BC. Thus, having ruled for just 86 days, the son of a slave who became the emperor of Rome was dead. Dio's epitaph in the immediate aftermath of the murder is particularly fitting:[60]

> 'Thus did Pertinax, who undertook to restore everything in a moment, come to his end. He failed to comprehend, though a man of wide practical experience, that one cannot with safety reform everything at once, and that the restoration of a state, in particular, requires both time and wisdom.'

Chaos now ensued in the palace. Both Dio[61] and the *Historia Augusta*[62] say the Praetorians cut off the old man's head and paraded it atop a spear down the Palatine Hill, though their bravado quickly left them and they quickly returned to their camp.

The *Historia Augusta* says they took Pertinax's head on the spear back with them, though this seems unlikely given the uproar this would have caused, especially as they only numbered 200–300.[63]

In the event, the head and decapitated body were recovered by his soon-to-be successor Didius Julianus, with Pertinax then quickly buried in the tomb of his wife's grandfather. An unfitting end for one of the great men of Roman history, certainly as viewed by contemporaries. However, by the end of the year this unfitting interment would be rectified by Severus, and in the most spectacular fashion.

ENTER SEVERUS

With the new emperor dead, Laetus and any other plotters were now faced with a big problem. Given there was no named successor, a power vacuum now existed in Rome. Thus, whether the assassination of Pertinax was planned or not, a new emperor was needed, and quickly.

Perhaps surprisingly, the first candidate to make a move for the throne was Pertinax's own father-in-law, Sulpicianus. He was still in the *Castra Praetoria* given the speed of events. The commander of the *cohortes urbanaes* and *vigilies urbanaes* clearly thought their support put him in a strong position to win over the guard. However, the Praetorians were wary of him given his familial links to Pertinax and only a few overtly supported him. One can sense a pause here as the guardsmen mulled over Sulpicianus while waiting to see if their actions would be punished, which they fully expected. However, when no reprisals came, they were emboldened and posted a notice outside the camp asking for bids for the imperial throne. In a very real sense, the Roman Empire was now up for sale.

At the time most of the Senators were still in the *curia* in the *forum Romanum* where they had gathered following Pertinax's earlier summons. Word had quickly reached them of the emperor's assassination, but the Senators waited there for official confirmation before making any move. News then reached them of the Praetorian's auction of the throne. Most reacted with shock and disgust. However, one man didn't. This was veteran Senator Didius Julianus, sitting in the chamber with his son-in-law, Cornelius Repentinus. The former soldier now saw an opportunity.

The *Historia Augusta* says Julianus was encouraged by two Praetorian tribunes called Publius Florianus and Vectius Aper, who had been sent to find another candidate for the throne.[64] The Senator encountered them as he left the *curia*. Herodian adds Julianus' wife Manlia Scantill, daughter Didia Clara and a 'mob of parasites' also urged him on.[65]

With this encouragement, Julianus raced to the Praetorian camp on the Quirinal Hill. When he arrived, his entry was blocked by supporters of Sulpicianus. So began Dio's 'most disgraceful business'.[66] Chaos reigned inside the camp, where Sulpicianus was still

AD 193: 'THE YEAR OF THE FIVE EMPERORS'

trying to convince the guard to support him. Julianus was at first unable to attract their attention and was reduced to writing messages on placards. Then, with the help of a guard officer called Maurentius, who had decided to switch allegiance from Sulpicianus, contact was made and an auction began between the two contenders for the throne. Julianus was still locked out, so the rival cash offers were made through Praetorian runners moving back and forth between Julianus at the gates and Sulpicianus inside, the latter most likely located inside the camp *principia*.

At some stage in the bidding process, Julianus managed to clamber up onto the wall of the camp where he gave a written promise to restore the rights enjoyed by the guard under Commodus, at the same time warning them not to trust Sulpicianus given his links to Pertinax. However, the counterbidding continued until it had reached Sulpicianus' upper limit of 20,000 *sesterces* per Praetorian. At that, Julianus' made a final reckless bid of 25,000 *sesterces*, holding up his fingers to show the amount, and shouting it in a loud voice. This at last won him the day and the guard acclaimed him emperor. The whole occasion shows the Roman Empire at its lowest, in the tawdriest fashion.

Nevertheless, Julianus was now emperor and had to secure his position. Towards the evening, the Praetorians scooped him up and headed in their thousands for the *forum Romanum* with their battle standards on full display. Given this show of force, there was no official interference, with the guard cavalry and urban cohorts wisely staying in their barracks. The citizenry certainly made their views known, though, with many hurling stones at Julianus as he passed and calling him a parricide. However, he soon reached the *curia*, untouched thanks to the Praetorians. There, many of the Senators had returned after bathing and dining. Julianus entered with a large body of guardsmen under the conceit he had simply come to address his fellow patricians. The remaining Praetorians stayed outside, surrounding the building. Dio, a direct witness to this coup, was particularly nervous given he'd recently prosecuted Julianus. However, the new emperor's attention was solely focused on gaining acclamation from his fellow Senators. He told them that, with the death of Pertinax, the imperial throne was vacant. Dio has him then say:[67]

> 'I see that you need a ruler, and I myself am best fitted of any to rule you. I should mention all the advantages I can offer, if you were not already familiar with them and had not already had experience of me. Consequently, I have not even asked to be attended here by the soldiers [clearly untrue], but have come to you alone, in order that you may ratify what has been given to me by them.'

With the Praetorians at his back, the nervous senators swiftly confirmed him in power. The *Historia Augusta* next describes an odd event happening, saying:[68]

> '... when the consul-elect, in voting on Julianus, delivered himself of the following: "I vote that Didius Julianus be declared emperor," Julianus prompted, "Say also Severus," the name of his grandfather and great-grandfather, which he had added to his own.'

Many later saw this as an ill omen given Severus would shortly prove Julianus' nemesis. For now, though, once his position was secured, he went to the palace on the Palatine to claim it as his own. The following morning many Senators went there to pay their respects, though Dio says they 'moulded their faces so as not to show their grief'.[69] In the same paragraph, he adds the wider population of Rome had no such qualms and were already plotting to remove Julianus from power, such had been Pertinax's popularity with the masses.

Julianus' situation was clearly precarious, with only the Praetorians keeping him in power. His first action, to sack Laetus, therefore seems strange. However, he clearly though the *praefectus praetorio* had form and chose not to trust him. The once mighty prefect was then replaced with two new incumbents chosen by the guardsmen themselves, who the *Historia Augusta* name as Flavius

AD 193: 'THE YEAR OF THE FIVE EMPERORS'

Genialis and Tullius Crispinus.[70] However, Julianus also knew he needed to widen his power base if he was to survive, and sought the support of the military more broadly. This included minting coins with the dedication 'Harmony with the soldiers'. He also pardoned Sulpicianus and retained him as city prefect, hoping the continuity would secure the support of the *cohortes urbanaes* and *vigilies urbanae*.

However, the key players who would determine the length of Julianus' reign weren't in Rome at all, but far away on the borders of the empire. These were Severus on the Danube, Niger in Syria, and Albinus in Britain. Between them, they controlled most of the elite troops in the empire. The only one Julianus thought might be a natural supporter was Albinus given the latter came from the same city as Julianus' mother, *Hadrumetum* in Africa Proconsularis. However, in the event all three contenders moved swiftly against him as soon as news of Pertinax's death and his elevation reached them. To recap, this would have taken five days for Severus, and eleven days for Niger and Albinus, using the fast horse relays and speedy maritime transport of the *cursus publicus*.

Clearly, Severus in Pannonia Superior had a major advantage here compared to Niger and Albinus, with both the latter based at the far extremes of empire. When the news reached Niger in mid-to-late April, he was in his provincial capital *Antioch-on-the-Orontes*. Knowing Rome would be in chaos, he sensed a unique opportunity. Gathering any nearby troops and a large crowd of citizenry, he addressed them about the situation in Rome, setting himself up to be acclaimed emperor. The tactic worked, with his troops robing him in imperial purple. He then began to plan his march west to secure the throne in Rome.

Meanwhile, when word reached Albinus in London (Roman *Londinium*), the result was the same, with the three British legions (II *Augusta*, VI *Victrix* and XX *Valeria Victrix*) promptly declaring him emperor, too. Albinus then began planning his own march on Rome, this time eastwards.

However, unsurprisingly the first mover against Julianus was Severus on the Danube, only five days away. There he sat with his veteran legions like a 'Sword of Damocles' poised above the Italian peninsula. When word reached him of Pertinax's demise at *Carnuntum*, his provincial capital and the lynchpin legionary fortress anchoring Rome's defences on the upper Danube, he reacted with cold fury. The fortress' incumbent *legio* XIV *Gemina Martia Victrix* proclaimed him emperor almost immediately. Contemporary sources say at first he tried to decline the offer in a traditional display of reluctance. However, these theatrics didn't last long, with the planning for his strike south beginning soon after. This took time, given Severus had to ensure the Danubian *limes* were secure before detaching troops for the new operation. Wisely, he decided to leave Pannonia Superior's *legio* X *Gemina* on the Danube to provide the core force defending the northern frontier there, then deployed large numbers of auxiliary troops from the provincial interior to replace *legio* XIV *Gemina Martia Victrix*. This elite legion, and one totally loyal to Severus, would lead his charge south. He then positioned Pannonia Inferior's *legio* II *Adiutrix* as a strategic reserve, ready to head south if needed to support his challenge for the throne or north if the *limes* were threatened. Severus also received pledges of support from all the other legions along the Danube and Rhine, including those in Moesia Inferior where the senior *legate* at the time was his brother Geta. Then, to secure his western flank, he sent an offer to Albinus saying if the latter supported his bid for the throne then the British governor would become his *caesar*, or junior emperor. Albinus received the courier seven days later and quickly accepted, realizing he was in no position to challenge Severus at that point given the latter's proximity to Rome.

Severus then set off, gathering *legio* I *Adiutrix pia fidelis* on the way. He soon reached Ravenna with his 11,000 men and crossed the Rubicon river separating Cisalpine Gaul from Italy proper, emulating Caesar's similar march south in 49 BC. The analogy would

AD 193: 'THE YEAR OF THE FIVE EMPERORS'

have pleased Severus. Once satisfied Julianus had not deployed an army to oppose him, he then headed straight for Rome. Travelling along the *via Flaminia* trunk road from Rimini, his lightning advance arrived in southern Etruria at the end of May. There, astride this key imperial trunk road, he camped 50km from the imperial capital, sending his scouts south to assess the situation.

In Rome, Julianus' shaky position was quickly deteriorating. With no support from the public and only nominal support from the Senate, he was totally reliant on the Praetorians to keep him in power. Soon, the guards began mocking him publicly, showing where the true agency in the relationship lay. Then word reached Rome that Severus had been elevated by his troops and was less than three days march away with his two crack legions. Shortly after, news arrived that Niger had also proclaimed himself emperor. For a short while, it was the latter who became the champion of the masses, in one incident a mob occupying the Colosseum and calling for him and his Syrian legions to come to Rome and save them from Julianus. However, the *Historia Augusta* says Severus' agents managed to intercept two key proclamations Niger had sent, one to the Senate and one to the Roman citizenry.[71] With news from Niger now withering, attention in Rome turned to Severus and what he would do next.

Julianus knew his situation was desperate. At this stage of the Principate, the legions were still based along its far-flung borders. He therefore had no strategic reserve to call on to help secure his position. With few viable options, he first tried to reason with Severus, sending the *praefectus praetorio* Crispinus north with an offer to share the throne. Severus executed him out of hand, suspecting the prefect had been sent to kill him. Julianus now panicked and ordered the Senate to declare Severus an enemy. The public met this with derision. Then, with Severus' legionary spearheads preparing to close on the imperial capital, Julianus ordered all military personnel in the region to come to his aid, though note none were legionaries. Dio, an eyewitness as Julianus' short rule descended into chaos, provides a detailed description of events:[72]

> 'The city during these days became nothing more nor less than a camp ... Great was the turmoil on the part of the various forces that were encamped and drilling – men, horses, and elephants – and great also was the fear inspired in the rest of the population by the armed troops, because the latter hated them.'

The mention of elephants is interesting given the last time war elephants were used in a battle involving the Romans was at Thapsus in 46 BC when Quintus Caecilius Metellus Scipio deployed them against Julius Caesar in North Africa. Those which accompanied Claudius at the close of his invasion campaign in Britain in AD 43 were either beasts destined for the arena, or from the emperor's own menagerie. That was the case here, too, though they proved a disaster, with Dio saying that when fitted with fighting towers they threw them off their backs.[73] Meanwhile, regarding the other emergency recruits, it is unclear who these were. Some argue they included marines and sailors from the *Classis Misenensis* Tyrrhenian fleet, usually based at Miseno on the Bay of Naples. These may have been the troops Dio says had forgotten how to drill, much to the amusement of the citizens.[74] It was also at this time Julianus executed Laetus, the former *praefectus praetorio*, and the unfortunate Marcia, his fellow conspirator in the assassination of Commodus. Julianus was clearly taking no chances, removing anyone close to the throne who posed even the smallest risk.

However, it was all to no avail as Severus now made his move. Marching at whirlwind speed, he soon arrived on the outskirts of Rome near the Flaminian Gate. This was a key entrance to the city through which the *via Flaminia* headed directly to the *forums* of Trajan, Caesar and Augustus, and the *forum Romanum*. From his camp, Severus sent word to the Praetorians that if they handed over the killers of Pertinax they would be unharmed. The guard knew

AD 193: 'THE YEAR OF THE FIVE EMPERORS'

they were no match for his Marcomannic War veterans and agreed immediately. At this point, Herodian then has Severus slipping small units of his legionaries into the city in disguise to prepare for his later formal entry.[75]

With the Praetorians switching sides, the Senate now realised Julianus was a liability. The new *consul* Silius Messalla quickly gathered any Senators not in hiding in the *athenaeum* to consider their next move, the location chosen so not to alarm Julianus. They voted unanimously to execute him, now calling him a usurper. At this point, the emperor was still in the imperial palace on the Palatine Hill bemoaning his fate and desperately seeking survival. He sent word to the Senate that he was willing to hand over imperial power to Severus. However, it was too late, with the Senate sending a military tribune to kill him. The soldier caught Julianus unawares in his private quarters, with Dio saying his last words '... but what evil have I done? Whom have I killed?'[76]

Julianus' body was handed over to his wife and daughter who buried it in his great-grandfather's tomb near the fifth milestone on the *via Labicana* road to Latium. Then, to make absolutely clear their change of heart, the Senate passed a *damnatio memoriae* motion against Julianus, officially wiping him from existence. There is no record of what happened to the troops gathered by Julianus in Rome, it being likely they headed out of the city as soon as possible.

Shortly afterwards Severus, still outside the city walls, moved west to east through the outer suburbs from the Flaminian Gate to the Praetorian camp beside the Viminal Gate. There, his response to their repeated disloyalty to his friend Pertinax and later Julianus was typically robust. With his Danubian veterans nearby, he ordered the Praetorians out of their barracks dressed only in their underwear. He then had them muster in their parade ground where he harangued them at length, saying they deserved to die 1,000 times over. Finally, he cashiered them, ordering them to strip naked. He then banished them, including the officers, to live at least 160km away from Rome for the rest of their lives. At the same time the murderers of Pertinax, earlier handed over by the guard, were brutally hacked to death. Dio says Severus also ordered that Narcissus, the wrestler who had killed Commodus, be tied up and thrown 'to the wild beasts'.[77] This was a day of reckoning indeed.

The next day, Severus entered the city proper through the Flaminian Gate. Based on the available historical data, the date was most likely 9 June AD 193. The *Historia Augusta* describes what happened next in detail:[78]

> 'Severus, armed himself and attended by armed men, entered the city and went up to the Capitoline Hill where the city's key temples were located; thence he proceeded, still fully armed, to the imperial palace on the Palatine Hill, having the standards, which he had taken from the praetorians, borne before him not raised erect but trailing on the ground. And then throughout the whole city, in temples, in porticoes, and in the dwellings on the Palatine, the soldiers took up their quarters as though in barracks.'

This was a textbook military coup, with the sequence of events very interesting. First, he visited the Capitoline's religious precinct to secure the backing of the priests there, as had Pertinax earlier in the year. Then, he moved into the palace to show clear intent to the political classes of Rome. Only on the following day, still fully armed and surrounded by battle hardened troops, did he travel down the Palatine Hill and through the *forum Romanum* to visit a by now very cowed Senate in the *curia*. The Senators swiftly acclaimed him emperor, which was no surprise given the massive military presence backing him. Dio, no fan of Severus, says the new emperor then gave an oath to the Senators that none would be put to death, though then adds that Severus soon went back on his word and executed any patricians who overtly opposed him.[79] Much later this included Julius Solon, the Senator who had actually framed the Senate's original conciliatory decree naming Severus emperor. Pertinax's earlier reign of discipline and order was over, replaced by Severus' new regime of iron and blood. To secure himself in power, Severus then trebled the number of *cohorts urbanae*, doubled the number of *vigils urbanae*, and reformed the Praetorian Guard with veterans from his own Danube legions, doubling it in size at the same time. He also doubled the size of the *equites singulares Augusti* imperial guard cavalry.

Pertinax now came to the fore again. Earlier, as soon as the fate of Julianus had been decided, the Senate immediately moved to rehabilitate the first incumbent in the 'Year of the Five Emperors', even before Severus had arrived in the city. The *Historia Augusta* then says that Pertinax was 'raised to the rank of the Gods', indicating the Senate deified him.[80] Then, once Severus was firmly in post as emperor, further recognition followed. The new emperor ordered Pertinax acclaimed yet again in the Senate. Dio then adds that Severus:[81]

'... commanded that his name [Pertinax] should be mentioned at the close of all prayers and all oaths; he also ordered that a golden image of Pertinax should be carried into the Circus Maximus on a cart drawn by elephants, and that three gilded thrones should be borne into the other amphitheatres in his honour.'

Severus then arranged a grand official state funeral for his former friend and mentor. Here, the *Historia Augusta* says that in place of the already interned body a wax effigy was used 'such as that used by censors', the latter referencing the practice of using an image in the state funerals of senior magistrate who'd died far away from Rome.[82] Of the actual event, Dio then gives a precise description that is worth reporting in full given the level of detail:[83]

'His funeral, in spite of the time that had elapsed since his death, was carried out as follows. In the forum Romanum a wooden platform was constructed hard by the marble rostra [public speaking platform], upon which was set a shrine, without walls, but surrounded by columns, cunningly wrought of both ivory and gold.

In it there was placed a bier of the same materials, surrounded by heads of both land and sea animals and adorned with coverlets of purple and gold. Upon this rested the effigy of Pertinax, laid out in triumphal garb; and a comely youth was keeping the flies away from it with peacock feathers, as though it were really a person sleeping. While the body lay in state, Severus as well as we Senators and our wives approached, wearing mourning; the women sat in the porticos, and we men under the open sky. After this there moved past, first, images of all the famous Romans of old, then choruses of boys and men, singing a dirge-like hymn to Pertinax; there followed all the subject nations, represented by bronze figures attired in native dress, and the guilds of the city itself – those of the lictors, the scribes, the heralds, and all the rest. Then came images of other men who had been distinguished for some exploit or invention or manner of life. Behind these were the cavalry and infantry in armour, the racehorses, and all the funeral offerings that the emperor and we senators and our wives, and the corporations of the city, had sent. Following them came an altar gilded all over and adorned with ivory and gems from India. When these had passed by, Severus mounted the rostra and read a eulogy of Pertinax. We shouted our approval many times in the course of his address, now praising and now lamenting Pertinax, but our shouts were loudest when he concluded. Finally, when the bier was about to be moved, we all lamented and wept together. It was brought down from the platform by the high priests and the magistrates, not only those who were actually in office at the time by also those who had been elected for the ensuing year; and they gave it to certain knights to carry. All the rest of us, now, marched ahead of the bier, some beating our breasts and others playing a dirge on the flute, but the emperor followed behind all the rest; and in this order we arrived at the campus Martius. There a pyre had been built in the form of a tower having three stories and adorned with ivory and gold as well as a number of statues, while on its very summit was placed a gilded chariot that Pertinax had been wont to drive.

AD 193: 'THE YEAR OF THE FIVE EMPERORS'

Inside this pyre the funeral offerings were cast and the bier was placed in it, and then Severus and the relatives of Pertinax kissed the effigy. The emperor then ascended a tribunal, while we, the Senate, except the magistrates, took our places on wooden stands in order to view the ceremonies both safely and conveniently. The magistrates and the equestrian order, arrayed in a manner befitting their station, and likewise the cavalry and the infantry, passed in and out around the pyre performing intricate evolutions, both those of peace and those of war. Then at last the consuls applied fire to the structure, and when this had been done, an eagle flew aloft from it.'

Severus later accepted the addition of Pertinax to his own name at the suggestion of the Senate, this recorded on numerous monuments, for example the inauguration stone in the public theatre at Minturno (Roman *Minturnae*) on the *via Appia*, the Arch of Septimius Severus in the *forum Romanum*, and atop the *propylaeum* of the *Porticus Octaviae* near the *circus Flamininus* as rebuilt by Severus and Caracalla.

Notably, the second dates to AD 202 at the earliest, the latter after AD 203. Thus Severus' association with Pertinax through nomenclature was no short term gesture. The new emperor also erected a permanent shrine to Pertinax on the Capitoline Hill, and then appointed the latter's son, also called Publius Helvius Pertinax, to be the *flamen* chief priest of a new cult dedicated to the newly deified Pertinax. Further, the Marcian brotherhood who led the worship of the deified Marcus Aurelius was renamed, at least temporarily, as the Helviani brotherhood in honour of Pertinax. Circus game days were also added to the Roman calendar to commemorate Pertinax's date of accession and his birthday.

So began the eighteen-year reign of Severus, the great warrior emperor. His first priorities now Rome was secure were to deal with Albinus in Britain and Niger in Syria. Given the former had already accepted the post of *caesar*, the emperor was free to first tackle the latter. So began a new round of full-scale civil wars of a scale to match anything in the later Republic, as three political titans fought to be last man standing.

5

Civil War

As AD 193 ended, Severus was in power in Rome, but not securely. Both Gaius Pescennius Niger in Syria and Decimus Clodius Albinus in Britain had also claimed the throne. Though the latter, as Severus' new *caesar*, was out of the running for now, Niger remained a major threat, and even now was casting his eyes west towards Rome. The new emperor therefore made the Syrian governor his priority and so began his two campaigns in the east. The first, huge in scale, featured the crucial AD 194 Battle of Issus where Niger was finally defeated, and a subsequent operation against breakaway vassal states. The second was even bigger, where he ultimately sacked the Parthian capital Ctesiphon in AD 198. Between them he faced Albinus' inevitable rebellion when the British governor made his final bid for power, leading to the titanic Battle of Lugdunum in AD 197. This was the largest civil war engagement in Roman history.

PESCENNIUS NIGER AND THE BATTLE OF ISSUS

The *Historia Augusta* says Pescennius Niger was born in central Italy to an equestrian family, his father called Annius Fuscus and his mother Lampridia.[1] No details are given of the year he was born, though based on his later career it was likely between AD 135 and AD 140. We also have no insight into his father's career, though his grandfather was a 'supervisor' in Aquino (Roman *Aquinum*). This was the key town controlling much of the *via Appia* trunk road between Rome and Capua. Niger also had a brother who shared his *cognomen* called Publius Pescennius Niger. We don't know if he was younger or older. Publius is recorded on an AD 183 inscription in Rome as a member of the *Fratres Arvalis* Arval Brethren, the important body of priests who offered annual sacrifices to guarantee good harvests.

As a young man, Niger enrolled in the military and was soon posted to join *legio* II *Traiana Fortis* in the province of Aegyptus. This began his long association with the east.[2] He was based at the legionary fortress of *Nicopolis* near the provincial capital Alexandria, initially as a junior centurion before rising steadily through the ranks with exemplary service. Eventually, he became the legion's *primus pilus*. This was a very senior post indeed, effectively making Niger fourth in command of the legion after the *praefectus castrorum* camp prefect, *tribunus laticlavius* second-in-command and *legatus legionis* legionary commander. Niger was then transferred to the Danube frontier where he continued to impress, playing a key role in the campaigns of Marcus Aurelius in the Second Marcomannic War.[3] Later, under Commodus, he was adlected to the Senate and as a newly promoted *legatus legionis* helped lead the Roman campaign against the Iazyges Sarmatians and Germanic Buri in Dacia. Here, he fought alongside fellow *legates* including Marcus Valerius Maximianus and Albinus, helping bring an end to the Third Marcomannic War. Again, Niger impressed, and as a reward Commodus appointed him a suffected *consul* in the mid-AD 180s (the exact year is unclear), around the same time the emperor took the title *Germanicus Maximus*. Niger performed well and was again suffected as *consul* in AD 190.[4]

Niger's next major promotion was again at the behest of Commodus, this time as governor of the key eastern frontier province of Syria in AD 191. It seems likely here the *praefectus praetorio* Laetus also had a hand in the appointment, with some contemporary accounts also suggesting the emperor's wrestling partner (and later assassin) Narcissus also played a role, though modern historians dismiss this.[5]

We have good descriptions of Niger at this point in his life, which describe him as tall but overweight, and with a liking for wine. He also had a booming voice that could carry across the courtyard of a legionary fortress *principia*. Meanwhile, his reputation as a successful military man continued to grow, and once in Syria he was soon winning victories again, this time in border skirmishers with the Parthians and their Lakhmid Arab allies. This stood him in good stead with his troops in the east, with whom he proved very popular.

Niger was still governing in Syria at the beginning of AD 193 when news came of the assassination first of Commodus, and then three months later of Pertinax. On both occasions, it took eleven days for the reports to reach him in his provincial capital *Antioch-on-the-Orontes*, six days longer than it had taken to reach Severus in *Carnuntum*. Thus, by the time he learned of Pertinax's demise, Severus had already been proclaimed emperor by *legio* XIV *Gemina Martia Victrix* for a week. Knowing time was against him, Niger quickly made his bid for the throne and was soon proclaimed emperor himself in *Antioch*. This is the moment Herodian has his soldiers drape him in imperial purple and give him tokens of imperial rank.[6] He also added a further *cognomen* to his name at this point, this *Justus* (the Just), hoping it would give him credibility with the wider public in the east. Back in Rome, Didius Julianus clearly thought him a real threat as on receiving news of events in *Antioch* he sent a centurion east with orders to assassinate Niger, though the plot came to nothing. However, the Syrian governor's attempts to communicate with the Senate and population in Rome were then thwarted by Severus who, as he approached Rome, intercepted Niger's two key the proclamations.

Events now moved quickly as Severus moved to secure his throne in Rome. First, after assuring the support of Albinus with his offer to become his *caesar*, Severus appointed his equestrian kinsman Gaius Fulvius Plautianus to be the *praefectus praetorio* in charge of his newly reformed Praetorian Guard (promoting him from his earlier role as Pertinax's *praefectus vehiculorum* in charge of the *cursus publicus*).

Plautianus was then ordered to capture Niger's children, these either resident in Rome at the time or on the family estates in Aquino. We do not know how many children he had, or their names, but they were now held hostage by Severus as collateral against Niger.

Meanwhile, the Syrian governor moved to secure his position, reaching out to his fellow governors in the Levantine provinces who all declared their support for him. This included Asellius Aemilianus, the highly popular proconsul of Asia and previous incumbent as Syrian governor before Niger's appointment there. Aemilianus had at first supported his own kinsman, Albinus, after Pertinax's assassination, but when the British governor sided with Severus, he switched to Niger given the latter's proximity in *Antioch*. Aemilianus then crossed from Asia to Europe across the Bosporus, the narrow waterway in northwestern Turkey linking the Black Sea with the Sea of Marmara. His target was Byzantium, which he occupied for Niger. This ancient Greek city had been founded in 657 BC by Byzas, ruler of the early Greek *poleis* of Megara in western Attica near Athens. As the location for his new settlement, Byzas chose a site on the south-western tip of the Bosporus defined by a pristine natural harbour created by a major inlet later called the Golden Horn. Crucially, by the late second century AD Byzantium also controlled access to the network of major trunk roads traversing the northern Balkans, and then on to the Danubian frontier and beyond. It was thus a key transport node which Aemilianus now secured for Niger, giving the Syrian governor an important foothold in Europe.

With his western flank secure, Niger next sent loyal troops from Syria to Egypt where *legio* II *Traiana Fortis* had yet to declare for any of the imperial candidates. Crucially, given it was the only incumbent legion there, it controlled the grain supply from Egypt to Rome. Severus realised the danger immediately and sent an urgent delegation to try to secure the legion's support, but it arrived too late, landing in Alexandria to find the legionaries had announced their support for Niger.

CIVIL WAR

Severus therefore deployed loyal troops in Cyrenaica to secure its eastern border with Aegyptus. The emperor then deployed naval assets to blockade Alexandria, preventing the rapid redeployment by sea of the Egyptian legionaries to support Niger back in *Antioch*.

This was a serious issue for Niger given he only had the support of six other legions. These were his own three in Syria, *legio* IV *Scythica*, *legio* III *Gallica* and *legio* XVI *Flavia Firma*, then *legio* III *Cyrenaica* in Arabia Petraea, and finally *legio* VI *Ferrata fidelis constans* and *legio* X *Fretensis* in Syria Palaestina. This compared to the sixteen, which, by this time, Severus had under his control along the Danube and Rhine. Realising he would likely lose a lengthy war given the disparity in numbers, Niger therefore decided to go on the offensive. His first move was to send a large force from Byzantium into the northern Balkans to secure the trunk roads there.

As they advanced, in late AD 193 his troops promptly defeated a small Severan army under the *legate* Lucius Fabius Cilo at *Perinthus* on the Sea of Marmara, causing heavy casualties.

This prompted Severus to intervene directly in the east, gathering a large army south of the Danube which he led in person. He also sent another *legate* called Tiberius Claudius Candidus ahead with an advance guard comprised of Danubian veterans. This was given the title the *exercitus Illyricus*, with *the legate* styled the *dux execitus Illyrici*.[7] When this crack force arrived at *Perinthus* they drove Niger's army back to Byzantium and then crossed the Sea of Marmara to Asia. Severus, following behind, stationed himself at *Perinthus*. From there, before launching his main offensive, he offered Niger the opportunity to surrender and go into exile. It is worth noting here there is no indication of personal animosity between Severus and Niger. Both had served happily together in the Marcomannic Wars and knew each other well. However, with the murder of Pertinax fate had intervened, after which *realpolitik* set in. Both were now being championed by their own supporters and troops, all of whom had invested in their success. Backing down was therefore not an option. Thus, Niger declined and vowed to fight on.

Severus, receiving Niger's rejection, then ordered Candidus to advance further west to the town of *Cyzicus* on the southern shore of the Sea of Marmara. There he found Aemilianus with a scratch force of eastern loyalists blocking his path. A meeting engagement ensued, with Niger's troops routed and Aemilianus captured. Dragged before Candidus in chains, he was promptly beheaded – a sad end for a long-time servant of the empire.

However, Byzantium remained loyal to Niger, the latter using the *Classis Syriaca* regional fleet to maintain communications with this key city. Its continued resistance proved a serious issue for Severus who soon took it under siege. However, against the odds the city held out tenaciously, and it took until the end of AD 195 before it finally fell. After this it was brutally sacked over a period of weeks, though Severus was later to rebuild much of it, including the famous Baths of Zeuxippus, the original hippodrome chariot racing circuit and the city's protective Hellenistic walls.

Meanwhile, whilst Byzantium held out, the emperor continued his advance and had soon crossed to Asia himself. There he quickly appointed Cilo as the new governor of Bithynia et Pontus and then advanced on the important city of İznik (Roman *Nicaea*) where Niger waited with another hastily gathered army. Another battle ensued, with Dio providing excellent detail:[8]

> 'Here a great battle took place between the two armies, with varying fortunes. Some fought in close order on the plain, others occupied the hills and hurled stones and javelins at their opponents from the higher ground, and still others got into boats and discharged their arrows at the enemy from a nearby lake. At first the followers of Severus, commanded by Candidus, were victorious, for they had an advantage in fighting from higher ground; but later, when Niger positioned himself at the head of his troops [presumably to rally them], the pursuers became the pursued, and victory rested with Niger's men. However, then Candidus seized hold of his legionary standard-bearers and forced them to turn round facing the enemy, at the same

time upbraiding the soldiers for their flight; at this his men were ashamed, turned back, and once more got the upper hand of their opponents. Indeed, they would have utterly destroyed them, had not the city [of İznik] been near and had not a dark night come on.'

For some reason, Candidus then failed to invest İznik. This allowed Niger to flee east into the Taurus Mountains where the bulk of his army awaited. There, he ordered the fortification of the mountain passes to prevent Severus and his army from targeting Syria directly as AD 193 ended. Niger himself then returned to *Antioch*, though by now his support in the Levant was beginning to fracture, with some of the key cities switching sides. These included *Laodicea* in western Anatolia and the important port of Tyre. Then, on 13 February AD 194, Aegyptus declared its support for Severus. Arabia Petraea followed soon after. Niger now only had direct control of Syria and Syria Palaestina.

Despite these successes, Severus was typically pragmatic as he gathered his forces over the winter months in eastern Anatolia for an assault on Syria. Though Candidus had defeated Niger at İznik, the Syrian governor had escaped and was now consolidating, ready for the new campaigning season. The emperor therefore dismissed Candidus for failing to prevent Niger's escape, though he was soon back in imperial favour. In the short term, Candidus' replacement was yet another *legate*, this time a highly experienced Illyrian called Publius Cornelius Anullinus, who Severus himself had previously served under.

In early Spring AD 194, Anullinus marched on the Cilician Gates, a key pass using the gorge of the Gökoluk River through the Taurus Mountains to link the Anatolian Plateau with the lowlands of Cilicia. The Severan advance quickly punched through Niger's garrison there, opening up the coastal route to *Antioch* and, beyond, to Syria. The final battle of the campaign took place in May AD 194 at Issus just to the north of Niger's provincial capital, this the narrow coastal plain near the modern Turkish town of Iskenderun

(Roman *Alexandretta*, or Little Alexandria). This had been founded by Alexander the Great after his famous victory there over the Achaemenid Persian king Darius III in 333 BC. The location was a superb defensive position, the plain only 2.6km wide between the Gulf of Issus and the surrounding mountains, with the usually shallow Pinaros River bisecting it east to west.[9] Here, Niger chose to challenge the Severan advance, though this time from the south bank rather than the north as Darius had centuries earlier. Sadly, the result was the same for the Syrian governor, the defender paying for a lack of battlefield initiative with total defeat.

On arrival at Issus, Anullinus chose to attack as soon as he saw Niger's army arrayed for battle. Here, he was helped by one of Niger's legions defecting in the build-up to the encounter. It seems likely Niger was outnumbered by the Severans anyway, especially after the emperor had earlier reinforced Anullinus with another army under a *legate* called Valerianus. However, with the defection, Niger was now seriously disadvantaged. Lacking the numbers to attack, he chose instead to rely on his defensive position and await the Severan assault. The result was a complete, humiliating defeat.

Niger fled south with his bodyguard to *Antioch* where he ordered the city to be evacuated, and then headed southeast at speed, hoping to reach the protection of the Parthian king Vologases V (AD 191–AD 208) at his court in Ctesiphon on the Tigris River. Vologases had been a vocal supporter of Niger's bid for power, hoping to gain territory along the eastern frontier in return. He had also moved to destabilise the Roman vassal states in the border region including Osrhoene, Adiabene and Hatra. However, Niger was captured soon after and swiftly decapitated, with his severed head taken first to Severus (by then in *Antioch*), and then to Byzantium where it was displayed on a pole in the hope it would encourage the city to surrender (though this failed, and the siege continued). Finally, Niger's head was sent to Rome, where his children had already been executed. His wife was also murdered, either with Niger, or in Rome after the Syrian governor's defeat.

The province of Syria was very wealthy, especially its capital *Antioch*, and Niger had ensured his time as governor proved highly profitable for his family. He'd accrued a large portfolio of rich agricultural estates there which, in a short time, made him one of the wealthiest men in the empire. Severus now took full advantage, confiscating Niger's estates in his own name. He also treated Niger's supporters in *Antioch* very harshly, particular the eastern Senators resident there, hoping to make an example of them, and also with an eye on more familial profit. Most of those targeted by Severus lost everything. Of note though, in what was the first of three Severan proscriptions of Senators and leading equestrians, most of those targeted in the east lived. As will be seen, that was certainly not the case after his defeat of Albinus in the west, and later triumphant return to Rome.

Some who fell foul of Severus' retribution chose to flee rather than answer one-sided accusations. The emperor dealt with these swiftly, appointing a back-in-favour Candidus to be his *dux adversus rebelles Asiae* tasked with tracking them down. He proved highly effective, and by early AD 195 Niger's remaining supporters in the east had been neutralised. Severus then moved to place his own supporters in key positions of power there, for example Quintus Venidius Rufus being appointed governor of Cilicia in Anatolia. He was a Severan loyalist whose kinsman Marius Maximus, the Senator who had earlier first acclaimed Pertinax emperor, was *legate* of *legio I Flavia Minervia pia fidelis* in Bonn (Roman *Bonna*). Rufus was later made governor of the key northern frontier province of Germania Inferior and, while there, played a key role transferring troops from the Danube and Rhine to support Severus' campaigns in Britain.[10] It was also at this point Severus initiated the division of Syria into two new provinces, Coele-Syria in the north and Syro-Phoenicia in the south. As first governor of the former, he installed a North African from Djemila in modern Algeria, Lucius Alfenus Senecio, later to play a crucial role in triggering Severus' campaigns in Britain at the end of his life. The emperor was also acclaimed *imperator* three times by his army to mark his three victories over the eastern governor.

Earlier, Severus had already ordered medallions and coins to be minted in Rome to celebrate Candidus' defeat of Aemilianus at *Cyzicus* and Niger himself at İznik. The prominence of North Africa in this coinage reflects its key role supplying grain to Rome. It also shows the importance Severus' home region was to play in his reign. This was an emperor very proud of his North African origins.

Next, after Anullinus' decisive victory at Issus, Severus ordered another issue of celebratory coins. These were the first he minted in *Antioch*, and here he followed a policy earlier instituted by Niger. This was to ensure the *denarii* had a higher silver content than the debased examples that had been in circulation since Commodus' reign. This proved highly popular, with Severus then ordering the other imperial mints across the empire to follow suit. This was a public relations exercise writ large, saying the good times of the earlier Principate were back. Further, Moorhead says Severus minted a far higher ratio of *denarii* to base coins than previously,[11] a policy Birley calls the ancient equivalent of printing money.[12]

With Niger now dead and his followers in Asia gone, Severus looked further east. In early AD 195, he gathered his army again and prepared to mount his first campaign there. His pretext came in the form of the vassal states Osrhoene, Adiabene and Hatra who, encouraged by Vologases V in Ctesiphon, had used the distraction of the eastern civil war to massacre the Roman garrisons in key border fortresses along the frontier. They then besieged the key city of Nisibis. Another motivation for Severus was the fact Byzantium had yet to fall, the city improbably hoping for an intervention by Albinus in far off Britain. Severus was reticent to turn his attention back west until the siege there had concluded. Further, he had to find a way to employ Niger's recently vanquished troops. Moving them east against a common threat was a good idea. Finally, Severus also knew that he now had the chance to emulate the great Trajan whose conquests in the east in the AD 110s, which he had led in person, expanded Roman control there to its furthest extent ever. Severus was a man of great ambition. Here was a chance to truly test his mettle, his aim to use the vassal state campaign as a springboard to target Parthia directly.

When Osrhoene, Adiabene and Hatra received word Severus was mustering his army against them, all quickly claimed allegiance to the new emperor. They argued their targets when attacking the Romans had been Niger's troops. However, the vassal states then gave their game away by keeping hold of the territory they had seized when Severus demanded they withdraw, no doubt with Parthia's continued encouragement.

In March, Severus crossed the frontier at Zeugma, his first target Urfa (Roman *Edessa*), the capital of Osrhoene. This surrendered immediately given the size of his army, with the vassal state then annexed and Gaius Julius Pacatianus installed as its new procurator. Notably, though, its ruler Abgar VIII was allowed to retain control of his capital and a small surrounding hinterland, at least for now, indicating Severus was hedging his bets on whether to create a new province or not while seeing how the rest of his campaign played out. This proved a shrewd move as, even though Osrhoene was indeed later made a province by Severus, Abgar proved a long-term supporter of the emperor and later visited Rome with a large entourage.

Once Osrhoene was pacified Severus swiftly moved on, capturing Erbil (Roman *Arbela*) in modern Kurdistan, the capital of Adiabene which then surrendered. Next, he advanced on Hatra which capitulated before the Romans arrived, saving the city from occupation by Severus. With Osrhoene, Adiabene and Hatra now back under Roman control the siege of Nisibis was lifted, with Severus then moving his army there to overwinter.

After the success of his campaign against the vassal states Severus adopted two new titles, *Parthicus Adiabenicus* and *Parthicus Arabicus*. Birley argues the latter's Arabian reference may refer to another success, perhaps diplomatic, further south of which today we have no record.[13] Meanwhile, we also know Julia Domna was with Severus given she was also awarded a title at the same time. This was *mater casotorum*, or matron of the camp. It is unclear if Caracalla and Geta were there, too, though this seems likely given the events which followed.

Back in Rome, when news of Severus' victories over Niger and the vassal states arrived, the Senate promptly voted the emperor a triumph. However, he declined the offer, saying he didn't want his first victories as emperor celebrated because they were in the context of a civil war. Interestingly, though, this didn't stop him building a triumphal arch in *Antioch*.

His army re-provisioned, and in early AD 196 Severus moved to test the Parthian frontier directly. He divided his army into three corps under the command of Candidus, the Italian patrician Titus Sextius Lateranus (*consul* the following year) and long-term Severan loyalist Julius Laetus. These targeted the Parthian fortresses along the border in a lightning campaign, which, despite dust storms and a shortage of drinking water, proved highly successful. All then returned to Nisibis. Severus knew Vologases would take time to respond given the distances involved, the fact that he was distracted dealing with rebellions in Persia and Media, and the feudal nature of his army. The emperor therefore ordered his three-army corps to deploy once more, this time commanded by Anullinus, Laetus again and another *legate* called Probus. More victories followed.

It was now late Spring and Severus headed back to *Antioch*. After his martial success he now took a series of administrative steps that had major implications for the wider empire. First, he proclaimed himself the son of Marcus Aurelius, and then issued celebratory coins on which he called himself the 'Son of the Deified Marcus Pius'. Second, he renamed his eldest son Marcus Aurelius Antoninus to reinforce Severan legitimacy through this new link with the Antonines (today known by his nickname Caracalla). Third, and most importantly, Severus announced that Antoninus was now his *caesar* and heir. This was a major development given Severus had already made Albinus in Britain his *caesar*. When the news reached Rome eleven days later, it caused consternation among many senators still unsure of Severus, the warrior who'd forced himself on them at the point of a sword three years earlier. Given Severus' treatment of many of their colleagues in the east after Niger's defeat, this is not surprising.

However, context is important here. Severus was always a careful decision maker, and never rash. It is thus highly likely that he knew exactly what he was doing in elevating Caracalla. Indeed, Herodian is explicit that Severus' earlier appointment of Albinus was a ruse to buy him time to deal with Niger.[14] The British governor, no fool himself, was equally aware he was being played by Severus. However, given his location in *Britannia*, when news of Pertinax's assassination reached him, he knew he was badly placed to act. Therefore, even though acclaimed emperor by his own troops, he instead accepted Severus' offer to be his *caesar* knowing it would also buy him time. In his thinking, this would allow him to see how things played out in the east before making his own decisive move. Therefore, when word reached him in London in June AD 196 of Caracalla's promotion, he was ready. A new and even more vicious round of civil war was about to begin.

CLODIUS ALBINUS AND THE BATTLE OF LUGDUNUM

Albinus declared himself *augustus* as soon as the news reached him from the east. The move was popular in Britain, with Herodian describing scenes of revelry.[15] This is unsurprising given his track record as a fine military and civilian leader, latterly in Britannia. Indeed, Kean and Frey say that of all the prime contenders for the throne in the mid-AD 190s, Albinus had the most prestigious pedigree.[16]

Albinus was born around AD 150 in *Hadrumetum* (also home of Didius Julianus), a port city originally founded by Phoenician colonists on the Gulf of Hammamet in modern Tunisia. The *Historia Augusta* says his father was a senator called Ceionius Postumus, while his mother was called Aurelia Messallina, adding he received a good education in Latin and Greek and showed 'signs of a haughty and warlike spirit' from a young age.[17]

Albinus began his progress along the *cursus honorum* early with a series of officer postings that saw him in the thick of the action along the frontiers of the empire. The *Historia Augusta* says his progress was helped by the patronage of three senior kinsman from North Africa called Lollius Serenus, Baebius Maecianus and Ceionius Postumianus.[18] It then provides detail about his early military service, saying:[19]

> 'In the capacity of a tribune he commanded a troop of Dalmatian horsemen; he also commanded soldiers of the First and the Fourth legions.'

Albinus proved an excellent soldier and entered the Senate with the patronage of Marcus Aurelius. After a series of further postings, all increasingly senior, he was promoted to become governor of Bithynia et Pontus in AD 175. There, he played a key role in ensuring this important province stayed loyal to the emperor during the rebellion of the Syrian *legate* Avidius Cassius the same year. Later, Albinus helped put down the usurpation. Afterwards, he was awarded two letters of merit from Marcus Aurelius. In one the emperor mentions Albinus' North African origins, but notably in the context of his pale skin, saying this didn't resemble that of his regional compatriots. The same letter also highlights the gravity of his character, saying it belied his young years.

Albinus then played a leading role in the Second Marcomannic War under Marcus Aurelius, and later under Commodus during the Third Marcomannic War. It was in this latter conflict he served alongside Severus and Niger. As a reward for his service, Albinus was made a suffect *consul* by Commodus in the mid-AD 180s, around the same time as Niger, though they never served in the role at the same time. Then, in AD 189, Albinus was promoted to the governorship of Germania Inferior, this the key frontier province on the lower Rhine. Here, he again impressed, leading troops north of the frontier on campaign against the Alamanni in Germania.

Albinus next appears in the primary sources holding a senior though unnamed magistracy in Rome, before a swift return to the Rhine again, this time to lead a legion. Again, he was successful, with Commodus holding games in his honour in Rome, where the emperor's spending on gladiators was notably lavish.

Next, at the suggestion of Laetus, Albinus was promoted a final time to become governor of Britannia in AD 192. It was there he heard of Commodus' assassination, with Kean and Frey saying he was complicit in some way, though given the distances involved this seems unlikely.[20] It was also there when he heard of Pertinax's murder three months later, after which his own legions proclaimed him emperor. Albinus then received Severus' offer to become his *caesar*, which he accepted after due consideration. At first this odd-couple arrangement worked for both parties. Severus was free to deal with his greatest threat, Niger in the east. Meanwhile, Albinus, in far off Britannia, gained additional legitimacy, and security too. This initial success is shown in coin issues minted in Rome at the time, with some featuring Albinus alongside Severus, and others Albinus alone. The British governor also shared the consulship with Severus in AD 194.

The *Historia Augusta* paints an evocative picture of Albinus at this time, saying he was:[21]

'... tall of stature, with unkempt curly hair and a broad expanse of brow. His skin was wonderfully white; many indeed think it was from this that he got his name. He had a womanish voice, almost as shrill as a eunuch's. He was easily roused, his anger was terrible, his rage relentless. In his pleasures he was changeable, for he sometimes craved wine and sometimes abstained. He had a thorough knowledge of arms and was not ineptly called the Catiline of his age.'

The reference to Lucius Sergius Catilina, better known as Catiline, is very interesting. Best known as the instigator of the Catilinarian Conspiracy, the failed attempt to violently take control of the Roman state in 63 BC, his name became a byword for villainy in Roman literature. Here again, we see the influence of later Severan propaganda.

There is no doubt Severus knew making Caracalla his *caesar* and heir would fracture his relationship with Albinus. However, the emperor was also keen the British governor make the first move, mindful of what today would be called the 'optics' back in Rome. Albinus duly did.

In London, the British governor launched his final bid for the throne in October AD 196. There, he'd gathered the *legates* and most *tribunes* from all the leading military units in Britain. This included his three legions, Caerleon-based *legio* II *Augusta*, Chester-based *legio* XX *Valeria Victrix* and York-based *legio* VI *Victrix*.

The officers proclaimed him augustus unanimously. Albinus then set out his plans to seize the throne, and soon his troops were readying to travel to Gaul.

In Antioch, Severus received the news Albinus had usurped a month later. Given this was the outcome he likely expected, he was ready to move immediately. First, he wrote to the Senate, chastising many there for encouraging Albinus. He then ordered the assembly to declare Albinus a public enemy. This went to a vote on 15 December, this date based on Dio's reference that it took place 'on the day of the last chariot race before the holidays'.[22] The senators voted unanimously in favour of Severus' demand.

The *Historia Augusta* records Severus' letter to the Senate at length. I detail it here in full given the insight it provides regarding his allegations of patrician support for Albinus. First, in a preamble, it sets the scene:[23]

> 'Albinus was beloved by the Senators as not one of the emperors before him. This was chiefly due, however, to their hatred of Severus, who was greatly detested by the Senate because of his cruelty.'

Here the *Historia Augusta*, usually more balanced in its view of the Severan Dynasty than either Dio or Herodian, reflects the anti-Severan primary sources used by the anonymous author. Next, it sets out the letter itself:[24]

'Nothing that can happen, O Conscript Fathers, could give me greater sorrow than that you should endorse Albinus in preference to Severus. It was I who gave the city grain [a reference to the North African cura annonae], I who waged many wars for the state, I who gave oil to the people of Rome [likely another North African reference], so much that the world could hardly contain it, and I who slew Pescennius Niger and freed you from the ills of a tyrant. A fine requital, truly, you have made me, a fine expression of thanks! A man from Africa, a native of Hadrumetum, who pretends to derive descent from the blood of the Ceionii, you have raised to a lofty place; you have even wished to make him your ruler, though I am your ruler and my children are still alive. Was there no other man in all this senate whom you might love, who might love you? You raised even his brother to honours [our first mention of this]; and you expect to receive at his hands, one a consulship, another a praetorship, and another the insignia of any office whatever. You have failed, moreover, to show me the spirit of gratitude which your forefathers showed in the face of Piso's plot, which they showed Trajan, and showed but lately in opposing Avidius Cassius. This fellow, false and ready for lies of every kind, who has even fabricated a noble lineage, you have now preferred to me. Why, even in the Senate we must hear Statilius Corfulenus proposing to vote honours to Albinus and his brother, and all that was lacking was that the noble fellow should also vote him a triumph over me. It is even a greater source of chagrin, that some of you thought he should be praised for his knowledge of letters, when in fact he is busied with old wives' songs, and grows senile amid the Milesian stories from Carthage that his friend Apuleius wrote and such other learned nonsense.'

For the record, there is no surviving evidence any Senator supported Albinus in the way Severus alleges. Further, one should note here there were no dissenters in the vote to outlaw Albinus when demanded by Severus. Indeed, the patricians would have been foolish to side against the emperor given the widely held view Severus was the better soldier. Their contemporary Dio provides context here:[25]

> 'Albinus excelled in family and education, but his adversary was superior in warfare and was a skilful commander.'

Before the year's end, Severus then began his march west for the final showdown with Albinus, knowing the British governor was the last obstacle to his undisputed hold on power. Here, Herodian emphasises the speed of Severus' advance:[26]

> 'The emperor himself set out on the march, through scorning heat and cold alike, and gave the army no respite for holidays or rest.'

His personal entourage included the imperial family, first and foremost Julia Domna, who made a strong impression on notables and the public alike as they travelled west through Anatolia.

Albinus also moved quickly, gathering his three British legions and most of the auxiliaries from the province. All were ferried to Gaul by the *Classis Britannica*. The most likely landing place was Boulogne-Sur-Mer, the British regional fleet's headquarters. Here Albinus aimed to gather a great army to challenge Severus, his bold move immediately rewarded when Lucius Novius Rufus (not the Quintus Venidius Rufus already mentioned), governor of the key province of Hispania Tarraconensis, declared for him. This gave Albinus another legion, the León-based *legio* VII *Gemina*, which quickly moved north through the Pyrenees to join him.

Severus then tried to assassinate Albinus, though the assassins were captured, tortured and confessed. Albinus responded by doubling the size of his bodyguard. He then moved to take the fight direct

The Severan Tondo, a contemporary tempura painting on a wood panel of the imperial family, now in the Altes Museum in Berlin. (Wikimedia Commons)

Arch of Septimius Severus, Leptis Magna. (Wikimedia Commons)

Late Roman soldiers on the Arch of Constantine, Rome. Severus began the series of military reforms which saw the classic Principate legionary evolve into this more flexible type of warrior.

Djémila, Roman *Cuicul*, in the Atlas Mountains in modern Algeria. A key city controlling access from the Mediterranean coast to the Saharan frontier during the Severan period.

Severan forum and Temple of the Gens Septimia in Djémila, seen through the Arch of Caracalla.

Theatre in Djémila, verdant backdrop provided by the Atlas Mountains. Djémila was a key stop on Severus' triumphal tour through North Africa when emperor.

Colosseum at the foot of the *forum Romanum*, Rome. Severus was resident in Rome four times when emperor.

Religion played a key role in defining Roman identity. Here, a wall painting from Pompeii shows Venus in a chariot being pulled by four elephants. Severus was a great believer in the classical pantheon, and notably superstitious, too.

The author in Rome researching the Severans, Colosseum in the background. Note the upper tier was rebuilt in the Severan period after a fire.

The *forum Romanum* in Rome, Arch of Septimius Severus at left.

Khemissa, Roman *Thubursicum Numidaru*, in the foothills of the Atlas Mountains in modern Algeria. Another important Severan city in Roman North Africa.

Rear of the Byzantine fort at Madauros, Roman *Colonia Flavia Augusta Veteranorum Madaurensium*, modern Algeria. Note it has been built from reused stone, here incorporating the Severan theatre as its rear wall.

Capitoline Temple, Timgad, Roman *Colonia Marciana Ulpia Traiana Thamugadi*, on the fringes of the Aures Mountains. A key anchor for the Severan defences along the Saharan frontier.

The groma built in the centre of the legionary fortress at Lambaesis, long term home of legio III Augusta near the Aures Mountains. Severus made it the capital of his new province of Numidia.

Above left: Bust of Septimius Severus, British Museum.

Above right: Roman *lorica segmentata* body armour, found in Kalkriese, Germany, a survival from the Varian disaster. Many legionaries at the time Severus became emperor were still wearing an evolved version of this thorax protection.

Right: Temple of Vesta, *forum Romanum*, Rome. As rebuilt by Julia Domna.

Above left: Commodus as Hercules, Capitoline Museum, Rome.

Above right: The unfortunate Geta, Capitoline Museum, Rome.

Arch of Septimius Severus, *forum Romanum*, Rome.

Theatre and Odeon, Lyon, Roman *Lugdunum*. Here, Severus was governor of Gallia Lugdunensis, married Julia Domna, and Caracalla was born.

 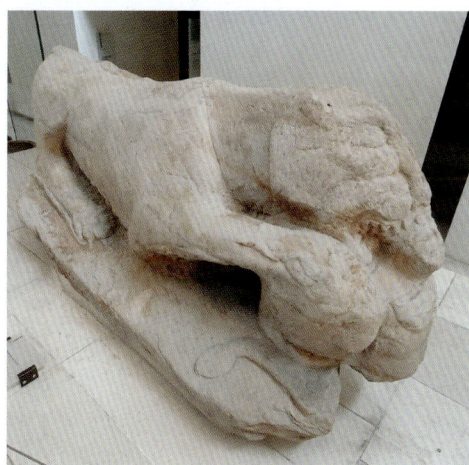

Above left: Bust of Julia Domna, Museum of Fine Arts, Lyon.

Above right: What the Romans really thought of the native Britons in the far north there. Cramond Lioness, National Museums Scotland.

Granary in Corbridge, Roman *Coria*. A key supply base for Severus' AD 209 and AD 210 campaigns in the far north of Britain.

The Multangular Tower in York, part of the later Roman defences of the legionary fortress there. Severus died in York in February AD 211.

Above left: Publius Helvius Pertinax, first emperor in the 'Year of the Five Emperors' in AD 193 and Severus' mentor.

Above right: Bust of Caracalla, Naples.

Caracalla with Parthian captive, Arch of Septimius Severus, Rome.

Septimius Severus and Julia Domna, Arch of the Argentarii, Rome.

Octagonal statue base in front of the Arch of Trajan in Timgad referencing the Concord of the Emperors, in this case Severus and Caracalla.

Monumental head of Septimius Severus, originally in the Temple of the Gens Septimia in Djémila and now on show in the museum there.

Larger-than-life bronze sculpture of Septimius Severus found in 1928 by a farmer ploughing his fields in Kythrea in the north of Cyprus near the ancient city of *Chytri*. Here, Severus is depicted heroically naked, in imitation of earlier sculptures of Hellenistic kings in the eastern Mediterranean and Levant.

to Severus, first heading north to the Rhine frontier. There he tried but failed to occupy the region, most likely because the legions there were Severan loyalists. He then turned south where his fortunes improved. Here Herodian says he won a series of small engagements against pro-Severan units in central Gaul.[27]

Severus, by now in the Balkans and still heading west, now sent his trouble-shooter Candidus ahead with an advance guard to Raetia and Noricum. These were the key provinces linking the Danubian and Rhine frontiers in the north. There, with the new title *dux adversus rebelles Noricae*, Candidus forcibly removed any supporters of Albinus from office. Severus appointed him suffect *consul* in absentia as a reward. Then, with Raetia and Noricum under control, Candidus advanced to the Rhine where Severan support remained strong. There, he found a ready ally in Cologne-based Virius Lupus, governor of Germania Inferior, who Severus now ordered to gather troops and head south to slow Albinus' advance through Gaul. A major engagement took place at an unknown location where the British governor was victorious, with Dio saying many Severan troops were killed.[28] Albinus then turned north again, besieging Trier. However, the city held out, its walls manned by the veterans of *legio* XXII *Primigenia pia fidelis* under its battle-hardened *legate* Claudius Gallus, another North African.

Albinus now looked south once more, first considering an ambitious plan to force his way into Italy through the Alpine passes. However, the idea was quickly abandoned when he learned Severus had strongly garrisoned them. He then switched targets to one he knew Severus couldn't ignore. This was Lyon in south-eastern Gaul, Severus' former provincial capital when governor of Gallia Lugdundensis and the key transport hub in the region. The city fell without a fight. On arrival Albinus declared it his capital, expelling the pro-Severan governor Titus Flavius Secundus Philippianus.

Albinus' first move once settled in Lyon was to issue coins to boost his legitimacy. Here he had the imperial mint at his disposal, one of the most important in the empire. Moorhead says his initial issues were silver *denarii* and a few gold *aurei*, with one issue of base metal *asses*.[29] These were all notable for four reasons. First, far fewer were minted than those in Albinus' name from Rome when he had been Severus' *caesar*. Second, the coins are poor in quality, using rough dies with crudely cut legends. This shows haste on the part of the *celators* (Roman die-engravers). Third, many of the coins have the legend *fides legionum*, referencing his army's loyalty. It is noteworthy Albinus felt the need to mention this at all. Finally, he is styled on the coins IMP CAE[sar] D[ecimus] CLO[dius] SEP[timius] ALB[inus] AVG[ustus]. Here, his use of *augustus* clearly shows he was now claiming to be a senior emperor.

At first, Albinus hoped he could find a new accommodation with Severus, the two perhaps sharing power as co-*augusti*. However, here he completely misjudged his opponent. Severus had no intention of sharing anything. He'd arrived in Rome by late summer AD 196. Legal documents requiring imperial attention give a clue to how long he stayed. Here, the Codex Justinianus preserves a large number of rescripts (replies to a legal question) from that year. Of interest, while there is only one from AD 195, one from January AD 196 and one from 30 June AD 196, ten are dated from 1 October to 29 December. This indicates Severus remained in Rome until the year's end. Then, early in January AD 197, he headed north to the upper Danubian frontier. There he knew his most loyal troops were based. Arriving in his old provincial capital *Carnuntum*, he installed Cilo as governor of Pannonia Superior, also leaving Caracalla in his care. This was near enough for his elder son to quickly join him if things went well in Gaul, but far enough away for short term safety if they didn't. It seems likely that, at this stage, Julia Domna and Geta had stayed in Rome.

Next, the *Historia Augusta* says Severus sought divine insight before moving further west.[30]

'In his anxiety, he consulted augurs in Pannonia, learning that he would be the victor over Albinus, and that his opponent would neither fall into his hands nor yet escape, but would die close by the water.'

The Gods onside, Severus then followed Candidus' earlier route through Noricum and Raetia, before finally arriving on the Rhine frontier. All the way he gathered troops to his banner, aiming to force a meeting engagement and finish Albinus once and for all. On arrival in northern Gaul he found the tide turning dramatically against the British governor, with the *Historia Augusta* saying:[31]

'Many of Albinus' friends soon deserted and came over to Severus; and many of his generals were captured, all of whom Severus punished.'

At this point, we then hear the unlikely tale of Numerianus, a former schoolteacher in Rome. For some reason devoted to Severus, when the emperor set off for the Danube he headed for Gaul pretending to be a Senator on official duty. Gathering a small force of volunteers on the way, he then began harassing Albinus' army camped around Lyon. Dio says he achieved a degree of success here, killing some of the usurper's cavalry and, more importantly, capturing 70 million *sesterces* (around $210 million in modern money) which he sent to a delighted Severus, by that time on the Rhine.[32] The emperor later rewarded Numerianus with a fine a country estate and a pension for his improbable exploits.

In Lyon, Albinus was now worried. Though his core support there remained strong, he was shaken by those deserting elsewhere. It was now clear a major showdown was looming, so he ordered all the provincial governors in Gaul and Spain to send him supplies. Herodian says that although some complied, many didn't.[33]

The end game of the campaign now began. Severus, secure on the Rhine, marched south at the beginning of February. This was notably early in the campaigning year, showing Severus was either very confident or needed a swift conclusion. The *Historia Augusta* next describes 'many operations being carried out in Gaul with varying success',[34] though despite any setbacks Severus' advance continued. Then a first major engagement took place at Tournos (Roman *Tinurtium*), 40km north of Lyon on the right bank of the River Saône. Here, Albinus tried to steer the Severan army away from his new capital, though failed given Severus won a hard fought, close victory. Indeed, it seems at one stage it was feared the emperor had been killed, with the *Historia Augusta* saying:[35]

> 'Through the fall of his horse, he was at one time in the utmost peril; and it was even believed that he had been slain by a blow with a ball of lead [slingshot], and the army almost elected another emperor.'

Somehow, Severus convinced his army he was still alive and won the day. Albinus then fled back to Lyon, setting the scene for the final titanic showdown which began on 19 February.

Given the claim *Lugdunum* was the largest civil war battle in Roman history, the size of the two armies has been much debated. As usually translated, Dio is very specific here:[36]

> 'There were 150,000 soldiers on each side, and both leaders were present in the conflict, since it was a life-and-death struggle between them.'

That would give an enormous total of 300,000 men engaged. Some have questioned this, arguing Dio meant 150,000 overall, but that his narrative has since been mistranslated. It is useful here to consider the overall size of the Roman army when Severus was emperor. The legions at the time still numbered 5,500 men each, this established as the norm by Augustus. There were at least 30 in existence at the time and may have been 33 given Severus himself created *legios* I, II and III *Parthica* for his eastern campaigns. It is unclear when these were formed, though Pollard and Berry say II *Parthica* certainly existed in AD 197 given an inscription in Rome references a recruit to the

CIVIL WAR

legion in that year (CIL 6, 3409).[37] Further, the dedication on a cinerary urn lid of a centurion from II *Parthica* buried near Rome, now on display in the Capitoline Museum, also indicates the legion had been formed by this time. Given the length of time it would take to establish and then man three new legions, and the fact Severus had already completed his first campaign in the east, here I work on the assumption they had been created by the time *Lugdunum* took place. This would give a nominal establishment of 181,500 legionaries across the 33 legions. We can add to this a similar number of supporting auxiliaries and naval *milites*, lifting the overall military complement at the time to over 360,000 men. Now, given Severus had been in the east when Albinus usurped and may have drawn troops from each region he passed through on his way back to the imperial centre, and the British governor had similarly added legionaries and auxilia from Spain to his three provincial legions, it is feasible that each had an army of 150,000. However, this seems highly unlikely given it would leave the frontiers of the empire significantly undermanned (as actually did happen in Britain, see below). Therefore, I think an overall total of around 150,000, comprising both armies, is far more likely.

What we can infer with a degree of certainty is the composition of the two armies given one was specifically from the east and one the west. As detailed, Severus had been campaigning on the eastern frontier when he learned of Albinus' usurpation. He knew this was a serious threat and most likely took significant numbers of legionaries and auxilia back with him from the Parthian frontier, including troops who had earlier supported Niger. In the case of the former, these would have been vexillations rather than whole legions as the border zone there still needed defending. However, given auxiliary units were smaller, they may have transferred west in their entirety.

Travelling west, Severus then called on more vexillations to join him, especially after travelling from Rome to the Danube frontier. Indeed, given his army at *Lugdunum* is referenced by Herodian as Illyrian, it seems likely the bulk of his army came from here, perhaps entire legions.[38] The principal formations there were still the veterans of the earlier Marcomannic Wars, with *legio* III *Italica concurs* in Raetia, *legio* II *Italica* in Noricum, *legio* X *Gemina* and *legio XIV Gemina Martia Victrix* in Pannonia Superior (the latter now fully reformed after being almost wiped out at the Battle of Carnuntum in AD 170), *legio* II *Adiutrix pia fidelis* in Pannonia Inferior, *legio* IV *Flavia felix* and *legio* VII *Claudia pia fidelis* in Moesia Superior, *legio* XIII *Gemina pia fidelis* in Dacia and *legio* I *Italica*, *legio* V *Macedonia* and *legio* XI *Claudia pia fidelis* in Moesia Inferior. These were some of the crack legions in the whole empire, battle hardened when earlier campaigning with Marcus Aurelius, and latterly with Commodus. It is highly probable Severus had already called on troops from this region to support his first eastern campaign, and, if so, these now returned with him before travelling on to Gaul. Severus also recruited troops from the four legions along the Rhine, these at the time *legio VIII Augusta* and *legio XXII Primogenia pia fidelis* in Germania Inferior, and *legio I Minervia pia fidelis* and *legio XXX Ulpia Victrix* in Germania Superior. As usual, to these legionaries from the Danube and Rhine we can add an equivalent number of auxiliaries, these also providing the main mounted component of his army. Finally, we know Severus also took the Praetorian Guard with him, and the *equites singulares Augusti* imperial guard cavalry.

Meanwhile, the *Historia Augusta* calls Albinus' army a 'mighty force'.[39] At its core were the three British legions, all highly experienced whose legionaries frequently campaigned in the unconquered far north of Britain. As detailed above, when he arrived in Gaul, Albinus was also joined by the Spanish *legio* VII *Gemina* under Rufus. As with Severus' army, the legionaries were joined by an equivalent number of auxiliary foot, though in this case fewer horse (though the latter did include the Lugdunum-based *ala* Asturum cavalry unit). Albinus also called on the Lyon-based *cohors I Flavia urbana* urban cohort.

On to the narrative of the battle, Severus pursued Albinus back to Lyon where Herodian says the usurper was to remain behind its strong wall circuit throughout the battle.[40] Given the course of the engagement this seems highly improbable and is most likely based on later Severan propaganda. Indeed, Dio's more balanced account makes it clear that both leaders fought in the battle with their troops.[41]

The Battle of Lugdunum was a two-day affair. As described by all primary sources, it was a heavy infantry engagement on a grand scale given the comparative lack of cavalry, especially in Albinus' army. The clash was a story of two wings, these dividing the battle line in half, rather than the more traditional clash with a centre and two wings. On his right, Severus deployed his more experienced legionaries and auxilia, with the less experienced troops on his left, and with the Praetorian Guard and most of his cavalry held in reserve under a *legate* called Laetus (this likely Julius Laetus, the army corps commander in Severus' recent eastern campaign, though his full name is not given). Meanwhile, Albinus placed the three British legions, these the most loyal to him, on his own right. His left wing comprised the Spanish legion, most of his auxilia and the urban cohort.

Severus opened the engagement by advancing his right wing, with Dio providing excellent detail.[42] He says soon the legionaries were in light *pilum* range, with volley after volley flying between the two lines, the auxilia joining in to throw their *lanceae*. Then, as the cohorts closed, the heavier *pila* were thrown at point blank range, clattering against raised *scuta* shields. Each legionary now drew his *gladius* and charged to a shuddering impact. The battle now became one of thousands of individual combats, each warrior seeking a killing blow against his opponent. This was civil war and no quarter was given, the fighting savage, with the *gladii* inflicting fearsome wounds. Eventually, the experience and morale of Severus' better troops told and Albinus' left flank legionaries and auxilia broke and fled for the safety of *Lugdunum*. The Severan troops pursued, only stopping when they reached the tents of Albinus' camp outside the city walls, which they then comprehensively looted.

The battle on Severus' left wing was far different and almost cost him his life. Here, the experienced British II *Augusta*, XX *Valeria Victrix* and VI *Victrix* had carefully prepared their position ahead of the battle. Crucially, Dio says they had strewn the ground to their front with concealed field defences.[43] These most likely included shallow trenches 1.5m deep with rows of sharpened stakes in the bottom, pits called *lilies* also with a sharpened stake in the bottom, and bands of *stimuli* wooden blocks embedded in the ground with an iron barb standing proud of the surface.

As Severus' left wing advanced, Albinus' legionaries lured them into the trap. Advancing as far as the field defences, they threw their lighter *pila*. Then, as the Severan troops closed with them, they pretended to withdraw in disorder. Their opponents broke into a full charge, thinking Albinus' right wing was breaking. The inevitable then occurred, with shocked Severan front rankers falling headlong onto the sharpened stakes and iron barbs of the concealed field defences. Propelled by the momentum of the charge, the second and third ranks followed in short order, adding to the carnage. Stunned rear rankers then shuddered to a halt amid shouts from centurions and *optios* trying to regain order. Soon, the troops on the Severan left wing began to withdraw, but the suddenness of the reverse to their front forced those at the very back into a deep defile where many lost their footing. Now, the whole wing was trapped between the field defences to the front and the defile at the back. The British legionaries then crossed their own field defences using pre-layed trackways, reformed on the other side and charged the mass of disordered Severan foot. Heavy *pila* were hurled as they closed, then *gladii* drawn. Archers and slingers joined in, a great slaughter following. Severus, watching in horror from the rear, realised the day might be lost if he didn't act immediately, especially as his victorious wing was still looting the enemy camp. He therefore mounted his charger and personally led the Praetorian Guard and *equites singulares Augusti* to rescue his beleaguered left wing. However, things didn't go according to plan and soon these elite troops found themselves drawn into the carnage between the field defences and defile. Dio says the guard were nearly destroyed, with Severus losing his horse again.[44] The wing then broke in full flight, with Herodian adding the three

British legions now began chanting their battle hymn to victory as they vigorously pursued.[45]

Severus now showed battlefield leadership worthy of Caesar himself. Tearing off his riding cloak, he mounted a new horse and led his own personal bodyguard into the mass of routers. Slowly and surely many troops began to rally, with Dio saying:[46]

> 'Severus was hoping either that they would be ashamed and turn back or that he himself might perish among them. Some indeed did turn back when they saw him in this attitude ...'

Eventually, the emperor managed to reform a battle line on his left wing, which at last stopped the rampaging British legions who were now exhausted from their pursuit. Then, having regrouped, Severus' troops began to push their opponents back.

With the two wings each fighting a separate battle, *Lugdunum* had to this point many parallels with another decisive encounter of the ancient world, Cynosophelae in 197 BC. There, Philip V's right wing pushed back Titus Quinctius Flaminius's left, and the latter's right the Macedonian left. The parallels now continued, with Laetus and his Severan cavalry reserve spotting an opportunity. Albinus' right wing had advanced far proud of where its own now routed left wing had been deployed, and its own left flank and rear were now exposed. Laetus fell on this with a savage cavalry charge, butchering many legionaries in the British legions before they could form a defence. The bloody engagement was soon over, though for Severus it was only a Pyrrhic victory given the scale of slaughter on both sides. Addressing these huge losses, Dio says:[47]

> 'Many, even the victors, deplored the disaster, for the entire plain was seen to be covered with the bodies of men and horses ... some of them lay there mutilated by many wounds, as if hacked in pieces, and others though unwounded, were piled in heaps, weapons were scattered about, and blood flowed in streams, even pouring into rivers.'

Confusion surrounds the fate of Albinus. Dio says he sought refuge in a house on the Rhone where he committed suicide,[48] while the *Historia Augusta* has him either stabbing himself or having a slave do so, but surviving.[49] The usurper, either dead of half alive, was then found by Severus. He was swiftly decapitated, his head sent to Rome and the body ritually desecrated by the emperor himself, who trampled it on his charger before the headless corpse was thrown into the Rhone. Albinus' family met a similar grim fate, his sons and mother murdered on Severus' orders, together with 29 senators unfortunate enough to choose the wrong side and find themselves in Lyon. The *Historia Augusta* says the latter had their bodies mutilated post-mortem to deprive them of a ritual burial, with their property and goods sold and the proceeds going to Severus' own coffers (including huge payments to his two sons), and to the imperial *fiscus* treasury.[50] Lyon itself was sacked and burned.

Meanwhile, Severus also targeted those who had provided financial support to Albinus, making use of the usurper's correspondence which he captured when Lyon fell. Numerous members of the local aristocracies in Gaul and Spain (outside of the Senators already killed) were executed, with their estates confiscated. Further, in southern Spain, much of the olive oil production fell into the hands of the state. Meanwhile, in Gaul, many of the factories producing Samian ware were destroyed, with their owners killed and property forfeited.

This was post-usurpation 'tidying' up on a grand scale, with Severus acting with his usual thoroughness. A whole series of administrative changes were then ordered before the emperor returned to Rome, retracing his circuitous route from the Rhine frontier through Pannonia. Before leaving he showered his loyal troops with rewards, with the *Historia Augusta* saying 'he gave his soldiers sums of money such as no emperor had ever given before'.[51]

First, Candidus was rewarded with the governorship of Hispania Tarraconensis where he replaced the unfortunate Rufus who was either killed in the battle or afterwards. The new incumbent's first task was to hunt down and execute any remaining supporters of Albinus in Spain not already purged. Sadly, for Candidus, his time as an imperial favourite soon came to a dramatic end. This was because, for some unknown reason, in AD 198 the Senate declared a *damnatio memoriae* against him, after which he was executed.

Severus' next regional appointment was to make Quintus Hedius Rufus Lollianus Gentianus, a leading Severan supporter who had played a key role in the campaigns against Niger and Albinus, governor of Gallia Lugdunensis. He thrived under Severus, becoming governor of Hispania Tarraconensis after Candidus' fall from grace, and in the early third century AD governor of the fabulously wealthy province of Asia.

Moving to Africa Proconsularis, Severus kept the existing governor in place, though appointed another supporter called Claudius Xenephon as a special *procurator ad bona cogenda* with orders to confiscate the property of those known to have supported Albinus. The proceeds were again split between the Severan family and the *fiscus* treasury.

Severan appointments in the aftermath of *Lugdunum* continued for some time. Next, Marius Maximus was promoted to become governor of Gallia Belgica, while Gaius Varelius Pudens was made governor of Germania Inferior, replacing Lupus who was made governor of Britain. For the latter, this was a major responsibility given he was replacing Albinus, the usurper himself, who as detailed had stripped most of the troops from Britain to support his bid for power.

On arrival Birley says Lupus faced an appalling task, with the north plundered by the native Maeatae who had used Albinus' distractions on the continent to raid across the frontier.[52] This huge confederation is first mentioned by Dio early in the reign of Commodus. Here, he details that, by that time, the various tribes in the far north had coalesced into two main 'races of Britons'.[53] These were the Maeatae, whose territory ranged from the Scottish Borders to the upper Midland Valley, and above them the Caledonians ranging north from there to the Scottish Highlands.

At the time Lupus arrived in late AD 197, he found the Maeatae not only still holding Roman captives and plunder from their recent raids, but also actively encouraging the Caledonians to join any future predation south of the frontier. With few troops with him, Lupus was forced to buy the Maeatae off with huge bribes to restore stability along the northern border.

The fortunes of Albinus' troops from Britain who survived the defeat at *Lugdunum* are not known, though as with *legio* VII *Gemina* in Spain the three British legions (together with supporting auxilia) were soon reconstituted given the need to re-establish a full military presence in Britain. They were later to play key roles in Severus' attempts to conquer the far north a decade later. The only major difference post-*Lugdunum* was with the regional fleet. Here, Frere interpreted an inscription in Rome from this time to suggest Severus amalgamated the *Classis Britannica*, *Classis Germanica*, *Classis Pannonica* and *Classis Flavia Moesica* into one command for a short while.[54] However, the British fleet was soon restored to its own individual command, certainly by the time Severus later campaigned in Britain.

Meanwhile, at the same time Lupus was restoring order in the north of Britain, Severus moved to quickly purge the more prosperous south of any surviving supporters of Albinus. Here, the emperor paid particular attention to the provincial capital London, sending military commissioners there who ordered the building of its first defensive wall circuit. Given there was no physical threat in Britain so far south, I have argued elsewhere that this 3.2km structure (which incorporated the existing Cripplegate vexillation fort) was built as a monumental statement of imperial power. This Roman wall circuit then later became the line of the medieval walls of London. Thus, the modern geographic outline of the 'Square mile', today's City of London, is still defined by a structure built by a North African Roman emperor as a message to its leading inhabitants to behave or else.

It was also at this point Severus began the process of physically dividing the province of Britannia in two, these Britannia Superior with its capital in London and Britannia Inferior with its capital in York. This replicated his similar reorganisation of Syria after earlier defeating Niger.

Despite this imperial attention, Birley says that for now Britain remained a sideshow after Albinus' fall.[55] Severus is next referenced in Germany on his return journey where he received an embassy from the Senate whose members were keen to declare their loyalty to him. Interestingly, the Senate chose a young patrician from Constantine in Numidia to lead the delegation, no doubt hoping to gain favour with Severus by acknowledging his North Africa roots. However, while the embassy was still with Severus on the Rhine, the emperor received urgent news from the east which was to shape his next few years in power. In his absence in Europe, Vologases and the Parthians had recaptured Rome's newly won border territories in Mesopotamia, besieged Nisibis again, and launched a large raid deep into Syria. A return to the eastern frontier now beckoned for Severus.

6

Imperator: Severus in the East and Egypt

With Albinus dead, Severus was now free to finally deal with the Parthians in the east, and he mounted an enormous two-phase campaign there from AD 198 to AD 200. First, though, he had unfinished business in Rome, clearing out any final supporters of Niger and Albinus. Then, after two years campaigning deep in the Mesopotamian interior, he visited Egypt in triumph.

BACK TO ROME

When Severus received news the Parthians were on the march again, he was still basking in the glory of Albinus' defeat.[1] The emperor acted immediately to secure the eastern frontier, knowing any sign of weakness against Vologases would undermine him in Rome. First, he sent Laetus, leader of the decisive cavalry charge at *Lugdunum*, east with orders to drive the Parthians out of Syria and Mesopotamia and lift the siege of Nisibis. Additionally, he was tasked with ensuring the continued loyalty of Armenia. Then, Severus ordered Claudius Gallus, the veteran *legate* of *legio* XXII *Primigenia pia fidelis* who had held Trier against Albinus, to lead an emergency force of vexillations drawn from the legions in the two German provinces to bolster the defences in the east.[2] With these two appointments, the emperor aimed to secure the eastern frontier while he first consolidated power back in Rome.

Severus then continued his travels to the imperial capital via Pannonia, hot on the heels of the Senatorial delegation. This had left Germany before him, seeking an audience with Caracalla in *Carnuntum*, our first indication the Senate was taking Severus' eldest son seriously as heir to the throne. Severus arrived shortly after, with all then heading south to Rome. On arrival there, he was greeted with cheering crowds, relieved the civil wars with Niger and Albinus were over. Severus then distributed bread to the population and made sacrifices in the Temple of Jupiter Optimus Maximus on the Capitoline Hill. Finally, he retired to the imperial palace on the Palatine Hill to consider his next moves, both domestically and abroad.

The following morning, Severus moved swiftly, first dealing with the Senate. There, many patricians thought he would try to win their favour now he was secure in power. Nothing was further from the truth. Instead, a furious Severus decided to teach them a lesson, terrorising the Senators in his first speech in the *curia* after returning. Here, he lambasted them for their treatment of Commodus, reminding them he was now the dead emperor's brother given his newly declared familial links with the Antonines. Dio, a direct witness to this tirade, heard him say:[3]

> 'For if it was disgraceful for him with his own hands to slay wild beasts, yet at Ostia only the other day one of your number, an old man who had been consul, was publicly sporting with a prostitute who imitated a leopard. But, you will say "Commodus actually fought as a gladiator." And does none of you fight as a gladiator? If not, how and why is it that some of you have bought his shields and those famous golden helmets?'

He ended the rant by praising Sulla, Marius and Augustus for the severity with which they had dealt with the Senate. The message here was clear. The Senate would now do his bidding, or there would be trouble.

To emphasise the point, Severus next ordered a final round of proscriptions, targeting any aristocrats he still thought a threat. Many were rounded up and executed without trial, with the *Historia Augusta* recording 46 unfortunate victims in the Senate. These were called Mummius Secundinus, Asellius Claudianus, Claudius Rufus, Vitalius Victor, Papius Faustus, Aelius Celsus, Julius Rufus, Lollius Professus, Aurunculeius Cornelianus, Antonius Balbus, Postumius Severus, Sergius Lustralis, Fabius Paulinus, Nonius Gracchus, Masticius Fabianus, Casperius Agrippinus, Ceionius Albinus, Claudius Sulpicianus, Memmius Rufinus, Casperius Aemilianus, Cocceius Verus, Erucius Clarus, Aelius Stilo, Clodius Rufinus, Egnatuleius Honoratus, Petronius Junior, the six leading members of the Pescennii *gentes*, Festus, Veratianus, Aurelianus, Materianus, Julianus, the three Cerellii brothers, Macrinus, Faustinianus, Herennius Nepos, Sulpicius Canus, Valerius Catullinus, Novius Rufus, Claudius Arabianus, and Marcius Asellio.[4] Potter is unequivocal here in calling out Severus' actions for what they were, mass murder.[5]

Among those listed were some of Rome's leading men, including Pertinax's father-in-law Sulpicianus, last recorded as Julianus' city prefect in AD 193, and the former *consul* Clarus, last detailed making a speech praising Severus when he came to power. The latter turned down the offer of a free pardon if he would turn informer.

Another high-profile victim, not named by the *Historia Augusta*, was Julius Solon, who four years earlier had drafted the Senate's decree declaring Severus emperor. Also not listed here, but detailed later in the *Historia Augusta*, was another important victim.[6] This was Gaius Cingius Severus, earlier governor in Africa Proconsularis and at the time of the proscriptions *curator aedium sacrarum* in charge of all public works, temples and sacred spaces in Rome. Severus accused him of trying to poison him and had him put to death, though notably it had also been Gaius Cingius Severus whose motion had condemned Commodus to *damnatio memoriae* after his assassination.

That was perhaps the real reason for his grim end, with some reports suggesting it was in the arena. Here, one can see a real attempt by Severus to rehabilitate Commodus. Notably, many of the latter's later statues and busts have intact features, indicting they date to this period rather than during his own lifetime when, post-mortem, most were defaced after his *damnatio memoriae*. A fine example of one badly damaged in this way can be found in the Sandwich Guildhall Museum in Kent. It was originally discovered near the later Saxon Shore site at Richborough, where it most likely adorned the earlier quadrifrons monumental arch there.

Severus then moved to restructure the equestrian class given many there had supported Niger, Albinus, or both. He appointed Marcus Aquilius Felix to revise those in the order, an ideal choice given the former centurion had ended his military service as a senior *frumentarii* secret service agent.[7]

Severus' final set of reforms in Rome before looking eastward were financial. Here, we see the Severan reset in full overt action, more akin to a hostile takeover than at any time previously. Opportunity was presented by many of his victims in the three proscriptions having helped run the *fiscus* imperial treasury. With few left to hold him to account, he had the Senate pass legislation legitimising his earlier appropriation of his victims' wealth. From that point, any monies accrued by the state in this way (or otherwise) were officially split between the Severan family and the *fiscus*. To ensure the new arrangement ran smoothly, the emperor then created a new layer of imperial administration to run the imperial finances. For the first time, this included officials based outside of Rome, at first in Italy and later elsewhere.

Many historians have commented on Severus' avariciousness here, with twentieth-century AD views shaped by the leading classical economist Tenney Frank, who wrote that:[8]

> 'I venture the opinion that if we had a reliable history of the third century AD, we should arrive at the conclusion that Septimius

Severus dealt the fatal blow to the empire by his confiscations and his centralizing of vast estates under imperial control.'

This view has proved tenacious, not surprising given Severus was clearly using his position as imperial strongman to line his family purse. What's more, he didn't care who knew.

Severus' wider restructuring of the imperial finances proved highly successful, despite his syphoning cash off for his own use. Crucially, he chose to share the good fortune with the military, knowing they were the real reason he was now secure in power. Further, he now also decreed that legionaries were able to marry legally while serving for the first time since the reign of Augustus. At the same time, he legalised any marriages his legionaries had earlier contracted illegally. This secured his enduring popularity with the legions.

Severus was likely still in Rome in June AD 197, based on an inscription found there dated the eighth. This records the return of three *equites singulares Augusti* from their service in Gaul. In the dedication, which names the emperor and his family, Caracalla is called *imperator destinatus*, meaning 'emperor designate'. Though still only a *caesar*, this took him a step closer to becoming a full *augusti* alongside his father. Plautianus is also mentioned, and is here given the title *clarissimus vir*, meaning right honorable. This indicates the *praefectus praetorio* had now been promoted to Senatorial rank for his service against Niger and Albinus.

Finally, Severus moved to ensure the behaviour of the Senate in the long term through the threat of direct military force. Here he stationed his elite founding *legio* II *Parthica* in a new legionary fortress at Albano Laziale (Roman *Albanum*) only 25km from Rome. To that point, all the legions of Rome had been based around its frontiers, with only the Praetorian Guard and *equites singulares Augusti* quartered as a militarised force in Rome itself. Despite the fact Severus had reformed both, the former with his own Danubian veterans, they retained their reputation for political unreliability. Further, both were always deployed with the emperor when on campaign. Now, here was a fully equipped line legion based so close to the imperial capital it could hold the patricians to account at a moment's notice if so ordered. With all now settled at home, Severus was free to turn his attention to Vologases and the Parthians in the east, in what became his most successful military campaign.

WAR IN THE EAST

Severus always intended to return east after dealing with Albinus. His motivation was martial glory. Despite his now declared association with the Antonines, the ambitious Severus planned to found a new dynasty. In that context, especially after the civil wars, martial glory against the enemies of Rome was the surest way to win support at home. Further, not only would conquest in the east set him on a par with Trajan (Lucius Verus' campaign in the AD 160s had also sacked Ctesiphon, but the emperor had not led it in person), it would also better Augustus, against whom all Roman emperors measured their success. Here, the late first-century BC poet Horace had written of the first emperor:[9]

> '... Augustus will be deemed a God on Earth when the Britons and the deadly Parthians have been added to our empire.'

Augustus achieved neither, giving his successors the opportunity to better him. Severus attempted both, succeeding in Parthia and only narrowly failing in Britain at the end of his life.

Severus' second eastern campaign featured two phases, one to consolidate the frontier zone after the initial Parthian aggression (the task already underway with Laetus and Gallus), the second a full-scale invasion of Parthian territory. Here, the primary sources indicate much of the emperor's journey east was this time by sea. The *Historia Augusta* reported 'Severus transported his army from Brundisium [modern Brindisi in southeastern Italy] and reached

Syria without breaking his voyage'.[10] His large entourage included his family, senior members of the court, Plautianus and much of the Praetorian Guard. They landed at the Cilician port of *Aegeae* in the southeastern Turkey and headed directly to *Antioch*. There, he mustered his army, with Dio saying he was also joined by a brother of Vologases, no doubt looking for Severan support to usurp his brother.[11] The *Historia Augusta* states that, while in *Antioch*, Severus was also briefly joined by his sister Septimia Octavilla and her son. It says:[12]

> 'His sister from Leptis Magna came to see him, and, since she could scarcely speak Latin, made the emperor blush for her hotly. And so, after giving the broad stripe to her son and many presents to the woman herself, he sent her home again, and also her son, who died a short time afterwards.'

Severus found much of the region already stabilised, with Syria cleared of the Parthians and the siege of Nisibis lifted by Laetus. The emperor therefore advanced to the frontier, joined on the way by the children of Abgar, the Osrhoene king still based in Edessa. Abgar also sent a contingent of royal archers to join the Roman army, showing his personal loyalty to Severus. There is no indication the royal offspring were hostages, unlike those sent to Severus shortly after by the King of Armenia who was also keen to show his fidelity. Crossing the Euphrates, the Romans soon reached Nisibis where Laetus was awarded honours by Severus. Dio next relates a strange tale, saying:[13]

> 'Severus, on reaching the aforesaid Nisibis, found there an enormous boar. It had charged and killed a horseman, who, trusting to his own strength, had attempted to bring it down, and it had been with difficulty caught and despatched by a large crowd of soldiers (the number taking part in the capture was thirty); then it had been brought to Severus.'

Whether a true story or not, the metaphor is clear. The Romans would win.

By this point, Vologases and his army had left not only Syria but also Mesopotamia. With no enemy to fight, Severus returned to *Antioch* where his troops proclaimed him *imperator* again. He then set to planning the second phase of his campaign, gathering a new army comprising his existing troops and many called to arms from across the region. When all was ready, Severus then launched a huge invasion of Parthia down the Euphrates and Tigris valleys, 'when the summer was well-nigh over' according to the *Historia Augusta*.[14] Soon, both Seleucia-on-the-Tigris and Babylon had been seized, having already been abandoned by the Parthians.

Severus then crossed the Tigris from Seleucia to Ctesiphon. This sat on the opposite bank of the river, 35km southeast of modern Baghdad. Here, it is clear once more there was no major Parthian resistance to the Roman advance, with Vologases having fled again. By the time Severus crossed the frontier, the Parthian king was dealing with yet another bout of internal unrest and was unable to gather an army in time to defend his capital. Dio provides detail about what happened next:[15]

> 'Upon capturing Ctesiphon, Severus permitted the soldiers to plunder the entire city, and he slew a vast number of people, besides taking as many as 100,000 captives.'

However, he chose not to pursue Vologaesus, nor occupy Ctesiphon. Instead, he returned to Roman territory, travelling along the Tigris valley, his campaign objectives met.

Victorious, Severus now celebrated as his army headed west. On 28 January AD 198, in a ceremony in front of his army, he took the title *Parthicus Maximus*, exactly as Trajan had done before. The date was carefully chosen as it was the exact centenary of Trajan's accession to the throne. More importantly, Severus also made the nine-year-old Caracalla his *augustus* co-emperor, with his youngest son Geta becoming his new *caesar*. Finally, Severus announced that Mesopotamia and Osrhoene would become new provinces of the empire (the latter broadly the territory of Trajan's short-lived province of Assyria), with Armenia signing new treaties confirming its ongoing alliance with Rome. Notably, Dio states that although Severus' two new provinces proved a success in the long term, with their territory remaining under Roman control well into the Dominate, they were expensive to man and proved a strain on imperial resources.[16] Each required a legion to hold the line, the idea being they would form a bulwark to protect Syria to the west. The legions were *legio* I *Parthica* based at *Singara* on the Tigris in the far north of Mesopotamia, and *legio* III *Parthica* based at *Resaina* in Osrhoene where Gordian III was to later fight the Sassanid Persians. Note, the location of each site within their respective provinces is a modern interpretation given we have little detail of the exact borders. Notably, Severus also installed another North African called Titus Claudius Subatianus Aquila as the first governor of Mesopotamia, the man's family from modern Algeria as was Senecio, governor of nearby Coele-Syria.

Though Severus could claim to have defeated the Parthians, he still had unfinished business as he returned west to *Antioch*. This was with Hatra, the key desert city in upper Mesopotamia which controlled mercantile traffic between the Roman west and Parthian east. One of the three vassals (along with Osrhoene and Adiabene) that had rebelled against Roman control after Niger's attempt to secure the throne, it was soon back under Roman control after Severus' first eastern campaign. However, it then rebelled again when Vologases invaded Mespotamia and Syria. Severus bypassed it in his second eastern campaign, prioritising the Parthians. Now, for reasons unknown, it continued to hold out against the Romans. Dio provides excellent detail about what happened next, including the downfall of two leading Severan supporters:[17]

'Severus now crossed Mesopotamia and made an attempt on Hatra, which was not far off, but accomplished nothing; on the contrary, his siege engines were burned, many soldiers perished, and vast numbers were wounded. He accordingly retired from there and shifted his quarters. While he was engaged in this war he put to death two distinguished men. One was Julius Crispus, a tribune of the Praetorians; and the reason was that Crispus, vexed at the war's havoc, had casually quoted some verses of the poet Maro in which one of the soldiers fighting on the side of Turnus against Aeneas bewails his lot and says: "In order that Turnus may marry Lavinia, we are meanwhile perishing all unheeded." And Severus made Valerius, the soldier who accused him, tribune in his place. The other man that he put to death was Laetus, for the reason that Laetus was proud and was beloved by the soldiers, who used to declare they would not go on a campaign unless Laetus led them. He tried to fasten the responsibility for this murder, for which he had no evident reason save jealousy, upon the soldiers, making it appear that they had been rash enough to commit the deed contrary to his will.'

This was a mighty fall from grace for Laetus, which Birley says was by far the more serious of the two unsavoury incidents.[18] The *Historia Augusta* provides context here, saying the *praefectus praetorio* Plautianus had been tasked at the time with another round of proscription against any remaining supporters of Niger.[19] This seems unlikely to me given the thoroughness with which Severus had earlier rooted them out. Perhaps, as Dio suggests, this simply was a case of jealousy. Notably, it was also at this time Candidus in Hispania Tarraconensis was executed, perhaps for the same reason. Birley suggests that in both cases Plautianus may have been exploiting Severus' superstitious beliefs, detailing that prophesies had highlighted both Laetus and Candidus as future potential rivals for the throne.[20]

Meanwhile, for Severus, Hatra still remained a problem, and he again besieged the city. Once more it proved an especially difficult target to capture, the city determined for some reason to resist

Severus. In particular, the use of flaming naptha by the defenders caused dismay in his troops, this a real terror weapon of the ancient world. Our main source is Dio, who glosses over the endgame of the siege, saying that after twenty days Severus left for the Mediterranean province of Syria Palaestina, providing no detail about how matters were resolved.[21] However, inscriptions in Antioch indicate Severus did indeed achieve his objective given they detail the emperor celebrating the submission of Hatra and its king, Barsemias. Certainly, a Roman auxiliary garrison, the ninth *cohort* of Moors, is recorded resident there a decade later.

After a brief visit to Syria Palaestina, where Dio says Severus forbade conversion to Judaism or Christianity,[22] the emperor then returned to Antioch. His final act there was to reorganise the frontier zone in the east, likely at the beginning of AD 199. This included greatly expanding the *limes Cappadocia* and the northern section of the *limes Arabicus* to incorporate the new provinces of Mesopotamia and Osrhoene, and similarly expanding the southern section of the *limes Arabicus*, the latter including the transfer of a significant part of Syro-Phoenicia to Arabia Petraea. The latter was a major undertaking, with Severus constructing a new sequence of fortifications in the Arabian Desert to bolster the *limes* there ranging from Basie to Dumata. Then, as the year progressed, Severus turned his attention to Egypt, his business on the eastern frontier successfully concluded.

ON TO EGYPT

Severus had a fixation on Aegyptus for three reasons, all key drivers for his visit there which lasted from late AD 199 to early AD 201. First, his passion for antiquities of the kind which proliferated in Egypt. Second, his desire to understand all things supernatural. Third, it was the last resting place of the classical world's greatest conqueror extraordinaire, Alexander the Great.

Severus travelled to Egypt via the land route through Palestine and the Nile Delta, stopping off at *Pelesium* when he arrived at the latter. This was a key city on the eastern extreme of the delta, 30km southeast of modern Port Said. Later, a Roman provincial capital and archbishopric in the dominate, it lay in a highly defensible position between the Mediterranean coast and the delta marshes. More importantly for Severus, it was the location of the tomb of Pompey the Great, the leading Roman statesman and general assassinated on arrival there in 48 BC after fleeing defeat by Julius Caesar at Pharsalus. Reverence for the dead was a key aspect of religious culture in Severus' Libyan homeland, and he spent a week there where he carried out sacrifices in honour of the great *optimates* champion. Here, the emperor was also following the example of Hadrian who had spent time there during his own extensive visit to Egypt earlier in the century when he had rebuilt Pompey's tomb around AD 130.

Severus entered Alexandria in early spring to great acclaim. The only event marring his arrival was an old inscription above one of the main city gates declaring Niger master of the city. Unperturbed, he quickly settled into the governor's palace, and once more we see the emperor's acquisitive trait come to the fore, a visit to the mausoleum of Alexander the Great swiftly following. We next have Severus granting the Alexandrians their own council for local government and allowing native Egyptians to enter the Senate for the first time. The emperor also invested heavily in the built environment in the city. This became a key feature of his time as emperor, with stone-built monumental building projects proliferating wherever he travelled. In Alexandria, this included the building of new public baths, a gymnasium and a huge new temple to Alexandria's mother goddess, Cybele. Severus also worshipped in the temple of Serapis, a God long associated with the former Ptolemaic dynasty and to whom Severus himself was a devotee. The *Historia Augusta* reports that of Severus' many fond memories of his Egyptian sojourn, this was his favourite.[23]

The imperial visit then followed the traditional grand tour upriver on the Nile, with Severus first viewing the pyramids and sphynx at Giza. Progressing further, he stopped at Memphis, and then at Lake Moeris where he viewed the great labyrinth with its twelve covered courtyards and 3,000 chambers. Moving on, at Thebes in upper Egypt, he visited the colossal statues of the eighteenth-dynasty pharaoh Amenhophis III in his mortuary temple. This was a favourite stop for Roman tourists because the statue was said to sing at dawn. Severus then continued upriver until he reached the southern *limes*, only stopping there, according to Dio, because of a plague outbreak.[24]

Of note, during Severus' visit to Egypt we see the *praefectus praetorio* Plautianus wielding real power for the first time in the imperial court. For example, shortly after the imperial party arrived in Alexandria, the provincial governor Quintus Aemilius Saturninus, who had gone to great lengths to ensure all was ready for the imperial visit, was promoted to become the joint prefect of the Praetorians alongside Plautianus. Having two *praefecti praetorio* was the normal state of affairs, so it is unclear why Severus had not earlier paired another prefect with his kinsman. More importantly, it is also unclear why he did so now. However, the result was dramatic, with Plautianus taking extreme exception and having Saturninus murdered within weeks. He appears to have gone unpunished, acquiring even more power.

Severus himself was still on the Nile in May AD 200 when he led the ceremony where the emperor (if present, though more usually a senior official) cast gold and silver gifts into a famous rock cave near Aswan (Roman *Philae*). This was to pray for the successful annual flooding of the river after the monsoon began in the Ethiopian Highlands that month. Severus then waited until the flooding season had ended before heading back downriver to the coast. This was because a local taboo forbade the ruler of Egypt to sail on the Nile while it was in flood, something the emperor, with his superstitious nature, would certainly have taken account of. He was still in Egypt at the end of August, though shortly after left with his entourage by ship from Alexandria, heading back to Antioch.

We have little detail of Severus' activities for much of AD 201, though he certainly remained in the east given early in the year he announced he and Caracalla would be joint *consuls* the following year. At the same time, he invested his eldest son with the *toga virilis*. This was the formal acknowledgment the thirteen-year-old was now a man. Severus and his elder son then inaugurated AD 202 as the new *consuls* while still in Antioch, the first time since AD 161 that two *augusti* had been joint *consuls* when Marcus Aurelius and Lucius Verus had taken the title. The emperor then announced his intention to return to Rome forthwith, where he planned to celebrate his *decennalia*. This was an important festival, with public games held by a sitting emperor to celebrate each ten years in power.

Severus' journey back to Rome was uneventful, though three anecdotes stand out. First, Dio can't resist adding more salacious tales about Plautianus, saying he had become a complete sensualist who gorged himself at banquets and freely indulged his other lusts.[25] Second, Julia Domna spent much time on the journey in the company of sophists, taking a great interest in the study of philosophy. One individual she engaged with was Philostratus, a noted pupil of Aerlius Antipater, the philosopher who was Severus' private secretary and tutor to Caracalla and Geta. Another writer she corresponded with at the time was Cassius Dio himself. Third, when travelling through Bithynia in northwestern Anatolia, Severus visited the tomb of another famous Libyan, Hannibal. Here, at Libyssa, he erected a white marble tomb to his great fellow countryman.

Severus then crossed to Thrace before travelling north to the Danube frontier, which he then followed west. Next, on reaching his old legionary fortress at *Carnumtum* in Moesia Superior, he appointed yet another North African called Titus Claudius Claudianus as its provincial governor. The emperor then headed south, arriving back in the imperial capital soon after. For the senators, this was a mixed blessing. For those who had survived his proscriptions, Rome now had a degree of political stability notably lacking over the past two decades. However, the nature of their emperor was now also clear. Severus was avaricious in the extreme, brutal, and determined to stay in power at all costs. The Severan dynasty was here to stay.

7

Imperator: Severus in Rome and North Africa

Severus spent much of the next six years in Rome, these his third and fourth stays in the imperial capital after becoming emperor in AD 193. Between the two, in a highlight of his reign, he returned to his native North Africa on a triumphal visit.

THE IMPERIAL CAPITAL

Severan Rome was the largest city in the world at the time, sprawling across seven hills. Here, today we still see the legacy of the Severan period, with around one third of the classical city visible dating to the dynasty.

There are abundant examples. Starting with the imperial palace on the Palatine Hill, Severus built a vast new suit of buildings which replaced Domitian's earlier *domus Augustana*. He dubbed it his *domus Severiana*, the new construction marking the final phase of expansion of the Palatine palace. It featured huge arched reception rooms, the whole topped with a viewing platform designed to give the emperor, his family and entourage a fine view of the *Circus Maximus* below. These structures are still visible today and are now known as the Severan Buildings. Severus also rebuilt the palace baths on the Palatine such that they now ran below his new reception rooms for ease of access.

Alongside the palace, Severus then constructed an enormous nymphaeum called the *Septizodium* which contemporaries called the most impressive of all the structures he commissioned. Completed in AD 203, this featured a majestic façade with columns, cascading gardens and fountains on several levels, built on the south-eastern side of the Palatine to provide a sensually overpowering scenic entrance to the palace from the *via Appia*. Its seven huge semi-circular niches, arranged in linear fashion perpendicular to the roadway, were based on the *scanae frons* of a Roman theatre and contained the statues of the seven planetary deities. These were Saturn, the Sun, the Moon, Mars, Mercury, Jupiter and Venus, with *Septizodium* translating as sevens suns. Nothing remains of it today except some foundation brick stumps below the Palatine palace, and its physical appearance is only known from Renaissance paintings. This is because Pope Sixtus V ordered its eastern façade demolished in 1588 to provide *spolia* for his numerous building works. Today, over ten significant structures in central Rome constructed at this time have been identified with stone and brick from the *Septizodium*.

Next, in the *forum Romanum* itself, Julia Domna rebuilt the Temple of Vesta after it had been destroyed in the AD 191 fire. This was an important temple which played a key role in the life of the city given it was here the vestal virgins tended the sacred flame which burned perpetually to symbolise Rome's life force. The only man able to enter at this time was Severus himself as *Pontifex Maximus*. The structure built in Julia Domna's name was round, the traditional shape for such a temple (based on the shape of the ancient huts of Latium), featuring a cylindrical cell decorated with half columns, the whole surrounded by an external ring of full-size Corinthian columns. Much remains today.

Severus also rebuilt all the public and private buildings along the *via Nova*, one of the two pre-imperial routeways through the *forum*, the other being the *via Sacra*. The *via Nova* separated the formal buildings in the *forum* itself from the imperial structures atop the

Palatine. Here, the arches evident today spanning the road were built in the Severan period to carry the upper stories of shops and houses for those practising commerce or living here. Recent excavations have uncovered a wealth of Severan-period artifacts associated with this construction phase, many now on display in the new museum inside the *domus Tiberiana*.

Severus also significantly upgraded the *Porticus Octaviae*, a late-first-century BC colonnaded portico which enclosed the temples of Juno Regina and Jupiter Stator near the *circus Flaminius* in the southern *campus Martius*. Here, after a fire in AD 203, the emperor and Caracalla sponsored not only its repair but erected a fine new marble *propylaeum* entrance surmounted by an inscription recording their largesse. This is still visible today as one enters the old Jewish Quarter in Rome.

Meanwhile, on the Caelian Hill to the immediate east of the *forum Romanum*, the remains of two other key examples of the Severan built environment are visible today. These are now located in the Parco Archaeologica del Celio. The first is the Temple of Fortuna Muliebris, goddess of good luck for women, originally built at the fourth milestone along the *via Latina* by the proconsul Verginius Tricostus Rutilius and dedicated in 493 BC. Specifically, the temple honoured the role played by the women of Rome in opposing the war led by the exiled Roman general Gaius Marcius Corioanus and his Volsci allies against the city in the early fifth century BC. The only architectural remains visible today are fragments from a marble slab which was found close to the mile marker, all now on display in the archaeological park. The inscriptions on these reference two phases of restoration, the first by Augustus' wife Livia and the second by Julia Domna. The latter appears to have been a significant reconstruction of what by then would have been a 700-year-old structure.

However, far more important on the Caelian Hill today are the remains of the enormous *Forma Urbis Romae* Severan map of the city. This measured 18m by 13m and was carved on 150 slabs of Proconnesian marble sourced from Marmara Island in the Sea of Marmara. It was commissioned by Severus himself. The map was originally mounted vertically in the Temple of Peace in the *forum* of Vespasian to the west of the location where its remains are displayed today in the new Museo della Forma Urbis on the Caelian Hill, forming a central focus for the Parco Archaeologica del Celio.

The *Forma Urbis Romae* was constructed at 1:240 scale, this detailed enough to show the floor plan outline and interior detail of almost all the city's monuments, palaces, bathing complexes, arenas and theatres of all kinds, temples, aquaducts and *insulae* at the time Severus was emperor. The road plan is also exceptionally clear. Of note, the boundaries of the structures as displayed on the map were not only decided by exact geographical location, but also the space available on the slab. Nevertheless, this was a true map rather than the more usual Roman travel itinerary, for example the famous Antonine example detailed in the Introduction. The *Forma Urbis Romae* is orientated south at the top to north at the bottom and includes the names of the public buildings, streets and private homes of the city's leading citizens at the time. In particular, the scale of the *Septizodium* on the map is startling. Meanwhile, specific symbols are used on the map to illustrate finer details, for example steps, staircases and monumental columns.

The *Forma Urbis Romae* was destroyed during the Middle Ages when, over time, the slabs were gradually removed from the ruined Temple of Peace to provide building material for new structures. Antiquarians then began the process of recovering the surviving fragments, with the ten per cent or so recovered to date now on display in the Museo della Forma Urbis set in a life-size horizontal recreation of the original.

The importance of Severus' *Forma Urbis Romae* lies not only in the intimacy it provides the viewer with his Rome, but also in the insight it provides into the emperor himself. Maps are equated today with power and territorial control, the earliest modern examples usually military initiatives, for example the original Ordnance Survey sequence in Britain. The Roman equivalent was the imperial trunk road network, with the building of new major roads always accompanying their campaigns of conquest. If a significant road was built, they intended to stay.

In that context, constructing the *Forma Urbis Romae* took Roman geographical control to a totally new level given the accuracy and detail. It was also typical of Severus, an emperor obsessed with physical control.

However, the two most visible structures in Rome today specifically linked to Severus are monumental arches. The first has already been detailed in the first chapter, this the 6.15m high *Arcus Argentariorum* Arch of the Moneychangers in the *forum Boarium* which was dedicated after his return from North Africa on his fourth visit to Rome, featuring its life-size sculptures of Severus and Julia Domna.

Far more dramatic, though, is the Arch of Septimius Severus in the *forum Romanum*, still today one of the *forum*'s most impressive features. This enormous triumphal arch was deliberately planted to the immediate northwest of the *curia Julia*, with its foundations straddling those of the Senate meeting house. Such deliberate placing was clearly designed to remind the Senators who the boss was. Severus' new arch also encroached on the *Umbilicus Urbis Romae* or *Mundus*, a small monument said to mark the centre of the city of Rome and also thought in the classical world an entrance to the underworld. Typically, Severus decided that rather than accommodate the latter as he built his own arch, he would rebuild this ancient monument, too, its remains still visible as a brick structure.

Severus' arch in the forum is imperial monumentalisation writ large. It was constructed of fantastically expensive alabaster-white marble, and was dedicated after his return from North Africa to commemorate the victories in his two eastern campaigns. As such,

Caracalla and Geta also share the emperor's limelight on the arch, though see below with regard to the younger son.

The arch is 23m high, built on a raised travertine base which was originally approached by steps from the forum, the central archway being spanned by a beautifully coffered semicircular vault with lateral openings on each side archway. The structure is 25m in width and almost 12m deep. Its three archways rest on piers, to the front of which are composite columns detached on pedestals. On its spandrels are carved reliefs of winged victories, while a staircase in the south pier leads to the top where originally there were bronze statues of the emperor, Caracalla and Geta riding a *quadriga* four-horse chariot, together with soldiers.

The arch has a detailed dedicatory inscription on both sides across the top which reads:

'To the emperor Caesar Lucius Septimius Severus Pius Pertinax Augustus Parthicus Arabicus Parthicus Adiabenicus, son of Marcus, father of his country, Pontifex Maximus, in the eleventh year of his tribunician power, in the eleventh year of his rule, consul thrice, and proconsul, and to the emperor Caesar Marcus Aurelius Antoninus Augustus Pius Felix [this is Caracalla], son of Lucius, in the sixth year of his tribunician power, consul, and proconsul (fathers of their country, the best and bravest emperors), on account of the restored Republic and the rule of the Roman people spread by their outstanding virtues at home and abroad, the Senate and the People of Rome.'

However, of most interest in a military context are the depictions on the arch of the Severan Roman military campaigns in the east on the four relief panels, two on each side of the arch. These show:

- Relief 1 on the left forum-facing panel, featuring preparations for the first campaign in the east, then a battle scene featuring many troops, and finally the liberation of Nisibis in the same campaign

IMPERATOR: SEVERUS IN ROME AND NORTH AFRICA

after Osrhoene, Adiabene and Hatra had all capitulated, with an enemy leader fleeing to the right. Sadly, it has been much worn but is still a useful source of data.

- Relief 2 on the right forum-facing panel is also damaged and shows the revolt of Osrhoene prior to Severus' first eastern campaign. In the upper register, we then see how Severus later announces the annexation of the city state after it surrendered.
- Relief 3 on the left Capitoline Hill-facing panel is better preserved and shows the second eastern campaign, specifically the second phase with Severus' assault on Parthia. Here, we see the Roman attack on Seleucia-on-the-Tigris, with Parthian troops fleeing left and right. The upper register then shows the citizens of the town surrendering.
- Relief 4 on the right Capitoline Hill-facing panel shows the sack of Ctesiphon as the invasion of Parthia came to a successful end. A siege engine is shown employed to breach the walls, and the city then surrenders. In the upper register we then see Severus declaring Caracalla his fellow *augusti*, with Geta named *Caesar*.

Also on the arch, other reliefs include statues of the four seasons and prisoners of war on the pedestals. We also see loot from the two eastern campaigns being transported back to Antioch.

One final note regarding the arch is how we see Geta on it today. As detailed, by the time the arch was constructed Severus was ruling jointly with Caracalla, and he is clearly mentioned in the dedication. However, in the text there is also a parenthesised section in the centre where Geta's name was also originally mentioned in the context of him being *Caesar*. This was later chiselled away when Caracalla declared him *damnatio memoriae* after his murder. Additionally, separate representations of the two brothers each holding a Parthian captive on the Capitoline Hill-facing piers of the arch are noteworthy given Geta's face has been chiselled away here too. Further, as he never officially existed after his *damnatio memoriae*, neither did his Parthian captive. Therefore, his face was removed, too.

Staying with Severus' elder son, we can finally look at the enormous public baths which still carry his name today and stand as a remarkable landmark to the Severan Dynasty. These are the Baths of Caracalla, constructed between AD 205 (some argue AD 212, but this is too late based on the latest archaeological data) and AD 216. At the time they were built, they were the largest public bathing complex in ancient Rome, and possibly the entire Roman world, and were only bettered in size by the later Baths of Diocletian. Planning for their construction was initiated by Severus himself. Indeed, some primary sources reference them as the Baths of Severus rather than Caracalla, though this is likely a mistranslation of Severan rather than Severus. Here, I stick with Baths of Caracalla to avoid confusion.

The site chosen for the new public baths, on the southern side of the city, was already an elite location in Rome. It was formerly occupied by a vast garden estate developed by the architect Gaius Asinius Pollio for Augustus called the *horti Asiniani*. Severus' idea here was to make his new vast bathing complex one of the first sites visitors saw as they approached Rome along the *via Appia*. Constructing the complex was a huge undertaking, with around 13,000 prisoners of war allegedly used to level the building site. Further, 6,000 artisans and tradesmen were employed every day for the actual construction work, which utilised more than 21 million specially made high-quality bricks and tiles. The whole complex was richly decorated with mosaics and fine marble, with 600 skilled workers required for the marble work alone, this using 6,300m³ of the fine building stone.

The bathing complex consisted of the huge bathhouse itself and a surrounding park, the latter created by the later Severan emperors Heliogabalus (birthname Sextus Varius Avitus Bassianus, later called Marcus Aurelius Antoninus, before adopting the nickname by which he is better known today) and Severus Alexander. The enormous quantities of water needed were supplied by a new branch of the *Aqua Marcia* aqueduct, named the *Aqua Antoniniana* after Caracalla's actual name.

Everything about the baths was monumental. The central building itself measured 214m by 114m and consisted of four levels, two above ground and two below. The largest room within was the *tepidarium* measured 52m by 25m and featured a vaulted dome 38m high. The *basilicae thermogram* entrance halls were in the northwest and southeast corners and were designed to impress, with the bathhouse symmetrically aligned along a northeast-southwest axis. Each entrance measured 50m by 20m. Modern estimates indicate 1,600 people could use the bathing complex at the same time in this ultimate testament to Severan grandiosity.

Later Severan dynasty additions to the built environment in Rome included a significant repair of the Colosseum after a fire around AD 217 when the upper storey visible today was constructed as part of the repair programme, and the huge temple of Heliogabalus atop the Palatine Hill overlooking the *forum Romanum*.

Severus, Julia Domna and their family spent the next six months in Rome. Cassius Dio, a spectator and sometime participant in the events he describes, usefully sets out an average day in the life of the emperor at the time:[1]

> 'He was always doing something before dawn and after that used to take a walk while talking and listening about the matters of the empire. Then he would have a judicial court, except when there was some festival or another. Then he would take a bath after engaging in some kind of exercise. Following this, he would have a meagre lunch either on his own or with his children. After lunch, he usually napped for a bit. When he rose, he then turned to the rest of his affairs and then used to spend time engaged in both Greek and Latin debates while walking again. Near dusk, he would bathe again and then dine with those who were attending him – for he did not frequently have a guest for dinner and

he would only sponsor expensive banquets on days when it was necessary.'

The reference to the emperor riding here is very interesting given the phrase 'as much as he was able', which is our first indicator of the long-term condition for which Severus is best known – gout. If Dio is referencing this illness, then it indicates at this stage he was still able to walk. I consider this subject now given Severus' foot problem was to trouble him for the rest of his life.

Shortly after, Dio mentions the illness by name for the first time, at least as translated today, saying that Severus 'eventually grew very weak from gout'.[2] The Greek word Dio uses is ποδάγρα, or podagra, meaning foot trap. This emphasises sudden pain experienced in the metatarsophalangeal joint of the big toe. The first writer to use the word gout itself to describe podagra was the Dominican monk Randolphus of Bocking, the domestic chaplain to the Bishop of Chichester from 1197 to 1258. He uses the phrase 'gutta quam podagram vel artiticam vocant', which translates as 'the gout that is called podagra or arthritis'. The actual term is derived from the Latin word *gutta*, which means drop, referring to the prevailing medieval belief that an excess of one of the four humours would, under certain circumstances, drop or flow into a joint, causing pain and inflammation.

In modern medicine, when a practitioner is confronted with the symptoms detailed by Dio, several alternative diagnoses might be made, depending on other symptoms. These include septic arthritis, cellulitis, pseudogout, other types of inflammatory arthritis including rheumatoid and psoriatic, plus a stress fracture. Of note, Severus is known to have fallen from his horse at least twice when campaigning against Albinus, which might certainly have caused injury. He was also physically active for much of his earlier life, even when not on campaign, which again might expose him to injury. If in either context this caused a wound to his foot, whether of the bone or otherwise, and it was not treated properly or healed badly, then that might have caused his longer-term health issue.

However, Severus' symptoms do certainly sound like a modern diagnosis of gout, especially when later in life in his campaigns in Scotland he is detailed being carried in a sedan chair as he was unable to ride a horse or walk. We know gout certainly existed in the Roman world given skeletal remains which show evidence of damage from uric acid crystals. Also, in terms of risk factors for the condition, Severus' gender, age, and socio-economic status would all have increased his susceptibility. As a final comment, long term chronic pain and an inability to walk would also have badly affected Severus' mental health later in life when he was notably short tempered.

When Severus returned to Rome in AD 202 after five years' absence, the event was celebrated in high style by the populace there. They were no doubt encouraged by his imperial largesse given he distributed ten gold pieces a head to the urban plebs, Praetorian Guard and *equites singulares Augusti*.[3] Here, Dio details that:[4]

> 'Severus took particular pride in this generosity; indeed, no emperor had ever before made such a large donation to the entire population of the city. The total sum amounted to 200,000 sesterces.'

This sum seems on the short side if every pleb and guard received the donative, so perhaps Severus' munificence was more targeted. Even so, it was still a vast amount of money which no doubt came out of the *fiscus* rather than Severus' own coffers.

More celebrations then followed with an imperial wedding. Here, the fourteen-year-old Caracalla reluctantly married Fulvia Plautilla, daughter of Plautianus, who now reached the peak of his influence within the Severan court as Severus' closest confidant. Syvanne says the *praefectus praetorio*'s ambition here was to unite the imperial family directly with his own, though this was always doomed to failure given Caracalla 'felt intense dislike towards his wife and her father'.⁵ Plautianus was certainly made to pay by the avaricious emperor for the marriage of his daughter to his eldest son, with Dio (who was a wedding guest) saying he gave as much for his daughter's dowry as would have been needed for 50 women of royal rank.⁶

The Severan family then moved on to their *decennalia* celebrations. For completeness, there is an issue here with the historiography given the year was still AD 202, while Severus became emperor in AD 193. That would indicate the celebrations were a year early. We have no indication why, though the timing may have been influenced by his plans to travel to North Africa later in the year.

We certainly know detail about what occurred during this festival, which involved extensive public sacrifices in the temple precinct on the Capitoline Hill, spectacles across Rome and victory games in the main arenas, particularly the Colosseum where hundreds of animals were slaughtered in beast hunts. Unusually, this included hyenas imported from India.

Of note, Severus was also offered another triumph by the Senate at this time but turned it down. The *Historia Augusta* states this was because 'the disease of his limbs made it impossible for him to stand up in a triumphal chariot'.⁷ This is our third reference to the gout-like symptoms detailed above by Dio, showing that on this occasion the illness was also affecting his ability to stand. Meanwhile, in his final act during this short visit to Rome, Severus appointed his younger son Geta and Plautianus as *consuls* for the following year. Then the entire imperial entourage was on the move once more, this time to Severus' homeland North Africa.⁸

BACK TO AFRICA

Severus arrived in Carthage in October AD 202 for what was to be a short eight-month visit to his North African provinces. He was the first emperor to visit the region since Hadrian early in the second century AD.[9] At his side for most of the trip were Julia Domna, Caracalla, Geta, Plautianus and Plautilla. Inscriptions also show Severan family members from the region joined the royal party on several occasions, for example a cousin of the emperor called Lucius Septimius Aper.

While in Carthage, Severus made the first of a series of administrative reforms in North Africa, declaring the provincial capital *ius Italicum*, this a great privilege meaning it was exempt from provincial taxation. Shortly after, the emperor bestowed the same honour on Utique (Roman *Utica*) to the north, which he may have briefly visited before returning to Carthage. Meanwhile, *Thugga*, *Thignica* and *Thibursicum* were given *municipia* mercantile status, giving them taxation benefits, too.

Early in January AD 203, the emperor then began a six-month circuitous tour of his North African territories, first heading west. As always with Severus, we get a sense of an emperor in a hurry, and this trip was no exception. His first stop was modern Annaba in Algeria, the key Roman coastal city of *Hippo Regius*. Notably, Severus' travels through North African are still visible today in the surviving Roman built environment, where one gets the sense of a local hero returning. In every city and town, the local magistrates strove to commemorate the occasion in grand style, with each trying to better their neighbours. Annaba is no exception, where today in the modern archaeological park can be found the majestic remains of the 'great north baths', a huge 4,500m^2 public bathing complex built to commemorate Severus' visit. This featured numerous religious statues made from highly polished Parian marble, whose inscribed bases are still visible *in situ* today. Several of the actual statues are on display in the museum there.

Continuing west, Severus next stopped at the *colonia* of Guelma (Roman *Calama*). Its finest surviving Roman monument is the theatre, with much of the structure visible today rebuilt in the French colonial period but still retaining its distinctive Roman form.

Construction began in AD 203 to coincide with Severus' visit, and he dedicated the new building project and its adjacent bathing complex in person. Under the Severans, Guelma was to become one of the richest Roman settlements in the region.

The imperial party next headed into the Atlas Mountains as they continued west, stopping at the mountain-top city of Constantine. Sadly, this is one of the few locations in the region where little remains of the Roman built environment, though inscriptions in the National Museum of *Cirta* (this a Latinised version of the city's original Numidian name) are Severan.

However, much is evident dating to the Severus' visit at the next stop on the emperor's journey west, this another Atlas Mountain site called *Cuicul*, today's Djemila in Algeria. This was a key Roman city linking the Mediterranean coast with the Saharan interior of Numidia. I have stood here in the 48m by 44m porticoed *forum* which dates to this time, and from there viewed the Temple of the Gens Septimia built later by Severus Alexander, through the Arch of Caracalla. The former, with an interior clad in fine marble, featured two monumental statues of Severus and Julia Domna. The heads of these are today displayed outside the fine museum at the site. My overall impression was one of huge scale, the Severan desire to monumentalise the imperial presence writ large.

Before the end of the month, Severus then headed south through the southern Atlas Mountains to the high plains where he next made one of the most important stops on his tour. This was at the legionary fortress of Lambaesis, home to *legio* III *Augusta*. There, he was briefed by its *legate* Quintus Anicius Faustus on the five-year campaign he'd unsuccessfully been leading against the Garamantes in the Libyan desert interior, trying to prevent their raiding of Tripolitania. While in Lambaesis, Severus also initiated the formal separation of Numidia from Africa Proconsularis, making the legionary fortress its new capital. In recognition, the latter's *canaba* civilian settlement was designated a *colonia* which put it on a par with nearby Timgad.[10]

IMPERATOR: SEVERUS IN ROME AND NORTH AFRICA

Severus' veteran commander Claudius Gallus then became the new province's first governor.

As elsewhere in North Africa, Severus' visit to Lambaesis is well recorded in the built environment. There can still be found today the fine three-bay Arch of Septimius Severus, a *Septizodium* modelled on that in Rome (though here far smaller and more akin to a grand fountain than a nymphaeum), and numerous Severan inscriptions. Of the latter, the best known is on a substantial statue base now in Lambaesis Museum in nearby Tazoult. Set up in honour of Severus and Caracalla, the text shows the shift in iconographic emphasis which was an emerging feature of the Severan reset. Specifically, here it emphasises militarism, martial valour and conquest as opposed to civic virtue and benevolence, the latter central features of Antonine inscriptions in the previous century.[11]

After Lambaesis, Severus visited nearby Timgad, where today its best-known monument is the three bay Arch of 'Trajan'. Its modern appellation is derived from an incorrect nineteenth-century AD dating. In fact, it was built at the time of Severus' North African visit. Thus, here we have yet another Severan monumental arch on the fringes of the Saharan *limes*. Further, two substantial octagonal statue bases in front of the arch reference the Severans, one of which featured a statue of Mars (reflecting the martial theme detailed above in the inscriptions from Lambaesis) and one the Concord of the Emperors (here Severus and Caracalla). These were set up by a local notable called Lucius Licinius Optatianus eager to thank the Severus and his son for being made Timgad's *flamen per-petuus* chief priest of the imperial cult. In the inscription on the base of the Concord statue, he proudly says that together they cost him 35,000 sesterces.[12]

Severus then headed east along the main trunk road through the high plains to Tébessa (Roman *Theveste*) in modern Tunisia. Today, its principal Severan association is the enormous *quadrifrons* (four bay) Arch of Caracalla. Construction of this imposing monument began while Severus was still emperor but was likely completed after his death given evidence from the keystone of each arch. These were originally intended to feature an individual portrait of each member of the emperor's close family. Portraits of the emperor, Julia Domna and Caracalla (now defaced) were completed, but that of Geta was not, dating events here to after the latter's *damnatio memoriae*. Interestingly, construction of the arch was not funded by the imperial *fiscus*, but by another individual donation, this time of 250,000 *sesterces*. This was given as a bequest in the will of Gaius Cornelius Egrilianus, a contemporary of Severus who had earlier been *legate* of *legio* XIV *Gemina* in Pannonia Superior and had been a leading native of Tébessa. Meanwhile, the Temple of 'Minerva' in Tébessa is also likely Severan and contemporary with his visit. Its incorrect attribution to Minerva was based on the nineteenth-century AD misidentification of avian images as owls, when in fact they are eagles. Blas de Roblès, Sintes and Kenrick argue the temple was dedicated to Bacchus and Heracles, who the emperor at this stage in his life claimed were his divine protectors.[13]

The imperial party next headed north back to the coast, on the way stopping at two more key cities in the southern foothills of the Atlas Mountains. The first was Madaure (originally *Colonia Flavia Augusta Veteranorum Madauerensium* when founded by Nerva and later called *Madauros*). This city featured one of the empire's leading law schools, much of which is still visible today. It was also the home of Apuleius, author of *The Golden Ass*, the only classical Latin novel to survive today. In Madaure can be found yet another Severan theatre dating to his time in North Africa, much of it surviving as the north wall of the Byzantine fort built much later following Belisarius' reconquest of Vandal North Africa. Again, the construction of the theatre was privately funded, this time by the *flamen* priest Marcus Gabinius Sabinus who spent 375,000 *sesterces* on the project.

Severus' final stop before reaching the coast was Khemissa (Roman *Thubursicu Numidarum*), located in a dramatic landscape of rolling green hills 950m above sea level and 40km southeast of Guelma. Here, the emperor bestowed the settlement with *colonia* status, though little remains in the built environment to record his visit.

By mid-March, Severus was back in Carthage. His first focus was to the west, where the local Mauri tribes were causing trouble in Mauretania Caesariensis and (farthest west) Mauretania Tingitana. Though the emperor didn't visit the region in person, he did order the southern extension of the *limes* there, building a new series of fortifications called the *nova praetentura*. A swift campaign to the south then followed under the *legates* Haius Diadumenianus and Sallustius Macrinianus, who targeted the mountainous region between the two provinces. Here, through the Taza Gap and the valley of the Mouloya river in the Atlas Mountains, raiding Mauri had found easy routes of access to the coast. Roman success followed, with a victory monument built at Bou Hellou, 90km east of *Volubilis*, the latter a former Mauritanian capital close to the Atlantic coast of modern Morocco. Both legates were then appointed joint governors of the two Mauritanian provinces for a short period while administrative changes were made to support the new, more southerly frontier. This included a new road building programme, with vexillations of *legio* III *Augusta* drafted in to carry out the task using local Berber labour for non-skilled work.

At the end of March, Severus then set off for the grandest part of this grandest of short tours, returning home to Leptis Magna. Birley identifies his route along the Carthage to Alexandria trunk road, stopping first at *Thapsus*, then Gabes (Roman *Tacapae*), next *Sabratha*, then Tripoli (Roman *Oea*), before finally reaching his *patria*.[14] On arrival, he found some things changed given it had been nearly 30 years since his last visit. These included a greatly expanded public bathing complex which had been restored and enlarged under Commodus, and the rebuilding of the Arch of Antoninus Pius.[15]

Much more pleasing to Severus, he found Leptis Magna full of recent statues and dedicatory inscriptions to himself, Julia Domna, Caracalla, Geta, Plautianus (later to become an issue, see below), Plautilla, and his own father, mother, grandfather, and first wife Paccia Marciana. While the latter might seem odd to a modern audience, it simply reflected the Roman concept of reverence for the dead, she in this case a native of Leptis Magna. The earliest Severan statue fashioned here after he became emperor dates to AD 197 and resided in the Temple of Liber Pater, God of viticulture, male fertility and freedom. Notably, amid a host of honorific titles, the inscription on its base also calls Severus *conservatori orbis*, the defender of the world. No doubt the statue was erected amid a rush following his final defeat of Albinus at *Lugdunum*, especially in his hometown. Meanwhile, on inscriptions for statues erected during the imperial visit, the citizenry of Leptis Magna changed their collective name on the dedications from the *Lepcitani* to the *Septimiani*.

While in Leptis Magna, Severus was keen to show beneficence to his home city. As with Carthage and *Utica*, he declared it *ius Italicum*. He also initiated a major public building programme to commemorate his visit. Ostensibly, this showed a serious level of imperial investment, though notably many of the new constructions were paid for by local public funds rather than his own *fiscus*. Here, Golvin details a new colonnaded *forum* and *basilica*, a *Septizodium* nymphaeum (again modelled on that in Rome and far larger than that in Lambaesis), and significant upgrades to the provincial palace and theatre.[16] However, the most significant monumental legacy to Severus's visit was the enormous quadrifrons arch built over one of the major crossroads in the city. Work on this had begun before the Severan visit but was now completed while he was there, the structure adorned with reliefs of the imperial family and Roman victories in the east during Severus' two earlier campaigns there.[17] A new artificial port was also built in Leptis Magna which rivalled that of Carthage in size and grandeur, and which today is the best preserved Roman port in the world.

The surrounding countryside around Leptis Magna was also extensively landscaped at this time, with a new 200m dam and canals being built to re-route the Wadi Lebda around the city. New residential areas also sprang up in fine suburbs built outside the city walls, with the population growing by the end of Severus' reign to over 100,000. By this time, the city had grown to 435 hectares in size.

Aside from detail of the route the imperial party took on its travels, there is only one mention of Severus' stay in North Africa in the literary record, this from Leptis Magna. It features in Flavius Philostratus' *Lives of the Sophists*, first published in the AD 330s.[18] He was a sophist who studied in Athens and later lived in Rome. In this work, he provides a treasury of anecdotes about notable sophists, painting a picture of their predominant influences. In this reference, he details a debate between two rival sophists in front of the imperial family in Leptis Magna, these Heraclides of Lycia and Apollonius of Athens. The latter was widely acknowledged to have outperformed the former.

The imperial party spent the winter months in Leptis Magna, where Geta and Plautianus began AD 203 as the new *consuls*. However, before he left, Severus had one last piece of unfinished business in Tripolitania. This was to deal with the Garamantian raiders who had caused *legio* III *Augusta*'s legate Quintus Anicius Faustus so much trouble. Here, this most warlike of emperors couldn't resist the opportunity to lead another campaign, this time south into the desert interior of the western Fezzān. Crossing the *limes Tripolitanus* in late January, a huge Roman column was soon deep in Garamantian territory, with the local Berber tribesmen unable to gather enough warriors to resist the invasion. One after another, their key oasis settlements fell to the Romans, including *Cydamus*, Bu Njem (Roman *Gholaia*, where an early AD 203 inscription details a Roman bath house being built), *Garbia*, and finally, the Garamantian capital Garama. This was over 600km south of Leptis Magna, indicating that while Severus may have personally led the initial stages of the incursion, he left Anicius Faustus to finish it. Then, when the campaign was successfully concluded, much of the captured territory was incorporated into Africa Proconsularis. The emperor then further refortified the border, extending the *limes Tripolitanus* to incorporate his newly conquered land, with a new more southerly sequence of *centenaria* fortified farmhouses built at the same time.

We know Severus was back in Leptis Magna by April given the legionary centurion Titus Flavius Marinus dedicated an altar there on the eleventh of the month to the emperor's birthday, celebrating Severus' safe return at the same time. Shortly after, the imperial party left for Carthage where in one last series of administrative reforms Severus annexed several settlements located just south of the Numidian *limes*. These included Mesaaad (Roman *Castellum Dimmidi*), Tabuda (Roman *Thabudeos*), Tobna (Roman *Thubunae*) and Zabi. At the same time, *Gemellae* and Biskra (Roman *Vescera*, the key frontier town south of the Aures Mountains), which for some reason had been lost to Roman control, were incorporated back into imperial territory. Finally, once more the fortified frontier was extended to incorporate these new territorial acquisitions. Thus, by the time the emperor reluctantly returned to Rome in June AD 203, the whole southern frontier of Roman North Africa had been significantly expanded and re-fortified.

Both Dio and the *Historia Augusta* conclude their brief commentaries of Severus' North African visit by detailing a falling out between Severus and Plautianus late in the trip. Dio says the cause was the number of statues erected in honour of the latter across the region, especially in Leptis Magna, with the emperor so angry he had some bronze statues of the *praefectus praetorio* melted down.[19] Meanwhile, the *Historia Augusta* is even more specific, saying the emperor was angry because 'Plautianus had placed his own statue among those of his kinsmen and relatives'.[20] It then adds that Severus declared Plautianus a public enemy. When word of this spread through the empire, those in position of power reacted accordingly, for example Racius Constans, the governor of Corsica et Sardinia, who ordered the statues of Plautianus there to be destroyed. However, Severus then wrong-footed all by relenting and reappointing his *praefectus praetorio*. Those who had sought his favour by following his earlier lead were then punished, including Constans. With the breach between Severus and Plautianus for now healed, even if only temporarily, the imperial party headed back to Rome.

ROME AGAIN

Severus' arrival back in the imperial capital was again commemorated with an altar inscription set up by *equites singurales Augusti* guardsmen, this dated 10 June, marking their successful return to Rome from what the dedication calls the African *expeditio felicissma*. Once more the emperor's return was marked by festivities, and also a minor triumph called an *ovatio* following his victory over the Garamantes. This was a celebration of victory against an inferior opponent, or one against whom the Senate had not declared war. The Arch of Septimius Severus, construction of which had begun during his previous visit in AD 202, was also now dedicated by the emperor given it was nearing completion. Two new *consuls* were then appointed for the following year, his friend Fabius Cilo (for the second time) and Annius Libo, grandson of Marcus Aurelius. Both took their posts as AD 204 began, the year when Severus presided over the Saecular Games in Rome. This was an ancient Roman religious celebration which lasted for three days and was held irregularly to celebrate the end of one era and the beginning of another. Severus chose AD 204 to mark the 220th anniversary of the Saecular Games held by Augustus, this a clear reference to the establishment of his own Severan dynasty. Then, later in the year, Caracalla and Geta were declared *consuls* for AD 205. Much to the annoyance of their father, both were now truly enjoying the high life in Rome.

As that year began, the issue of Plautianus' influence over Severus and his power in the imperial court again became a problem. For some time relations between the *praefectus praetorio* and the other imperial family members had been in rapid decline, especially Julia Domna and Caracalla. The latter, still bitter at being forced to marry Plautilla, was particularly antagonistic, with Dio stating:[21]

> 'Antoninus, in addition to being disgusted with his wife, who he thought a most shameless creature, felt resentment against Plautianus as well, because he kept meddling in all his undertakings and rebuking him for everything that he did; and so he conceived the desire to get rid of him in some way or other.'

Caracalla now took matters into his own hands. By January AD 205, he felt confident enough to make a decisive move. First, he persuaded a freedman called Euodus, who had been his tutor in early boyhood, to recruit three centurions. Then, on 22 January, while the imperial family was having dinner, the three soldiers appeared before Severus. They informed him that they, together with seven other troopers, had been ordered by Plautianus to murder both emperors. They then read out a letter which appeared to confirm their story.

Of note, only Herodian argues there is some truth in Caracalla's accusation, saying Plautianus was aware of his hostility to Plautilla and because of this feared for his life, and so started plotting against the imperial family.[22] However, most dismiss this, and I agree.

This was an audacious plot by the young Caracalla, and it worked amazingly well, helped by the emperor's superstitious nature. This was because the night before he'd had a dream that Albinus was still alive and plotting against him. He ordered Plautianus before him immediately, alone and with no Praetorians at his side. Severus then laid out the charges, clearly and without showing any emotion. The incredulous *praefectus praetorio* denied everything immediately, with Severus then offering him the opportunity to defend himself. However, Caracalla forced the issue, seizing Plautianus' sword and punching him in the face, saying he would kill him with his bare hands. The emperor quickly moved to restrain his elder son, though to no avail as Caracalla now ordered one of his attendants to slay the *praefectus praetorio*.

The brutal deed done, an interesting precursor to Caracalla's later murder of Geta, another courtier plucked some bloody hairs from Plautianus scalp and took them to a nearby room where Julia Domna and Plautilla were waiting. When presented with the gruesome evidence, the latter was understandably grief-stricken, though Julia Domna remained impassive.

Sadly, for Plautilla, without her father to protect her from Caracalla's animosity, her life would now become a misery. Meanwhile, the dead prefect's body was thrown to the dogs in the street, though the remains were later recovered on the emperor's orders and given a private burial. Of Plautianus' grisly fate, de la Bédoyère compares him to Tiberius' *praefectus praetorio* Lucius Aelius Sejanus though argues Severus' prefect was even more ambitious and scheming given his successful (to that point) manipulation of an imperial marriage.[23] Of final interest here amid this breathless and dramatic episode, it is noteworthy Severus has very little voice or presence while the events were taking place in his own court. This is unusual for such a commanding emperor, and though there is clearly an issue here with historiography, it is significant nevertheless.

Having seemingly learnt his lesson regarding command of the Praetorians, Severus now returned to the traditional two-prefect system for the guard, appointing the leading equestrian Quintus Maecius Laetus and his friend and senior jurist Aemilius Papinianus to the twin posts. The latter was a relative of Julia Domna and an ultra-reliable Severan loyalist. There they were to remain for the remainder of Severus' reign.

Little is recorded of the Severans in Rome for the next two years. The one subject the primary sources do comment on is the deteriorating behaviour of Caracalla and Geta, with Dio saying:[24]

'The sons of Severus, that they had got rid of a pedagogue in Plautianus, now went to all lengths in their conduct. They outraged women and abused boys, they embezzled money, and made gladiators and charioteers their boon companions, emulating each other in the similarity of their deeds, but full of strife in their rivalries; for if the one attached himself to a certain faction, the other would be sure to choose the opposite side. And at last they were pitted against each other in some kind of contest with teams of ponies and drove with such fierce rivalry that Antoninus fell out of his two-wheeled chariot and broke his leg. Severus, during his son's illness that followed this accident, did not neglect any of his duties in the least, but held court and attended all the business pertaining to his office. And for this he was praised.'

Dio's insight becomes even more important now given that, after Plautianus' death, the senator was promoted to become a member of Severus' *Consilium Principis*. He says the emperor now spent most of his time worrying about the behaviour of his sons, taking an interest in legal matters, and composing his autobiography. Meanwhile, Julia Domna continued to champion her favourite philosophers and sophists.

Then, in January AD 207, Severus had another chance to test his martial skills. This was regarding an outlaw called Bulla who had spent the previous year 'ravaging Italy in the presence of a great host of soldiers'.[25] The *bagaudae* leader, also called Felix by contemporary writers, had been joined by a host of runaway freedmen and slaves, some from the imperial house itself. Birley suggests he may also have teamed with some of the Praetorians Severus had discharged in disgrace when he came to power in AD 193.[26] The emperor now took matters in hand, personally leading a campaign which soon captured

Bulla, who was condemned to a grisly death through *damnatio ad bestias* in the Colosseum.

However, Severus remained frustrated. He never felt settled in Rome and still had no time for the Senate and imperial high politics. The ageing warrior now longed for another chance of real military conquest. Then, in late Spring AD 207, his final chance came. This was in the form of a highly alarming letter from far off Britannia, the wild northwest of his empire, where the governor told of impending doom there. Soon, Severus was on the march again, for his last and mightiest campaign.

8

Imperator: Arrival in Britain

In Rome, Severus was bored. This most military of men was never happy in the imperial capital, with its constant political machinations and temptations. However, he was to have one last chance at martial glory with his *expeditio felicissima Brittannica*. Here, he led by far the largest force ever to campaign on British soil, in Rome's final attempt to conquer the far north of Britain. Given the scale of his two invasions there in AD 209 and AD 210, I break down the narrative into two chapters. In this chapter, I firstly discuss the reasons behind Severus' *expeditio felicissima Brittannica*, then consider his planning for the campaigns and arrival in Britain, before finally detailing the battlespace in the far north. This includes an in-depth description of Severan York, his imperial capital for the last three years of his life.

WHY DID SEVERUS JOURNEY TO BRITAIN?

Virius Lupus remained governor in Britain until early AD 201 after securing peace in the north by paying huge subsidies to the Maeatae and Caledonians in the aftermath of *Lugdunum*. While in post, he was assisted by a new procurator appointed directly by Severus with orders to ensure the province's economic recovery continued after Albinus' revolt. This was Sextus Varius Marcellus, a Syrian patrician and later father of the Severan emperor Heliogabalus. It was

Marcellus who now began planning for the formal separation of Britannia into two provinces.

For much of his term in office, Lupus focused on restoring the military infrastructure in the north of Britain. This included repairing the trunk road network there and rebuilding the various fortifications south of Hadrian's Wall, though at this stage not the wall itself. He also played a key role in reconstituting the three British legions after their defeat with Albinus in AD 197. Under his watchful eye, soon vexillations from *legio* II *Augusta* in Caerleon, *legio* XX *Valeria Victrix* in Chester and *legio* VI *Victrix* in York were again manning the northern *limes* in Britain. Lupus then disappears from history, with some arguing he was killed on campaign while others believe he died of natural causes in office. Whatever his fate, there was certainly no disgrace involved given his sons Lucius Virius Agricola and Lucius Virius Lupus Julianus were *consuls* in AD 230 and AD 232 respectively.

More confusion follows regarding Lupus' replacement. Birley argues there was at least one more governor in post in Britain before the arrival of Gaius Varelius Pudens in AD 202.[1] This makes sense given the dating evidence we have from inscriptions and dedications, and the gap between Lupus disappearing and Puden's arriving. One candidate was a friend of Severus called Pollienus Auspex, who Birley says was noted in court for his sarcastic humour.[2] However, the evidence used to argue his case for the posting is marginal at best. Another often listed as the short-term stand-in between Lupus and Pudens is Marcus Antius Crescens Calpurnianus. He was earlier Lupus' *iuridicus* legal expert in his *officium consularis*. Once more, though, despite inscriptions from Ostia which some claim are definitive proof, we have no completely reliable data to support his case.

With Pudens we are on much firmer ground, his tenure as British governor widely reported in the primary sources. Pudens was a Severan favourite who we last met replacing Lupus as governor of Germania Inferior after the latter's appointment to Britain in

AD 197. He was another North African, this time a native of Djemila in the Atlas Mountains in modern Algeria, who'd been suffect consul the year after Severus became emperor. In Britain, he proved a great success, later spending time in senior posts in Rome before finally becoming governor of Africa Proconsularis in AD 210.

Pudens' key legacy in Britain was to continue the rebuilding process of the northern frontier started by Lupus. Here, we are fortunate, given several inscriptions recording this survive. A key one is that at the outpost fort at Risingham (Roman *Habitancum*) on Dere Street in Northumberland. This can be firmly dated to Puden's term in office, based on references to Caracalla which give specific dates. Another, better known, is an inscription from Bainbridge (Roman *Virosidum*) in North Yorkshire which records a new barrack block being constructed under his governorship. Other fragmentary inscriptions from Ribchester (Roman *Bremetennacum Veteranorum*) in Lancashire and Caernarvon (Roman *Segontium*) in Gwynedd also reference Pudens sponsoring military rebuilding work there, but these are more fragmentary.

Pudens' tenure as British governor ended in AD 205. His replacement was Lucius Alfenus Senecio, last mentioned as the first governor of Coele-Syria after Severus had separated the original province of Syria into two. As with Pudens, Senecio was a North African, also from Djemila. He had made steady progress along the *cursus honorum*, becoming procurator of Gallia Belgica and later Mauretania Caesariensis before his Syrian promotion to governor. The inference here is that, at least earlier in his career, he was a specialist administrator rather than military leader.

The situation Senecio inherited on the northern frontier was complex. Rome had already weathered severe agitation there after Albinus' usurpation, with Lupus stabilising the frontier through the huge subsidies he paid the native leaders to cease their predation across the frontier. He then began to reassert Roman authority there. However, notably this had not included Hadrian's Wall itself, only the surrounding infrastructure, especially to the south. One should note here the enormous statement of Roman power Hadrian's Wall represented. There has been a debate for decades about the purpose of the fortification. I am firmly on the militaristic side of the discussion. In that regard, I believe not only was it a physical military barrier separating *Romanitas* from *barbaricum*, but that it was also built with the psychological impact on the local Brigantes in mind. When constructed, it smashed through their territory, with no regard for the devasting political, economic and societal shock caused to regional native society. This was Roman power writ large, paying no attention at all to any local concerns. Now, almost 90 years later, it still held that same shocking hold on the natives living there. That made it a target every time the Maeatae and Caledonians challenged the *limes*, their slighting the wall an overt signal they did not accept the rule, or even influence, of Rome. The fact Lupus had failed to initiate repairs after the damage caused to the frontier in the wake of Albinus' revolt acknowledged this. The Romans would only begin its full repair once their military strength along the frontier had returned to some kind of near normality. From that point they could then ignore any localised challenges to their authority. Clearly, with Senecio's appointment, normal service had now resumed as it was he who began its repair.

We are fortunate that British inscriptions reference Senecio more than any other Roman governor in the province. Soon after his arrival, these begin to appear, showing restoration work underway on the northern *limes*. These include inscriptions showing legionaries and auxiliaries carrying out building and repair work at the large wall forts of Birdoswald (Roman *Banna*, where a new granary was built), Housesteads (Roman *Vercovicium*) and Chesters (Roman *Cilurnum*). Meanwhile, other rebuilding work occurred at sites north and south of Hadrian's Wall at the same time, all part of the Roman system of defence in depth in the north. This included construction of a new gate and walls at Risingham following the earlier restoration work there under Pudens, and the building of a new annexe at Bainbridge (Roman *Virosidum*). The latter was a key fort in today's

North Yorkshire, where, again, Senecio continued the earlier work of Pudens. Other work was similarly carried out at Corbridge. Of note, some of the inscriptions recording this building activity mention the involvement of the provincial procurator, Marcus Oclatinius Adventus, who had earlier replaced Marcellus. Key examples include Chesters and Risingham. Indeed, at the latter he may have taken direct charge of the work alongside the military tribune Aemilius Salvianus, also referenced in the inscriptions and directly appointed to the work by Senecio. Adventus was an interesting appointment to become the procurator in Britain at this time given he was formally a senior officer in the *frumentarii* imperial secret service. This has led some to suggest he was in post specifically to inspect the state of the northern *limes* in Britain on the direct orders of Severus.[3]

This extensive (and no doubt intrusive) construction activity, particularly on Hadrian's Wall itself, soon incurred the ire of the natives north of the frontier again. Evidence now begins to appear of renewed military activity along the *limes*. This includes an altar with a 'victory to the emperors' dedication set up by the *Ala* I *Astorum* cavalry unit at the fort of Benwell (Roman *Condercum*) on the western outskirts of modern Newcastle, specifically mentioning Senecio and calling him the '*consular*'. This hints at his direct military involvement. Further, Dio references victories in Britain in AD 206.[4] In addition, Julius Julianus, then *legatus legionis* of Caerleon-based *legio* II *Augusta*, set up an altar near Corbridge at the same time to celebrate military success. The latter is firm evidence the legions in Britain were back to their regular rotation of vexillations on the northern frontier. Meanwhile, another altar found in the late sixteenth century AD at Greetlands in the Pennines, likely from the nearby fort site at Slack (Roman *Cambodunum*), gives thanks to 'Goddess Victoria Brigantia'. Again, this suggests military activity given the native deity was associated with Minerva, the Roman goddess of military strategy.

Interestingly, when word of renewed conflict in Britain reached Severus, his reaction wasn't admiration for his fellow North African's martial success. Instead, Dio says he was irritated that Senecio was leading a serious military campaign while he, stuck in Italy, was reduced to fighting Bulla and his bandits for want of a better opponent.[5] Then, conveniently, early in AD 207, the emperor received a shocking letter from Senecio out of the blue. This said the whole of Britannia was in peril, with Herodian our principal source. He states:[6]

> '... the governor of Britain informed Severus by dispatches that the barbarians there were in revolt and overrunning the country, looting and destroying virtually everything on the island. He told Severus that he needed either a stronger army [usually interpreted as a request for more troops] for the defense of the province, or the presence of the emperor himself. Severus was delighted with this news: glory-loving by nature, he wished to win victories over the Britons to add to the victories and titles of honour he had won in the east and the west.'

There is some debate about whether this letter existed or not. However, for me, there is a degree of detail and suggested jeopardy in the passage that rings true, even if only in part. To that end, and taking Herodian's story at face value, as I cautiously do from this point, context becomes very important. That is because the letter is so often the starting point for narratives on the Severan *expeditio felicissima Brittannica*.

In the first instance, we have already seen Senecio's rebuilding work along Hadrian's Wall caused friction with the natives in the north, resulting in conflict and initial Roman military success. However, Senecio's language points to a dramatic change in fortunes, needing immediate imperial intervention. A blunt reading seems to indicate the threat Senecio details was sudden, very real, and that when presented with the opportunity to intervene Severus couldn't wait to get stuck in. In that regard, the reference to the emperor's 'delight' seems clear cut, especially in the context of his concerns about the behaviour of his sons in Rome, and his own boredom there. We are therefore left with a broad range of factors which may have been behind Severus' *expeditio felicissima Brittannica*.

IMPERATOR: ARRIVAL IN BRITAIN

First, Severus was itching to get away from Rome and return to the field, whether Senecio's letter existed or not. In that context, he may have been looking for an opportunity for new martial endeavour, and in the most extreme interpretation manufactured one. One should not forget Britain was always a magnet for those looking for military glory within the imperial system, with its far north truly the wild west of the empire. Thus, even if Senecio's letter was real, the events it narrated could have been made up by the imperial administration to give the emperor an excuse for his final campaign. To be clear, we have no direct evidence this was the case.

Second, Severus was obsessed with his legacy, especially given his age and ill health. He would certainly not have wanted to leave unfinished business in the form of unrest in Britain, if that had indeed occurred. In that regard, all Roman emperors, no matter how successful, knew they would be judged against the glory of Augustus. Here, Severus was keenly aware of the words of Horace regarding the first Roman emperor and the conquest of Parthia and Britain, or lack of in Augustus' case. In that context, from Severus' perspective, he had dealt with the Parthians. All that was left were the troublesome northern Britons.

Third, even after the attention of the emperor's *legate*s following Albinus' revolt, and the reformation of the British military establishment under subsequent governors, all may still not have been well with the garrison there. The rebuilding of infrastructure along the northern *limes* had certainly been taking place given that was the trigger for the renewed tension there, but some argue Hadrian's Wall was still undermanned. This theme has been developed to suggest this was a deliberate move by Severus because he still feared an internal threat in Britain rather than an external one from the north. Notably, the later Latin chronicler Paulus Orosius calls the unrest Severus dealt with in Britain a rebellion.[7]

Finally, and a factor much overlooked by many commentators, the motivations and behaviour of the protagonists. The Maeatae and Caledonians had already been heavily engaged along the border throughout the previous generation at various times from the AD 180s and had been bought off with enormous quantities of portable wealth in the late AD 190s by Lupus. That in itself must have caused enormous friction among their own elites, already coalescing into larger and larger political units through the cultural impact of the close proximity of the empire. Most likely their leaders were now permanently on the lookout for a military distraction to the south, and in that context saw the opportunity for a profit-making raid to keep their warriors occupied. Further, another factor for consideration here involves a possible harvest shock (crop failure) in their home territories. Given the emergence of the two confederations detailed above in the late second century AD, it seems reasonable to suggest that the population in the region was growing and there were more mouths to feed. We also know, as I detail below, that the weather at the time of the two Severan campaigns in the far north was unusually poor. We might therefore speculate that the latter could have impacted crop yields, leading to a need for the native leaders north of the frontier to head south to feed their growing populations.

My own view here is we are looking at a combination of factors, presenting all of those involved with a unique set of circumstances which together led to what followed. The warrior confederations north of the border were getting a taste for vast wealth and looking for an opportunity for easy plunder and may also have been hungry. Meanwhile, the northern border may still have been undermanned for whatever reason. Finally, Severus was on the prowl for war and mindful of his legacy. Whether triggered by the arrival of Senecio's letter or provincial news in another form, and whether real or engineered, the scene was now set for imperial shock and awe writ large in arguably the most devastating campaign ever fought on British soil.

PLANNING AND ARRIVAL

Whatever the reason behind Severus' reaction to the news from Britain, he didn't need a second invitation and jumped at the chance to take the field one last time. Birley says the emperor's first action was to gather any in elite imperial circles with knowledge of Britain to provide close council.[8] These included Calpurnianus and Pudens, both now back in Rome. Others included Gaius Julius Asper, ceremonial patron of Britannia in the imperial capital, and Polus Terentianus, Severus' ally in the 'Year of the Five Emperors' when governor of Dacia. He had earlier been *legate legionis* of *legio* II *Augusta* in Caerleon. Another former commander of this legion was also close to hand, Silius Plautius Haterianus, a fellow North African from Leptis Magna.

As the year progressed, Severus now began the detailed logistical planning for his *expeditio felicissima Brittannica*. The first step was to bring together the key military leaders and advisors who would accompany him. There is no evidence he took any of those detailed above, perhaps preferring a younger team to join what he knew would be an arduous expedition. Those we do know accompanied him included two Senatorial *comites* imperial companions with military experience, both from his *Consilium Principis*. These were called Julius Avitus Alexianus and Gaius Junius Faustinus Postumianus. The former, brother-in-law of Julia Domna, had been the *praefectus annonae* in charge of the grain supply in Rome at the time Pertinax was emperor. Meanwhile, the latter had recently been governor of Lower Moesia, and before that Hispania Tarraconensis. He was another North African and would take over as governor in Britain on the expedition's arrival, joining the still in post procurator Adventus. We have no idea why Senecio was removed, though perhaps the emperor was still jealous of the governor's military success in the province. As we have seen, the emperor was not one to share the limelight with anyone. Meanwhile, also accompanying the emperor was one of the two *praefecti praetorio*, Aemilius Papinianus. He was to play a key role in the two campaigns in Scotland, and also in the aftermath of Severus' death in York.

We also know of two others on Severus' senior military team from inscriptions which detail their job titles but not their names. The first is detailed on a sandstone altar found at Corbridge set up by the man assigned the key role of managing the granaries and logistics base there for the campaigns. This is an important individual in our story given it is his inscription (RIB 1143) which gives us the name *tempore expeditionis felicissi(mae) britanic(ae)*, or *expeditio felicissima Brittannica*. In full, the inscription reads:

'[...]norus [...pr]aep(ositus) cur(am) agens horreorum tempo[r]e expeditionis felicissi(mae) Brittannic(ae) v(otum) s(olvit) l(ibens) m(erito).'

This translates as:

'[...]norus..., officer in charge of the granaries at the time of the most successful expedition to Britain, gladly and deservedly fulfilled his vow.'

The other inscription comes from Rome, with the individual the *praefectus classis* admiral of the *Classis Britannica* regional fleet. Notably, this is the same individual who was earlier detailed commanding the amalgamated *Classis Britannica*, *Classis Germanica*, *Classis Pannonica* and *Classis Flavia Moesica* in the wake of Albinus' defeat. It is unclear if the fleets were still combined by this time, or had by then been separated, with our candidate now in charge of the one fleet. Either way, he and his navy were to play an important role in the Severan campaigns. Overall, the emperor's military team leading the expedition would have been huge, the appointment of the logistics manager at Corbridge very instructive in showing the scale of the pre-planning.

Severus knew he would be away for years with the *expeditio felicissima Brittannica* and planned to run the empire from Britain while there. To do this, he also took with him his senior administrative team. This included other members of his *Consilium Principis*, for example the *ab epistulis* head of secretariat and the *Princeps*

Peregrinorum head of the *frumentarii* secret service. Both are sadly unnamed. More importantly, he also took with him much of the *fiscus* imperial treasury to fund his expedition, and the *a rationibus* high ranking financial officer who ran it.

To these, Severus added his own personal retinue of imperial freedman and slaves from his *familia Caesaris*, of whom we know specifically of two. These were Castor, the court chamberlain, and Euodus. The latter was Caracalla's former tutor, who had played such a key role in the downfall of Plautianus. The emperor was also joined by his close family including Julia Domna, Caracalla and Geta, the latter two probably the first on his list to travel with him given his keenness to remove them from the sensual diversions of Rome. Key senators who were not already part of his military team also joined to ensure the smooth running of the imperial administration.

Ever the meticulous planner, Severus' next step was to ensure stability throughout the empire while he was away in Britain, especially given his hostile relationship with the Senate. We have some detail here, with his planning again heavily focused on North Africans. This was the final step in the Severan reset of the empire, with key provinces not already run by his appointees now put in the hands of kinsmen, supporters and friends. For example, Pannonia Superior was placed under the governorship of Egnatius Victor, and Germania Superior under Aiacius Modestus Crescentianus. Both were important postings anchoring the *limes* on the Danube and Rhine respectively, with both men experienced military leaders. Meanwhile, Severus appointed Marius Maximus governor of Coele Syria to hold the eastern frontier against the Parthians, promoting him from governing Gallia Belgica where he had been based since Albinus' defeat. Further, Maximus' kinsman Quintus Venidius Rufus was reappointed governor Germania Inferior. Additionally, Severus' friend Gaius Julius Septimius Castinus was appointed *legionis legatus* of *legio* II *Adiutrix pia fidelis* in the key Danubian frontier province of Pannonia Inferior. All the above were North African, with Severus' plans clearly successful given that, even after his death in York in AD 211, the empire within and outside its borders remained remarkably quiet, despite Caracalla's immediate purge of his father's inner circle.

At the beginning of January AD 208, Caracalla and Geta then took over as *consuls* in Rome, the final piece in Severus' political jigsaw before heading off to Britain. Coins were then minted showing the emperor riding off to war, though we know from the primary sources that he was carried in a litter for the land-based part of his journey given the gout or other condition he was suffering from. The sources indicate that his two sons reached Boulogne-sur-Mer in north-western Gaul before him, probably with their own entourages. The majority of the huge imperial party took things more slowly given the enormous administrative and financial baggage train travelling with the emperor. All used the same route, by sea from Ostia to Marseille in southern Gaul, then picking the Rhone on the Mediterranean coast and travelling upriver to Lyon. From there, they then headed further north up the Saône to central Gaul, at which point they transferred to the imperial road network for the final stretch to the Gallic coast.

Severus and his sons would certainly have entered Britain through the imperial gateway at Richborough, essential given he would have wanted to put his stamp on the formerly recalcitrant province from the word go. The image of the ageing and ailing emperor being carried through Domitian's quadrifrons arch there in a sedan chair is an enigmatic one, though one wonders if he might have made the effort to hobble through under his own power given the importance of the expedition to him. Either way, he had arrived and the *expeditio felicissima Brittannica* was underway. Sadly, we don't have a specific date, but it was most likely early spring.

His exact route north is also unknown, though with archaeological data, analogy and informed anecdote we can begin to piece it together. In the first instance, travelling west on Watling Street through northern Kent, he would have passed through a variety of settlements including Rochester (Roman *Durobrivae*) and Springhead (Roman *Vagniacis*), before reaching the provincial capital *Londoninium*. Here,

I work on the informed assumption that, while Severus had initiated the separation of the province into two (these Britannia Superior and Britannia Inferior) after the defeat of Albinus, the process had yet to be completed. Thus, we are still dealing with one united Britannia, and one capital.

Having spent some time in London, Severus then headed north along Ermine Street, his target York. Along the way his entourage passed through the key settlements on this major trunk road, often overnighting. This was the Roman equivalent of a medieval Royal procession, with the hosts at each stopover close to bankrupted as they strove to impress the Severans and their retainers. Likely resting places on the route included Godmanchester (Roman *Durovigutum*), Water Newton (another Roman *Durobrivae*), Ancaster (Roman *Causennae*), Lincoln, and then either Brough-on-Humber (Roman *Petuaria*), if Severus chose to cross the Humber by ferry, or Castleford (Roman *Lagentium*) and Tadcaster (Roman *Calcaria*), if they chose the inland route.

Two other sites have also been suggested recently as potential Severan stopping places on the emperor's journey north. First, Upex has argued the monumental building known as the *praetorium* at Castor (Roman name unknown) 1.5km north of Water Newton may have been a likely location for the Severan imperial entourage's stay (as opposed to *Durobrivae*) given its immense size.[9]

With its commanding views of the Nene Valley and fine mosaics, this would certainly have made an acceptable stand-in imperial residence, even if only for a short time. The term *praetorium* was first used for the site by local antiquarian Edmund Artis in the nineteenth century AD, who argued it had a military or administrative function given its scale. However, more likely it was the centre of a very grand villa estate.

Meanwhile, a reference on a curse tablet found in Leicester (Roman *Ratae*) to a Septizodium there has led to speculation that part of the journey may have switched west to the Fosse Way at some stage. It seems more likely the structure in Leicester, if indeed it was located there and the curse scroll doesn't originate elsewhere, celebrated a later visit by the Severans or their representatives, either during the British campaigns in the north, or later.

What is clear is that by the late summer at the latest, Severus and his entourage had arrived in York, the key city in the north of Roman Britain which anchored the northern *limes*. Improbably, this frontier settlement on the far fringes of the empire now became the imperial capital for the last three years of Severus life.

BATTLESPACE: YORK AND THE FAR NORTH OF BRITAIN

York was one of the great towns of Roman Britain, not as large as London but featuring its third longest permanent bridge after that in the provincial capital and the Medway crossing at Rochester. The town's Roman name *Eboracum* means 'place of the yews', this a Latinisation of an earlier Brythonic name.[10]

York was founded by *legio* IX *Hispana* as part of the conquest campaigns of the Roman governor Quintus Petillius Cerialis. He arrived in Britain in AD 71 with orders to target the north of Britain, and specifically the Brigantes. This huge confederacy of tribes resided in what is now Yorkshire (excepting part of the east coast, the territory of the Parisi regional tribe there), Lancashire, Cumbria, Northumberland and (possibly) southwestern Scotland. They wielded considerable power, with their pre-Roman tribal capital located at Stanwick in North Yorkshire.

Tacitus says that Cerialis immediately headed north on his arrival to set about the Brigantes.[11] In the first instance, he ordered the veteran *legio* IX *Hispana* out of its legionary fortress at Lincoln into modern Yorkshire where the troops constructed a new fortress on the northern bank of the point where they crossed the River Ouse. This was a very defensible location given the specific spot chosen was where a large tributary, the River Foss, runs into the Ouse.

IMPERATOR: ARRIVAL IN BRITAIN

This provided riverine protection on two sides of the fortification. The fact the recently arrived *legio* II *Adiutrix* immediately moved into the vacated fortress at Lincoln indicates there were no plans for the famous ninth legion to return there, and that it was now based permanently in its newly founded fortress in York.

The original legionary fortress in York was classically playing card in shape and very large, enclosing an area of over 20 hectares and able to host the 5,500 men of the legion. Its original defences were a ditch and 3m high turf/clay rampart topped by a palisade, with wood-built towers and gates. However, from around AD 110 (earlier for the gateways, see below) the whole was replaced by a stone-built structure with tile bonding layers.

At the centre of the fortress was the parade ground featuring the *principia* headquarters building which housed the senior base commander and his staff. On one side of this parade ground, perpendicular to the *principia* itself, stood an associated *basilica* great aisled hall. The scale of the latter, certainly from the time of Severus' arrival, was immense. By way of example, we have a single column recovered in 1969 during excavations of the *basilica*. This, the only survivor of the many that would have featured in the huge structure, is 7.6m tall and constructed of magnesian limestone and millstone grit. It now stands in Minster Yard in front of York's Minster School. This and other archaeological finds when investigating the *basilica* show it would have been at least 68m long, 32m wide and 23m high heigh, the latter just short of the height of today's Minister. As such, it would have been an improbably imposing structure to the natives in the north, a classic example of the Romans using monumentalisation in the built environment to shock and awe.

From the *principia* the legion based in York was administered, while it was from the *tribunal* podium at one end of the adjacent *basilica* that the commanding officer addressed his troops and received visiting dignitaries. Meanwhile, in the *principia* itself, a row of rooms served as offices, the central one the *aedes* which was the legionary shrine and the spiritual heart of the fortress. It was here the legionary standards were kept. The *aedes* also had a more practical function in that beneath its floor sat a vault in which the legionary pay chest was kept.

Other buildings near the *principia* included the *praetorium*, the commanding officer's house which was built in the same manner as a fine town house, this used for business as well as domestic purposes. The southwest corner of that at York is thought to be part of the Roman structural remains exposed in the undercroft of the Minster today, and the origin of the plaster wall paintings on display there, too. The *praetorium* in the legionary fortress at York was quickly occupied by Severus and the imperial family on their arrival in AD 208 and effectively became the imperial palace until his death there in February AD 211.

As a final comment on legionary fortress, I reference the unit that garrisoned it. As we have seen, the founding legion was *legio* IX *Hispana* which remained there until the early second century AD. This is last mentioned in an inscription dated to AD 108 when the fortress gateways were being rebuilt in stone, after which the legion disappears from the written record. Whatever its fate, in AD 122 it was replaced by *legio* VI *Victrix* which arrived with Hadrian on his visit to the northern *limes* in Britain. This legion then participated in the building of Hadrian's Wall and was still resident in York at the time of Severus' expedition.

North of York, Dere Street was the principle Roman trunk road from the city northwards to the frontier and beyond, ultimately passing through the modern Scottish borders and reaching the Firth of Forth. One can follow much of its route today given some sections are tracked by the modern road network, for example the A1 south of the River Tees and the A68 north of Corbridge. The road owes its name to the Germanic Kingdom of Deira which lasted from AD 559 to AD 664, covering a region ranging from the Humber to the River Tees, and westwards to the Vale of York. The kingdom itself possibly derived its own name from the Brythonic original of the River Derwent. Dere Street corresponds roughly with the first British route identified in the Antonine Itinerary. Intriguingly, this shows Dere Street also heading slightly further south from York, 19km to a place called *Delgovicia* (today unknown) and then a further 36km to a '*Praetorium*' (again unknown).

Travelling north from York along Dere Street, the first place of note is Aldborough (Roman *Isurium Brigantum*) in North Yorkshire, the regional *civitas* capital in the former territory of the Brigantes. The site also featured a fort, one of many scattered across the region dating to the time of Cerialis' campaigns against the Brigantes, this guarding the point where Dere Street crossed the River Ure.

Heading further north one next reaches Catterick (Roman *Cataractonium*), again in North Yorkshire, site of the Roman fort guarding the Dere Street crossing of the River Swale. Mattingly says this base was the key long-term transit camp for Roman troops heading north to the frontier and beyond.[12] Piercebridge (Roman name unkown) follows, where a Roman fort existed at this Dere Street crossing of the River Tees from AD 70. Continuing onwards, Binchester (Roman *Vinovia*) in County Durham is the next site, to the immediate north of Bishop Auckland. This was the location of yet another fort, this time guarding the Dere Street crossing of the River Wear.

Moving on, one next reaches Ebchester (Roman *Vindomora*) in County Durham, an auxiliary fort protecting the Dere Street crossing of the River Derwent. Finally, before reaching the *limes*, just short of the wall, we then come to Corbridge in Northumberland at the junction of Dere Street and the east-west Stanegate military road which predated Hadrian's Wall, with Corbridge its eastern hub. This town was the most northerly in the Roman Empire, originally the site of a fort established around AD 85, which, by the time of Severus, had been replaced by a large urban settlement. During the Severan campaigns two walled military compounds were built within the town boundary, both visible today, reflecting Corbridge's key role as a logistics base. Dere Street then travelled through Hadrian's Wall at the Portgate, before continuing north into *barbaricum*.

Finally, when considering the north of Roman Britain, two other sites need consideration given the key roles they played in the *expeditio felicissima Brittannica*. The first is Brough-on-Humber to the southeast of York on the northern shore of the Humber. This site was originally a fort founded in AD 70 and then abandoned around AD 125. However, its *vicus* civilian settlement developed independently into a substantial town, which, after the decline of the fort, became the *civitas* capital of the Parisi. This town featured a substantial port and ferry-crossing, as detailed above, providing a swift link from Lincoln to York along the original route of Ermine Street. It was to play a major logistics role in the *expeditio felicissima Brittannica* as one of the main ports of access for troops arriving to join Severus' vast campaigning force.

The second site is South Shields in modern South Tyneside, Tyne and Wear. This vexillation fort site, on the south side of the mouth of the River Tyne, was massively enlarged by Severus to serve as one of his key logistics bases for the *expeditio felicissima Brittannica*.

Back to the northern frontier, travelling north through the Portgate on Hadrian's Wall one entered *barbaricum* proper. There, the Romans often stationed small garrisons in forts north of the *limes* to keep the frontier region under tight control. Examples include Risingham where in this narrative Adventus had recently been involved in building work, and High Rochester (Roman *Bremenium*), both in modern Northumberland.

Then, as one continued north along Dere Street into the modern Scottish Borders, one began to enter a true Conradian heart of darkness as far as the Romans were concerned. The empire never fully conquered the far north of Britain, only coming close twice. The first was under the great warrior governor Gnaeus Julius Agricola in the AD 80s when he ultimately led Rome's legions to the Moray Firth and ordered the *Classis Britannica* to circumnavigate the main island of Britain. It is in this campaign Tacitus sheds true light on how the Romans viewed the far north when Agricola addressed his troops prior to the AD 83 Battle of Mons Graupius against the Caledonians. Here, he has the governor say:[13]

'And, if we must perish, it would be no mean glory to fall where land and nature finally end.'

However, the emperor at the time was Domitian, who was far more concerned with conflict on the Danube and had no interest in far off Britain. He ordered Agricola back to Rome, despite his immense military achievements, and soon the northern frontier had fallen back to the line of the Solway Firth-Tyne. The second time the Romans came close was under Severus, as we will see.

Why the Romans never committed to fully incorporating the far north of Britain into imperial territory is much debated. For one thing, campaigning so far north and then staying there was incredibly expensive, in a region some argue was not as economically viable as some of the lands to the south. For another, it is clear the natives there proved particularly difficult opponents for the Romans, having no interest at all in accepting *Romanitas* in any form if it required submission to the emperor. Also, climate and terrain played an important role, particularly in a Severan context as we will see.

The fact the region of modern Scotland wasn't conquered by Rome meant that it was a real place of difference when compared to the Roman province to the south. Particularly, this meant there was no stone-built Mediterranean-style urban settlement which was such a key feature of the Roman experience. Indeed, most of our evidence for the Romans in the far north is military in nature, and the only towns as the Romans would recognise them the *vicii* of fortifications. These forts, some stone-built and some not, are our key evidence of short-term attempts to stay in the region, often over decades, though the number of sites decreases as one goes further north.

A typical example of a far northern vexillation fort can be found at Newstead (Roman *Trimontium*) in the Scottish Borders, built at the point where Dere Street crossed the River Tweed. This Flavian and Antonine fortification featured an extensive *vicus* and amphitheatre, with an excellent visitor centre in nearby Melrose telling its story today.

Similar forts were constructed along the length of the Antonine Wall, built along the Clyde-Forth line during the reign of Antoninus Pius when, for a brief period, the *limes* in Britain were driven even further north by the North African-born governor Quintus Lollius Urbicus. Construction of this new frontier began in AD 142 and took about twelve years to complete, with the final wall protected by sixteen such forts. The best-known today is Rough Castle near Falkirk. Small fortlets were positioned between them in a similar manner to the system used on Hadrian's Wall. This wall was abandoned after only eight years of occupation, with the garrisons for the most part relocating back to Hadrian's Wall. Notably, the Antonine Wall was then refortified and manned as part of Severus' *expeditio felicissima Brittannica* was underway.

Other key Roman military sites in the far north included the fortified harbours and supply bases at Cramond on the Forth and Carpow on the Tay, both to play key roles in Severus' expedition as part of a littoral maritime logistics network anchored on South Shields to the south. Meanwhile, on a far grander scale was the huge legionary fortress at Inchtuthil on the Tay, the most northerly such fortress by some distance in the Roman world. This was built around AD 82 by *legio* XX *Valeria Victrix* as part of Agricola's campaigns of conquest, though was never completed and quickly abandoned when the Romans headed south again after the governor was recalled by Domitian.

Finally, in terms of the Roman presence in the far north of Britain, we have marching camps. These temporary fortifications are our main evidence of the various Roman campaigns in the region, given one or more were built by each military force at the end of every day's march in enemy territory. As such, when we match the size of a sequence of forts with the archaeological record and the estimated size of a campaigning army, they provide a site-by-site plot across the landscape of the campaign itself. In Britain, such marching camp sequences are especially well preserved in Wales and, most usefully here, Scotland.

IMPERATOR: ARRIVAL IN BRITAIN

In terms of native settlement north of the British *lime*s at the time of the *expeditio felicissima Brittannica*, first a note on the geology which in Scotland is unusually varied. The four main geographical sub-divisions there, south to north, are:

- The Southern Uplands lying to the south of the Southern Uplands Fault, comprising largely Silurian formations. Today, much of the Scottish Borders can be found here.
- The Central Lowlands, a rift valley comprising mainly Palaeozoic formations. Geographically, today this is called the Midland Valley, with the Southern Upland Fault its southern border and the Highland Boundary Fault its northern border. The Clyde-Forth line runs through the centre of it.
- The Grampian Mountains, often named as part of the Highlands and Islands.
- The Highlands and Islands.

In this work, the former two are the Scottish Lowlands, the latter two the Scottish Highlands. The key geological feature is the Highland Boundary Fault running southwest to northeast from the Isle of Arran to Stonehaven on the North Sea coast. This is because, as will be seen, it marked the northern boundary of the Severan campaigns there. For clarity, there is no evidence, archaeologically or historically, that Severus penetrated the Grampians or the Moray and Buchan Lowlands just south of the Moray Firth as did Agricola earlier.

Meanwhile, all the primary sources covering Rome's occupation of Britain comment negatively on the climate in this most northwesterly outpost of the empire. For example, Tacitus calls the weather 'foul, with frequent rains and mist'.[14] Meanwhile, Strabo states:[15]

> 'Their weather is more rainy than snowy; and on the days of clear sky fog prevails so long a time that throughout a whole day the sun is to be seen for only three or four hours about midday.'

Indeed, it is no coincidence that one of the exports Britain was best known for in the Roman world was the *birrus* rain-proofed hooded wool cloak.

Climate was an even bigger issue for Severus given the fact the weather in Britain is generally poorer the further north and west one goes, particularly as one moves from the Lowlands to the Highlands. Further, according to the primary sources, the weather experienced by Severus' troops as their legionary spearheads headed north in AD 209 and AD 210 was particularly poor, so overall climate would have had a major impact on the campaign.

Native settlement in the campaigning region of the *expeditio felicissima Brittannica* in the Southern Uplands and Central Lowlands of modern Scotland had distinct similarities to settlement in the north of the province of Britannia. The was especially the case the nearer the settlements were to the Roman *limes*. For example, the round houses of south-eastern Scotland used dry stone walls in their construction, with an internal ring of posts utilised to support an 'attic' to give extra living space. This was also the most common type of dwelling in Brigantian territory south of Hadrian's Wall, not surprising given the kinship between the natives north and south of the frontier before the arrival of the Romans. One key point of difference were hillforts, long out of use in Roman controlled territory but still very much a feature of the landscape north of the *limes*. Mattingly highlights the well-known examples at Burnswark Hill, Traprain Law, Dryburn Bridge and Broxmouth.[16] Interestingly, these all featured round houses within their 6m high ramparts, showing they were designed for long-term habitation during times of crisis.

In terms of these people living north of the British *limes*, by the time of the Severan incursions the tribes there had coalesced into the Maeatae and the Caledonian confederations, the former in the Southern Uplands and Central Lowlands, the latter in the northern Central Lowlands, Grampian Mountains, and Highlands and Islands. When first describing them in the context of conflict at the beginning of Commodus' reign, Dio provides excellent detail:[17]

> 'The Maeatae live next to the cross-wall which cuts the island in half [likely a reference to Hadrian's wall given the Antonine Wall had by this time fallen out of use], and the Caledonians are beyond them. Both tribes inhabit wild and waterless mountains and desolate and swampy plains, and possess neither walls, cities, nor tilled fields, but live on their flocks, wild game, and certain fruits. Their form of rule is democratic for the most part, and they choose their boldest men as rulers. They go into battle in chariots, and have small, swift horses; there are also foot soldiers, very swift in running and very firm in standing ground. For arms they have a shield and a short spear, with a bronze apple attached to the end of the spear shaft, so that when the enemy is shaken it may clash and terrify the enemy; and they also have a dagger. They can endure hunger and cold and any kind of hardship; for they plunge into swamps and exist there for many days with only their heads above water, and in forests they support themselves upon bark and roots, and for all emergencies they prepare a certain kind of food, the eating of a small portion of which, the size of a bean, prevents them from feeling either hunger or thirst.'

The hunger-preventing food described here has been identified as the heath pea (*lathyrus linofolius*) by Dr Brian Moffat of the Soutra Aisle research centre.[18]

As Dio suggests, this was clearly a very hardy enemy, capable of sustaining military campaigns for a long period in the worst climatic and geographical conditions. However, both Severan incursions in the north were met with intense guerrilla resistance rather than any kind of attempt at a meeting engagement as earlier faced by Agricola at Mons Graupius. This was likely because of the specific strategy the Romans used. Meanwhile, the extension of Maeatae territory north of the 'cross-wall' is based on now well understood etymological evidence regarding place names in the Scottish Lowlands. For example, two large hills in the region have long been associated with the confederation. The first is Dumyat Hill in the Ochils overlooking Stirling, where the name of its hill fort, Dùn Mhèad, is a Gaelic derivative of the original Brythonic for 'hill of the Maeatae'. The second is Myot Hill near Falkirk.[19]

9

Imperator: The Severan Campaigns in Britain

Severus launched his two, immense campaigns to conquer the far north of Britain in AD 209 and AD 210. He came very close to success, but his death in February AD 211 in the freezing cold of a British winter quickly ended Roman interest in the region. Here, I narrate this fantastical story as he led the largest campaigning force ever on British soil into the unconquered far north in Rome's last attempt at this extraordinary feat.

SEVERUS' MILITARY FORCE IN BRITAIN

Orders to mobilise the military units making up Severus' huge force for the *expeditio felicissima Brittannica* were sent out across the western empire in late AD 207. Soon, dispatches were speeding in all directions along the *cursus publicus* from Rome.

We can build a confident picture of the vast force Severus assembled using the primary sources, inscriptions set in place after the campaigns had concluded, analogy and reasonable anecdote. First, the three British legions were put on alert that the emperor was coming to the province in person and planned to finally conquer the far north. Their 16,500 legionaries would form the core of Severus' army as, despite their earlier support of Albinus, they had now been fully reformed and had enormous experience campaigning in the planned battlespace in modern Scotland. The British legions seem to have performed well during the Severan campaigns there, for example *legio* VI *Victrix* being awarded the commemorative title *Britannica Pia Fidelis* (based on tile stamps from Carpow) and *legio* XX *Valeria Victrix* being similarly styled *Antoniniana* by Caracalla after the death of his father. Similarly, all the auxiliary units in Britain were also put on standby.

Next the Praetorian Guard and *equites singulares Augusti* would accompany Severus to Britain, leaving only a small cadre back in Rome. It was unthinkable the emperor would go on campaign without both, with the Praetorian prefect Papinianus a key part of his military command team as detailed. By this point, after being reformed by Severus, the former numbered around 5,000, the latter around 1,000. Severus also took in its entirety the legion he had come to think of his own, *Albanum*-based *legio* II *Parthica*. One of the cohorts from the *cohortes urbanae* in Rome may also have joined the emperor on the expedition.[1]

Meanwhile, other units receiving notification in late AD 207 to prepare to journey to Britain were those based along the northern *limes* on the Rhine and Danube. These were likely vexillations of legionaries rather than entire legions, and units of auxiliaries. The latter were a key component of this campaign, with Moorhead and Stuttard estimating their numbers at a huge 35,000 including their British counterparts.[2] We know specifically of one such unit who fought with Severus in Britain – the auxiliary foot *cohors* V *Gallorum*, whose presence is recorded in inscriptions at South Shields and Cramond where its troops helped support the emperor's logistics operation in the far north.

Overall, a reasonable estimation of this gathering of military units from across the western empire implies a total force of around 50,000 troops mustered for the *expeditio felicissima Brittannica*, this figure corresponding to the calculation by Moorhead and Stuttard that the granaries at the rebuilt fort at South Shields could hold enough grain to feed 50,000 men for two months (they were increased in number by a factor of 10 at this time),[3] and also the seemingly random figure chosen by Dio when referencing casualties in the campaign.[4]

To this figure of 50,000, we can then add the 7,000 naval *milites* of the *Classis Britannica* which, whether now independent again or still under a joint command structure with its Rhine and Danubian counterparts, played several vital roles in the campaigns in the far north. These included controlling the littoral and riparian flanks of the legionary spearheads, scouting, patrolling and, perhaps most importantly, transporting men and supplies.

Notably, the army Severus led to Britain was different to that he had commanded in his earlier eastern and North African campaigns. This was because, as part of the Severan reset of the wider empire, he also initiated the first series of big reforms of the Principate military. This set in place the initial changes which later allowed Diocletian and Constantine I to carry out their much wider series of military reforms in the Dominate.

The most visible of the Severan military reforms was regarding the legions. Not only did he increase their number to 33 with his three Parthian foundings, but he also initiated a reform of their equipment. When he came to power, his legionaries were still readily identifiable as the classic Principate type earlier led by Trajan and Marcus Aurelius. Think of *lorica segmentata* banded iron armour, large rectangular *scutum* body shields, imperial Gallic helmets, the pilum lead-weighted throwing javelin and the gladius stabbing sword. However, this traditional legionary panoply began to alter at the beginning of the early third century AD. This was largely a response to a change in the nature of the opponents the Romans had faced in the Antonine and early Severan periods. Previously, the legions had most often faced a similar infantry-heavy force, excepting the Parthians in the east. However, they were now tackling a multitude of threats, many of a differing nature, for example the Sarmatians on the Danube frontier. This required a more flexible response.

This change in the panoply of the legionary is shown in real time on four monuments set up in Rome by four great warrior emperors. These are Trajan's Column, the Column of Marcus Aurelius, the Arch of Septimius Severus, and the Arch of Constantine. The latter is particularly important given it is in effect a time machine, built in AD 315 to celebrate Constantine's victory over Maxentius at the Battle of Milvian Bridge in AD 312. At the time, the imperial *fiscus* treasury was running low as it had been used by Maxentius to fund his failed defence of Rome. Therefore, Constantine's architects sourced panels for the new arch from existing monuments to complement its new and contemporary depictions of his martial success. These included four panels called the Great Trajanic Frieze which comprised slabs from a monument to celebrate Trajan's Dacian victories, and four panels from a lost Arch of Marcus Aurelius to celebrate his successes in the Marcomannic Wars (four additional surviving panels are on display in the Capitoline Museum).

The change in the equipment of the later Principate legionary was initially evident in his weaponry. First, from the later reign of Severus the longer cavalry-style *spatha* sword began to replace the shorter *gladius* for all Roman foot soldiers. This weapon was up to 80cm in length. The new sword was suspended from a baldric on a Sarmatian-type scabbard slide, and came to dominate Roman military equipment in the west until the empire's end there, continuing in use in the east afterwards. It seems likely the adoption of this weapon had its origins in the need for more reach to tackle armoured mounted opponents.

A similar change is also evident in the use of the *pila*, these gradually replaced by a *hasta* thrusting spear of between 2m and 2.7m in length in the same period. This change is visible, taking place on the four monuments detailed above. Thus, on Trajan's Column, the Column of Marcus Aurelius and the reused panels on the Arch of Constantine the legionaries shown in *lorica segmentata* are mostly armed with *pila*, while on the Arch of Septimius Severus and on the contemporary panels on the Arch of Constantine they have been replaced by spears. Again, this was a response to the experiences fighting mounted opponents more frequently, as with the longer sword. A legionary spear wall made much more sense engaging such opponents than the use of *pilum* impact weapons, with one such legionary phalanx depicted on the left forum-facing panel of the Arch of Septimius Severus, there countering Parthian cataphracts.

Moving on to the defensive panoply, this change is also evident with the shield. In the early third century AD, the traditional *scutum* began to be replaced by a large flat (and sometimes slightly dished) oval body shield, confusingly still called a *scutum*. This new design was of simple plank construction, with stitched-on rawhide, and was strengthened with iron bars. The two types appear to have been used side by side for some time, with examples of both found at the fortified frontier-trading town of Dura-Europos in Syria dating to AD 256. This transition is also very evident on the four monuments detailed above, with many of the large round shields featuring on the Severan arch, and even more on the contemporary panels of the Arch of Constantine. Once again, this change seems to have been associated with the type of opponent more commonly faced by the Romans, the round shield perhaps more suited to dealing with a mounted threat. It certainly gave greater freedom of movement for the new swords and spears coming into use with their greater reach and would also have been cheaper to produce.

Not surprisingly, a change is also evident in the body armour of the legionary as the Principate approached its end. Thus, on Trajan's Column and the Column of Marcus Aurelius most are wearing *lorica segmentata*, as they are on the reused panels on the Arch of Constantine. However, on the Arch of Septimius Severus there is a much higher proportion wearing *lorica hamata* chainmail and *lorica squamata* scalemail, this proportion increasing yet again on the contemporary panels of the Arch of Constantine.

Meanwhile, as the Principate progressed, legionary helmets also became increasingly substantial, with the early imperial

Italic type disappearing entirely by the early third century AD. The imperial Gallic style did continue in use, but was increasingly supplemented by heavier, single bowl designs reinforced by cross-pieces and fitted with deep napes, leaving only a minimal T-shaped face opening. These helmets provided exceptional levels of protection.

A final change in this period was the appearance a new type of legionary. This was the *lanciarii* light trooper, armed with a quiver of javelins and wearing lighter armour than their front-rank line-of-battle equivalents. Such troops, who operated like the *velites* of the Polybian legions, skirmished forward to deter mounted bowmen and other lightly armed missile troops. They are first attested on gravestone epigraphy serving in the ranks of *legio* II *Parthica* in the context of Caracalla and Macrinus' AD 215–AD 218 Parthian War campaign in the east.[6] It is unclear if these were in use a few years earlier when Severus campaigned in Scotland, but it seems likely given the flexibility *lanciarii* provided the more rigid formations of legionary heavy infantry.

It is also worth noting that artillery played a major role in the Severan attempts to conquer the far north of Britain. It was the legionaries who provided this key component of Roman armies when on campaign. Such weapons included the light *scorpio* dart-thrower and the larger *ballista*, the latter firing large bolts and shaped stones. When at full strength, each cohort fielded one of the latter and each century one of the former. This gave an impressive total of ten *ballistae* and 59 *scorpiones*.

By early AD 208, all the units making up the *expeditio felicissima Brittannica* were on the move, coinciding with Severus' departure from Rome. Meanwhile, the vessels of the northern regional fleets gathered in the Rhine Delta and off the major ports on the continental coast of Gaul, ready to start ferrying troops to Britain. Those from the Danubian and Rhine *limes* travelled either down these major river systems or their adjacent military trunk roads, then gathering in holding camps to await the journey across the North Sea.

Here, recent archaeological research in the modern Netherlands has shown this process in action. At Ockenburgh and Scheveningseweg in The Hague (near the Roman municipium of *Forum Hadriani* in Germania Inferior), new data indicates the location of a number of these Severan transit camps. Here, de Bruin provides the latest detail, saying:[5]

> 'During the Severan period, two sites in the Hague [detailed above] functioned as military settlements. The occupation consisted of irregular, mounted units (numeri). At Ockenburgh beneficiarii might have been stationed as well. The suspected presence of Frisian auxiliaries in The Hague and other surrounding military settlements is mirrored by the influx of Frisian troops in northern Britain in the [early] third century. Possibly, the Frisian units were stationed in the Lower Rhine area before being transferred to Britain.'

The *numeri* he details were part of the auxiliary component of the *expeditio felicissima Brittannica*, with Frisian cavalry noted for their ferocity. Meanwhile, the *beneficiarii* if present were likely seconded to the staff of the governor of the province to help administer the huge troop transfers to Britain. This was Quintus Venidius Rufus as earlier detailed, with two inscriptions found near the fort at Leiden (Roman *Matilo*) indicating the role he played gathering the legionaries and auxilia for Severus' expedition.

By early summer AD 208, military units began arriving in Britain from the continent, to join the three legions and auxiliaries already there. All the key ports along the east coast of the province were used, including Wallsend and South Shields on the Tyne, Brough-on-Humber, Caistor St Edmunds in north Norfolk (Roman *Venta Icenorum*, then the *civitas* capital of the Iceni and a port on the Great Estuary), London, Richborough and Dover. The legionaries and auxilia then headed inland to York, to be joined by Severus and the imperial entourage when they arrived there in late summer.

STRATEGY AND ROUTE OF THE EXPEDITIO FELICISSIMA BRITTANNICA

On arrival in York, Severus received an embassy from the leaders of the Maeatae and Caledonians seeking a peace deal with the emperor. Assuming this did take place, noting our only sources are Roman, it isn't surprising given the overwhelming force they were now aware was about to be unleashed on them. Their spies and other sources in the south would have certainly told them of Severus' grim reputation when dealing with his enemies, and even friends when it suited him. However, the emperor was in no mood for compromise, this not realistically an option given the size of the military force he was gathering. Herodian says that, instead, he wanted to:[6]

> '... prolong his time in Britain and not return hurriedly to Rome, while entertaining his ambition to add to his victories and titles by a campaign against the British, so he sent the delegates away empty-handed, and put everything in order for war.'

They were lucky to leave with their lives.

Now fully settled in the *praetorium* of the legionary fortress in York, Severus set about running the empire from the town which was to be his capital for the next three years. No doubt he felt more at home in this military setting than back in Rome, especially given a new temple to Serapis had been erected there in his honour by Claudius Hieronymianus, *legate legionis* of *legio* VI *Victrix*.

As for York itself, either shortly before Severus' arrival or during his stay there, the *canaba* civilian settlement on the south bank of the River Ouse was given the status of a *colonia* veteran settlement. This significantly improved its commercial standing, important given the role it was now to play as the mercantile hub for Severus' campaigns of conquest in the far north. While the legionary fortress was certainly improved during the emperor's stay, particularly the *principia*, *praetorium* and *basilica*, archaeological data also shows significant change taking place in the new *colonia*. One can imagine the happy chaos there as the local populace got used to having the Severans in residence across the river, and the enormous army gathering nearby. Soon, merchants from across the empire were arriving to sell the widest range of goods imaginable, with the locals no doubt making the most of this once in a lifetime opportunity.

We have our best insight into the workings of the Severan imperial administration in York in the context of Geta, his youngest son, who early in AD 209 was elevated by Severus to become joint-*augusti* with he and Caracalla. The key reason was because when Severus later left to campaign in the far north with his eldest son, it was Geta who was left behind in York to run the empire with his mother Julia Domna. Here, Geta is specifically recorded in the role on an inscription from *Aenus* in Thrace. This details that on 12 September the following year, Geta heard an embassy from the town in York. This was led by a senior magistrate called Diogenes, with its success recorded on a fine white marble plaque in the Thracian town. The imperial presence in York is also traceable through archaeological data of another kind, this time face pots for cosmetic creams. Such containers dating to the Severan stay in York have been found in excavations there, these decorated with female figures featuring Julia Domna's famous crimped coiffure hairstyle.

Moving on to Severus' overall strategy for the *expeditio felicissima Brittannica*, this was very specific to the battlespace in question, and brutal in the extreme. The emperor's aim was clearly to finish off the far northern Britons once and for all.

In the first instance, logistics underpinned the entire operation, this crucial to the keeping of such a huge military force in the field in enemy territory for what became two campaigning seasons. To that end, the eastern maritime flank was vital, with a never-ending conveyor heading north from South Shields with food and supplies. This stopped off at Cramond on the Forth and Carpow on the Tay as required, the carried materials then being transshipped to smaller riverine vessels which made use of the regional river systems in the Southern Uplands and Central Lowlands to transport their goods to the troops on the front line and in the rear. The vessels would then return with any booty, prisoners soon to be slaves, and the wounded (of which there were many in these two campaigns), before the whole process began again.

Once his lines of supply were set in place, the emperor then planned a *'Severan surge'* across the northern *limes*, following the line of Dere Street to Inveresk on the Forth. This onslaught was designed to hammer through the Scottish Borders as one massive homogenous force, cauterising all before it. Once on the line of the old Antonine Wall, having reactivated the fortified harbour and supply base at Cramond and the wall itself (the former as a key supply centre, the latter to protect his rear), Severus then planned to bridge the Forth. Next, he planned to divide his force into two, with the younger Caracalla leading two thirds of his army along the line of the Highland Boundary Fault southwest to northeast, building forts to seal off each glen as he passed. This would isolate the Grampian Mountains and Highlands and Islands from the Scottish Lowlands battlespace. This force was to include all three British legions and the majority of the British auxiliaries given their experience operating in this most hostile of battlespaces. Once Caracalla reached the coast, where the Highland line met the North Sea, any Maeatae and Caledonians to the south would be hopelessly trapped, especially given the regional fleet had orders to secure the coast and prevent any native access to the sea. At that point, Severus then intended to launch his own third of the army across the Forth, through Fife and into the soft underbelly of native British resistance. This involved reactivating the Antonine fortified harbour and supply base at Carpow on the Tay, crossing this fast-flowing river and then smashing into the upper Midland Valley from below. Severus' force was elite indeed, including the Prateorian Guard, *equites singulares Augusti* and *legio* II *Parthica*.

Overall, this was a very sound strategy given the nature of the opponent, terrain and climate, and the emperor expected a swift victory given the scale of the operation.

THE SEVERAN CAMPAIGNS IN SCOTLAND IN AD 209 AND AD 210

Severus launched his first savage assault on the far north of Britain in Spring AD 209, the local tribes in the Scottish Borders suing for peace as quickly as possible given the vast asymmetry between the Roman and native forces there. The results of this initial phase of the *expeditio felicissima Brittannica* are visible today at the Stanegate fort of *Vindolanda*. There, at some stage between AD 208 and AD 211, the Antonine fort structure was demolished and a new fortlet built to the immediate west at a location previously utilised for extramural occupation. The Antonine fort platform was then reused to build some 250 circular huts laid out back-to-back in rows of 10, within a Roman-style road grid, and with drains between. The purpose of this dramatic change is unknown to us today, but some now argue it was a concentration camp for natives from the Scottish Borders forcibly removed from the battlespace to the north. This seems a reasonable hypothesis given what came next.

As the vast Roman force advanced, with its enormous supply train, outriders from auxiliary cavalry *alae* ranged far and wide to protect the flanks of the legionary spearheads and to scout ahead, raiding any recalcitrant native settlements foolish enough to resist. At the end of each day's march, a huge 67 hectare marching camp was then built, effectively making the Roman force untouchable as it advanced. Today, we can track the line of these camps given their high state of preservation in the archaeological record. Specifically, they were located at:[7]

- Newstead V
- St Leonards (slightly larger at 70ha, the largest in the Roman world)

- Channelkirk
- Pathhead III

Once at Inveresk on the Forth, the 'Severan surge' then turned west, aiming to bridge this huge estuary at a convenient crossing point. Cramond was also now reactivated as a key supply base, with Roman troops then fanning out along the old Antonine Wall line, though probably in limited numbers given the vast majority were needed for the assault on the farthest north.

At some point on the south shore, a bridge was then built to allow the force to cross the Forth. The exact location of this crossing has never been found, and there is some debate about where it was and what form it took. The principal data showing the use of a bridge or bridges in the Severan campaigns in Scotland is numismatic. The specific coins in question are a gold aureus, bronze asses and bronze medallions, all of Severus, all dating to AD 208 and all featuring the image of a permanent bridge, and a small coin or medallion of Caracalla dating to AD 209 which features a bridge of boats.

The bridge was most likely located on a line between South and North Queensferry as with the three modern bridges across the Forth there, but what form did it take? A permanent monumental bridge seems highly unlikely given the length required to bridge the Forth at this point, even with Inch Garvie playing a role, with today's railway bridge on the same alignment an impressive 2,467m long. By way of comparison, the longest bridge in Roman Britain was that across the Thames in London at 280m in length, with the Medway crossing at Rochester second at 183m. Further, there is no physical evidence of any permanent Roman bridge over the Forth, at this point or elsewhere. Reed reached the same conclusion in his detailed analysis, arguing instead in favour of an enormous bridge of boats.[8] Again, this makes sense, as Reed suggested the AD 209 coin of Caracalla celebrates its construction. Here, he estimates over 500 vessels would have been required to bridge the Forth at that point, impressive considering the overall size of the *Classis Britannica* was 900 vessels. The scale of this astonishing feat of engineering cannot be underestimated.

Once the bridge was ready, Caracalla crossed with his larger force. He then led it in a lightning strike along the Highland Boundary Fault, building the well-known sequence of 54 hectare forts as he went to cut the Maeatae and Caledonians living in the Midland Valley off from the Highlands. These well-known sites, often described as marching camps, were likely designed for longer use given each was specifically built to cut a Highland glen off from the lowlands. They are located at:[9]

- Househill Dunipace near Falkirk, possibly a stopping off point before crossing the Forth
- Ardoch 1 at the fort site on the southwestern end of the Gask Ridge
- Innerpeffray East
- Grassy Walls
- Cardean
- Battledykes, Oathlaw
- Balmakewan
- Kair House

A further hypothesis here sees the Flavian Gask Ridge system of watchtowers and signal stations brought back out of retirement to act as a link between the Caracallan forts on the Highland line and Roman reserve forces on the Forth.

Caracalla's advance was unrelenting, with Dio showing Roman military engineering at its superb best when he describes the legionaries and auxilia 'cutting down forests, levelling heights, filling up swamps, and bridging rivers'.[10]

Finally, and after very tough fighting in which Dio says the Romans 'experienced countless hardships', Caracalla's legionary spearheads reached Kair House. There, the final fort in his

54 hectare sequence was built on Bervie Water, 13km south west of Stonehaven on the North Sea Coast.[11] With the Highland line visibly converging with the ocean there, this marked the most northerly point reached by the Romans in the Severan campaigns. Of note, Severus was only able to follow this strategy of lowland isolation because of the vast number of troops available to him. Agricola, with his smaller force of 30,000, was unable to do this. That is why the latter had to pursue his enemy much further north, with his Flavian route tracked by a string of 44 hectare marching camps, with the most northerly at Muiryfold north of the Grampians. Thus, Severus' planning for his campaigns is shown in its true light, one of meticulous organisation and execution which, but for his untimely death in AD 211, may well have succeeded.

With the Highland line and lowland Scottish coast secure, Severus himself now launched his own legionary spearheads over the Forth, heading directly northeast through Fife. This region was heavily settled by the Maeatae who the emperor targeted directly, building two 25 hectare marching camps. The first was at Auchtermuchty which, as earlier detailed, is on the direct line of march from North Queensferry on the Forth to Carpow on the Tay, this likely his main route of advance. Supporting archaeological evidence for this line of attack includes a coin of Pertinax found at Auchterderran to the northeast of North Queensferry, and a Severan hoard of 600 coins found at Loch Leven in the parish of Portmoak slightly further north. Severus' second camp in Fife was further east at Edenwood, this off the main axis of advance and likely marking a localised pacification action there. The smaller size of both camps when compared to Caracalla's glen blocking forts along the Highland line reflects the modest size of Severus' force compared to that of his son.

The emperor's advance through Fife was a short exercise given the asymmetry of the forces involved, with Severus quickly reaching the River Tay at Carpow. There, the Flavian and Antonine fortified harbour and supply base was reactivated to become the third key logistics node on the east coast after South Shields and Cramond. The initial Severan phase of this 11 hectare fort was first identified in the 1961–62 excavations by R. E. Birley and later confirmed by the subsequent excavations of J. D. Leach and J. J. Wilkes. This dates to the AD 209 campaign. The fort walls were built from turf, with stone used to construct the gates and principal internal buildings. These included a fine *principia*, *praetorium*, bath house and granary, these occasionally visible as crop marks. The site then received a second Severan upgrade during the AD 210 campaign. Here, over 200 stamped roof tiles from this later phase indicate the presence of *legio* VI *Victrix* and *legio* II *Augusta* (notably, in AD 209, both had been with Caracalla further north). Further, an AD 210 inscription found on fragments of carved stone originally atop the east gate (RIB 3512) features a few well-carved letters. These were part of a celebratory imperial inscription and are usually interpreted as a reference to Caracalla, though by another interpretation it could also reference both Severus and his elder son. The inscription also indicates the presence of *legio* II *Augusta* given imagery on one of the fragments features two *pegasi* confronting a Capricorn, both symbols associated with the legion. Note that when dating the Severan reoccupation of Carpow, some argue it occurred earlier in his reign at the end of the second century AD. However, there is no real data to support this hypothesis. Others have suggested the second phase of building work at Carpow may have taken place after the death of Severus, when the site could have been used to evacuate Roman troops from the far north. Again, there is no real evidence to support this, and it seems likely Carpow was abandoned soon after the emperor died in York.

However, the key to this location was not the fortified harbour and supply base, but the second major Severan bridge in modern Scotland. This was built here by the emperor in AD 209 as he viewed the upper Midland Valley north of the Tay. Once it was ready for use, Severus then struck north into the midst of the trapped Maeatae and Caledonians, driving hard to meet up with the larger force under

Caracalla. Kamm argues a likely place for the two armies to finally meet was at Inverbervie on the coast near the marching camp site at Kair House,[12] though the region around modern Stonehaven to the north is also a possibility.

One cannot overstate the brutality of this campaign strategy, which the emperor and his elder son followed to the letter. It is clear the Maeatae and Caledonians trapped south of the Highland line had literally nowhere to run from the enormous Roman military forces hammering their way through their homelands along two brutal axes. In such circumstances, the native Britons had no chance of coalescing into a single homogenous fighting force, with resistance to the Romans reduced to localised, vicious guerrilla warfare as the only means of defence. For them, this was Faulkner's experience of Roman conquest as robbery with violence writ large.[13]

In terms of such hardships, although the Roman strategy clearly worked, the experience of battle for all protagonists was grim in the extreme. The weather was worse than usual, even in the far north of the islands of Britain, and the terrain proved particularly difficult for the Romans. Our best account comes from Dio when he described the AD 209 campaign:[14]

> '... as Severus advanced through the country ... he fought no battle and beheld no enemy in battle array. The enemy purposely put sheep and cattle in front of the soldiers for them to seize, in order that they might be lured on still further until they were worn out; for in fact the water caused great suffering to the Romans, and when they became scattered, they would be attacked. Then, unable to walk, they would be slain by their own men, in order to avoid capture, so that a full 50,000 thousand died [clearly a massive exaggeration, but indicative of the difficulties the Romans faced]. But Severus did not desist until he approached the extremity of the island.'

Herodian's account also highlights the difficulty Severus and Caracalla faced in forcing a major meeting engagement with the Britons:[15]

'... frequent skirmishes occurred, and in these the Romans were victorious. But it was easy for the Britons to slip away; putting their knowledge of the surrounding area to good use, they disappeared in the woods and marshes. The Romans' unfamiliarity with the terrain prolonged the war.'

Both these narratives show that no major battle took place. Indeed, only one primary source specifically details engagements at all, this the later Latin chronicler Paulus Orosius, who, in his brief reference to the campaign, speaks of 'great and serious battles'.[16] However, he wrote his *Seven Books of History Against the Pagans* in the second decade of the fifth century AD, his main sources including other late Latin historians such as Flavius Eutropius, Aurelius Victor and Jerome. As such, his narrative regarding the Severan campaigns and other events in the second and third centuries AD, written hundreds of years after the event, is riddled with errors. Here, our best source is clearly once more Dio, Severus' contemporary, who is explicit in saying no major battle was fought in the campaigns. I choose to follow his narrative.

A final note considering this gruesome campaign, and that of AD 210, is the belligerence of their opponents. This is evidenced by Dio's quote regarding the hardiness of the Maeatae and Caledonians. They were clearly far more experienced to a life living rough in their indigenous terrain when required than the Romans, with Herodian saying they dispensed with breast plates and helmets 'which would impede their movement through the marshes'.[17] Further, the natives of the far north of Britain were some of the toughest opponents the Romans ever faced, with their elites showing no interest at all in joining the Roman world as part of an enhanced province.

We have no first-hand accounts which detail the native experience of the Severan onslaught, not surprising given all our primary sources are Roman or pro-Roman. However, we can turn to analogy and the archaeological record for insight, specifically in the context of recently published research regarding the 7 hectare hillfort site at Burnswark in Dumfresshire in the Scottish Borders. Here, a debate has taken place as to whether data previously considered (from antiquarian and 1960s archaeological excavations) showed an actual Roman siege at the site (either Hadrianic or early Antonine in date) or that the site was an example of a Roman siege training exercise. The key items of interest in that regard were the north and south Roman siege camps there, and a plethora of ballista bolts/balls and lead slingshots found at the site. To reach a conclusion either way, the Trimontium Trust recently carried out a new review of the existing research and also secured fresh data, the latter based on a systematic metal-detecting survey to identify more lead sling shots (with a view to plotting their scatter) and also experimental archaeology regarding the use of slings in siege warfare.[18] The results of this research suggest a particularly grim interpretation, with the two camps now seen as a real-world tactical response to the topography in the context of a full siege, and the widespread scatter of sling shots and other missiles (and their quality) suggesting deadly intent.

As Reid says, the evidence shows that:[19]

> '... there was a massive missile barrage at Burnswark. This was not just restricted to the gateways, but extended along a full half kilometre of native rampart. The simplest explanation for this distribution is that the defenders on the hilltop were suppressed by a hail of sling bullets with an accurate range of 120m and the stopping power of a modern handgun, as well as ballista bolts, and arrows. This presumably covered an attacking force sweeping out the three huge gateways and storming the hilltop. Such a combination of missile troops and conventional infantry is likely to have been brutally effective.'

Further, one additional factor adds even more insight into the awful experience of the native Britons on the receiving end of this devastation. This is because some of the slingshots were hollowed out with a 4mm hole through their centre, this designed to make a screeching noise when slung. Thus, here we have an early example of psychological warfare on the battlefield.

Soon, the AD 209 campaign reached its endgame, and despite the ferocity of their opponents and the issues with terrain and climate, total victory soon followed across the battlespace for Severus and Caracalla. Dio says that once the emperor reached the most northerly point of his advance, he:[20]

> '... observed most accurately the variation of the sun's motion and the length of the days and the nights in summer and winter respectively. Having thus been conveyed through practically the whole of the hostile country (for he actually was conveyed in a covered litter most of the way, on account of his infirmity), he returned to the friendly portion, after he had forced the Britons to come to terms, on the condition that they should abandon a large part of their territory.'

There is much to unpack in this important quote. First, we have a classical world reference to the differential in sunlight hours in the far north of Britain when compared to the provincial south. Second, Severus was clearly involved in the campaigning battlespace throughout the AD 209 campaign. Third, we have our main reference to the emperor being an invalid while in Britain, carried as Dio describes in a litter rather than riding with his guard. Fourth, the natives in the far north were forced to unconditionally surrender (the phrase 'forced the Britons to come to terms' is very specific), which included giving up a large part of their territory. This no doubt included the prime agricultural land in the Scottish Borders, Fife and the upper Midland Valley, the heartlands of Maeatae confederation, which Severus planned to add to his British province. Here, Hodgson, in his 2014 analysis of the Severan campaigns in Scotland, emphasises that given the region was so terribly damaged, it would have taken time and the full political commitment of the imperial centre to reboot the regional economy to ensure its speedy contribution to the *fiscus*.[21] Finally, Dio makes clear that with matters in the campaigning theatre seemingly resolved, Severus headed back south to overwinter in York, leaving garrisons to hold the key fort and supply base sites in the far north including Caracalla's glen blocker forts, Cramond and Carpow. Notably, Dio makes no mention of any circumnavigation attempt for the regional fleet as detailed by Tacitus at the culmination of Agricola's Flavian conquest in the far north in AD 84. Dio goes on to provide important detail about the one-sided peace settlement process, which includes his mention of an attempted patricide by Caracalla:[22]

> 'Antoninus [Caracalla] was causing him alarm and endless anxiety by his intemperate life, by his evident intention to murder his brother if the chance should offer, and, finally, by plotting against the emperor himself. When both were riding forward to meet the Britons, in order to receive their arms and discuss the details of their surrender, Antoninus attempted to kill his father outright with his own hand. They were proceeding on horseback, Severus also being mounted, in spite of the fact that he was weakened by infirmity in his feet, and the rest of the army was following; the enemy's remaining force were likewise spectators. At this juncture, while all were proceeding in silence and in order, Antoninus reined in his horse and drew his sword, as if he were going to strike his father in the back. But the others who were riding with them, upon seeing this, cried out, and so Antoninus, in alarm, desisted from his attempt. Severus turned at their shout and saw the sword, yet he did not utter a word, but ascended the tribunal where the surrender was to be signed, finished what he had to do, and returned to headquarters. Then he summoned his son and ordered a sword to be placed within easy reach. He then upbraided the youth for having dared to do so such a thing at all and especially for having been on the point of committing so monstrous a crime in the sight

of all, both the allies and the enemy. And finally he said: "Now if you really want to slay me, put me out of the way here; for you are strong, while I am an old man and prostrate. For, if you do not shrink from the deed, but hesitate to murder me with your own hands, there is Papinianus, the prefect, standing beside you, whom you can order to slay me; for surely he will do anything that you command, since you are also emperor." Though he spoke in this fashion, he nevertheless did Antoninus no harm, allowing his love for his offspring to outweigh his love for his country; and yet in doing so he betrayed his other son, for he well knew what would happen [once he himself was dead].'

If this isn't a literary device by Dio, who was later very critical of Caracalla, then the narrative seems clear that here Severus only just survived an assassination attempt. The surrender was signed nevertheless, and on terms highly favourable to Rome, with the native Britons ceding plentiful territory to the empire as Dio earlier detailed. Severus next proclaimed a famous victory, with he and his two sons being given the title *Britannicus* and with celebratory coins being struck to commemorate the event. Campaigning, at least for the short term, was over, and to apparent imperial satisfaction. Dio even adds an anecdote here about Julia Domna, saying that after the peace had been agreed she had a conversation with the wife of a Caledonian leader named Argentocoxus in which they compared the sexual customs of their cultures.[23]

On their way back to York the imperial party stopped at key locations to celebrate victory, sometimes on the direct line of march and sometimes not. This included a journey west along Hadrian's Wall, which has a notable Severan rebuilding phase which may date to the beginning of the AD 209 campaign, but more likely post-dates Severus' death in York when it once more became the northern frontier in Roman Britain. Indeed, this reconstruction was so significant that the *Historia Augusta* and some of the later Latin chroniclers (no doubt using the former as their key source) attributed the initial building phase of the wall to Severus rather than Hadrian. Specifically, the *Historia Augusta* says:[24]

> 'Severus protected Britain, and this was the greatest glory of his reign, with a wall led across the island to the Ocean at both ends; in recognition of this he also received the title Britannicus.'

Later, Aurelius Victor said:[25]

> '... after driving out the enemy, Severus protected Britain, as far as it was useful, with a wall led across the island to the Ocean at both ends.'

Similarly, Orosius wrote:[26]

> 'The victorious Severus was drawn to Britain ... He thought that the recovered part of the island should be separated from the other, unconquered tribes by a wall. He therefore led a great ditch and a very strong wall, fortified as well with frequent towers, for a hundred and thirty-two miles from sea to sea.'

This Severan association with the creation of what we now know as Hadrian's Wall persisted into the antiquarian period, with the fortification's true attribution only generally accepted from the mid-nineteenth century AD.

The *Historia Augusta* next provides interesting detail regarding Severus' visit to the western section of Hadrian's Wall, with a story again highlighting the emperor's superstitious nature:[27]

> 'On another occasion, when he was returning to his nearest quarters from an inspection of the wall at Luguvalium [modern Carlisle] in Britain, at a time when he had not only proved victorious but had concluded a perpetual peace, just as he was wondering what omen would present itself, an Ethiopian soldier, who was famous

among buffoons and always a notable jester, met him with a garland of cypress-boughs [sacred to Pluto, God of the underworld]. And when Severus in a rage ordered that the man be removed from his sight, troubled as he was by the man's ominous colour and the ominous nature of the garland, the Ethiopian by way of jest cried, it is said, "You have been all things, you have conquered all things, now O conqueror, be a God."'

Again, there is much to unpack here. First, the exact location of the event. Birley suggests the wall section visited here by Severus was the fort at Burgh-on-Sand (Roman *Aballava*) to the west of Carlisle, given we know there was a Moorish auxiliary unit based there in the third century AD called the *numerus Maurorum Aurelianorum*.[28] Second, and more importantly, the Historia Augusta's reference to the Ethiopian's skin colour. It is of note that the vulgar Latin *Aethiop* (as used here in the original text) had multiple meanings in the Roman world. For example, it could reference those specifically from Nubia, or anyone with an especially dark skin. Some have suggested the *Historia Augusta's* use here is appearance-based racism. However, as previously stated, racism in the Roman world was different to that in ours, particularly the modern West. Instead, especially given Severus himself was dark skinned, here I believe the reference is purely based on the actual colour black and its association with bad luck. Of note, the text in the *Historia Augusta* sits amid a wider passage which addresses Severus' obsession with his own mortality as he grew older. This section narrates four near contemporary omens which foreshadowed his death in York in February AD 211, which in addition to the above details three others:

- A dream by the emperor regarding his own deification.
- An episode at a games in honour of victory in the north, which Birley suggests may have been at Carpow.[41] Here, three plaster figures of the goddess Victory were set up, one each for Severus (in the centre, carrying a globe inscribed with his name), Caracalla

and Geta. That of the emperor was unceremoniously blown over by a gust of wind.
- An animal sacrificial event, relevant here given it also relates to the colour black. Here, I detail the *Historia Augusta's* narrative in full:[29]

'And when finally reaching the town [either Carlisle or York] Severus wished to perform a sacrifice. However, through a misunderstanding on the part of the rustic soothsayer, he was taken to the Temple of Bellona [the Sabine goddess of war], and, in the second place, the victims provided him were black. And then, when he abandoned the sacrifice in disgust and betook himself to the palace [supporting the York interpretation], through some carelessness on the part of the attendants the black victims followed him up to its very doors.'

Interestingly, Severus' visit to Carlisle was commemorated in the stone-built environment, given a huge new bath house or imperial *mansio* was constructed at the time atop an earlier, much smaller Hadrianic predecessor. This was first discovered in 2017 and, given the finery of its construction, was clearly built with the imperial entourage in mind. In particular, two monumental, sculptured busts may feature Julia Domna. Excavations there are ongoing and have revealed the main structure was an enormous 60m by 60m in size. Of note, the vaulting tubes used in the roof of the complex were North Africa in style, perhaps reflecting the emperor's own architects participating in the construction process. Hilts says the finery and scale of the site certainly 'hint at a rich non-military clientele', a view backed up by the finding of large amounts of roof and hypocaust tile featuring an imperial stamp there.[30]

Severus, Caracalla and the military leadership overwintered in York and were still there in May AD 210, when Birley highlights a letter sent in the emperor's name in response to an inquiry by a lady called Caecilia.[31] This was dated to the fifth of the month. However, as always with the Roman experience north of the provincial border, the comparative calm there following the first campaign was not to last. Here, clearly the terms which had so satisfied the Romans in AD 209 were not so agreeable to the Maeatae and Caledonians, particularly the former. They had been the recipients of the most extreme experiences of the first campaign and as AD 210 progressed they revolted again. One of the reasons for the renewed aggression was likely because one of their key tribal centres may have been near to the later Pictish capital at Abernethy, very close to the Roman site and bridge at Carpow. Here, it may have latterly dawned on the surviving native Britons that the Romans were set to stay for the long term, settled there in the Maeatae heartlands.

One can only guess at the sad fate of the Roman garrisons in the region as the revolt gathered pace, and Severus once more determined to march north, this time to finish the job. However, on this second occasion his ill health got the better of him, with the ensuing campaign led by the apparently forgiven Caracalla. The emperor was less forgiving to the natives, though, especially when the Caledonians soon predictably joined in, as at this point he gave the genocidal order to kill all the Britons which I detail at the beginning of the book.[32] To be clear, the Romans always took an unforgiving attitude with recalcitrant natives who they slaughtered or enslaved without qualms as a natural response to rebellion.

Even so, Severus' specific order to leave no one alive for this second campaign was at the more extreme end of Roman retribution. This new campaign in AD 210 was a direct re-run of the first, using the same tried and tested strategy, though this time with genocide added. Once more, from a Roman perspective, it was totally successful, with commemorative coins of Caracalla and Geta celebrating victory in Britain minted in Rome. Once more a brutal peace was forced on the Maeatae and Caledonians, and once more the Romans manned their far northern garrisons, and the imperial party headed back to York for the winter. However, even after this second success, nothing was to remain as Severus had intended. This was because, in the freezing cold of a northern British winter, he died in York.

DEATH OF AN EMPEROR

Severus was clearly active to the end of his life, even when suffering from the fatal illness which finally carried him away. It is at this point Dio also has Severus give his famous death-bed advice to Caracalla and Geta saying 'be of one mind, enrich the soldiers, and despise the rest'.[33] The emperor then finally died on 4 February AD 211 aged 65, with the Historia Augusta saying:[34]

> 'In the eighteenth year of his reign, now an old man and overcome by a most grievous disease, he died at Eboracum in Britain.'

As to the nature of this fatal illness, modern narratives most often refer to gout, hence Severus' need for a litter on campaign in AD 209. As previously mentioned, though gout itself isn't usually a life-threatening illness, if untreated it is linked with subsequent kidney and heart disease. Also, one can't rule out a pulmonary condition given his age, the time of year and Severus' location when he died given his origins in the heat of North Africa.

Additionally, Dio and Herodian suggest Caracalla may have played a role in Severus' death. The latter is more nuanced:[35]

> 'Caracalla began to persuade the army to look to him alone, and was canvassing for the position of sole ruler by every means, slandering his brother [note by this time Geta had also been elevated to an Augustus]. But his father, ill for a long time and being slow to die, seemed to him a burden and a nuisance. He tried to persuade both his doctors and attendants who were caring for him to mistreat the old man, so as to be rid of him sooner. But finally, though slowly, Severus, for the most part destroyed by sorrow [because of his elder son's treachery], did expire, having had a life of greater distinction, as far as warfare is concerned, than all other emperors.'

Meanwhile, Dio is more explicit:[36]

'... his disease carried him off ... with some assistance from Antoninus [Caracalla] as well, it is said.'

Note that, as previously mentioned, both authors were no fans of Caracalla, or indeed any of the later Severans. Yet even then, though they both imply Caracalla's ill intentions towards his father, there is no smoking gun to be found here, or elsewhere. To that end, on balance it seems most likely that Severus died purely of natural causes, carried off by the cold of a bitter winter at the northern extremity of his empire while suffering from circulatory problems.

Severus was succeeded by his two sons as joint *augusti*, who he hoped to his last breath would rule the empire harmoniously together. As we will see, that was never going to happen. Next his body was cremated in York after a series of funerary ceremonies which lasted days. Finally, his ashes were placed inside an urn of 'purple stone'.[37] This had been ordered before his death. It is not clear if this came from Britain, very unlikely (although some say it could have been Derbyshire 'Blue John'), or if it had travelled with him from Italy. If the latter, it shows a degree of foreknowledge on his part that he wouldn't return. From Dio's description, if the urn was from the Mediterranean, it was most likely made of porphyry, a rare and very hard volcanic rock consisting of quartz, feldspar and mica whose name means purple. In the Roman world, urns of this material were thought fitting resting places for the ashes of an emperors given the colour association.

At this point, a dramatic divergence now began to appear between Severus' long-term plans for the far north of Britain and those of his sons. In short, neither could wait to get away from York and return to Rome. Separately, they began to make hasty preparations to leave, aiming to secure their respective power bases when back home. First, the harsh peace forced on the surviving Maeatae and Caledonians after the AD 210 campaign was hastily formalised, their numbers greatly diminished by the two savage Roman campaigns, particularly the last. The emperors then made it clear they had no intention of honouring their father's wishes to maintain a military presence in the far north. Soon plans were being set in place to begin evacuating Roman troops from the region, with the northern frontier again being reset on the line of Hadrian's Wall. For a time, garrisons may have been left behind at key sites such as Cramond and Carpow, though even they were soon abandoned one last time.

Caracalla and Geta now eyed their imminent return to Rome. Relations between the two brothers, never good, deteriorated rapidly in York after their father's death. Caracalla certainly didn't intend to rule alongside his brother for long, and now aggressively reset the imperial court in his own favour given he was the senior *augusti*. First he dismissed Papinianus, who we should remember was Caracalla's relative on his mother's side. Some argue that in his will Severus had tasked his *praefectus praetorio* with maintaining harmony between the brothers. This was clearly an impossible job, costing Papinianus his post. Next Caracalla executed many of his father's most devoted freedmen, including Castor the court chamberlain and Euodus, his own former tutor who had helped him bring down Plautianus. Again, these were men the dying emperor would have encouraged to keep the imperial family together. The order was also sent out at this time to execute Caracalla's former wife, the unfortunate Plautilla. He also put to death Severus' court doctors, likely because they had refused to speed his passing if Herodian is correct. Caracalla then tried to force the army to recognise him as sole emperor given the majority of the senior leadership was still in York. One apocryphal story here has him planning to kill Geta there and then but failing because his younger brother looked too much like his father, which made him popular with the troops. For now, the army stayed loyal to the dead emperor's dying wishes, maintaining support for both brothers.

By early Spring AD 211, after the death of the emperor, his funeral and cremation, and Caracalla's first round of proscriptions, the imperial party made ready to leave for Rome. At this point Julia Domna and the remaining imperial *comites* made a final concerted effort to reconcile her sons. Caracalla conceitedly responded with a public display of affection for Geta. Unsurprisingly, this wasn't to last, with the brothers having separate quarters on their journey home, and some arguing they took completely different routes with their respective entourages.[38]

Once back in Rome, matters worsened again, with Geta refusing to act as Caracalla's junior and both running their own separate courts where their supporters jockeyed for favour and position. The final event the brothers jointly participated in as *augusti* was the burial of their father in the Mausoleum of Hadrian. After this the imperial government ground to a halt due to their constant bickering, the brothers hardly speaking to each other. In the end they divided the imperial palace on the Palatine Hill between themselves, so they didn't have to physically meet.[39]

By this time some in their respective courts suggested Caracalla and Geta split the empire between them, with Geta taking control of the east. However, this quickly fell through at the instigation of Julia Domna who was keen to maintain the empire's integrity.[40] After this, with tensions continuing to rise, matters quickly came to a head. By now Caracalla's closest supporters were urging him to have Geta murdered, especially given many in the Senate and among Rome's literary elite were openly supporting the younger brother.[41]

At this point, Caracalla finally gave in to the demands of his supporters and ordered his brother's assassination, with a first attempt made during the Saturnalia celebrations in mid-December AD 211. For some reason, this failed, though another on 26 December finally succeeded.[42] Here, Dio provides the detail:[43]

> 'Many soldiers and athletes were now guarding Geta, both abroad and at home, day and night alike. Therefore, Caracalla induced his mother to summon them both, unattended, to her apartment, with a view to reconciling them. Thus Geta was persuaded, and went in with him; but when they were inside, some centurions, previously

instructed by Caracalla, rushed in and struck down Geta, who at sight of them had run to his mother, hung about her neck and clung to her bosom and breasts, lamenting and crying: "Mother that didst bear me, mother that didst bear me, help! I am being murdered." And so she, tricked in this way, saw her son perishing in the most impious fashion in her arms, and received him at his death into the very womb, as it were, whence he had been born; for she was all covered with his blood, so that she took no note of the wound she had received on her hand.'

Such was the sad end for Severus' youngest son. Meanwhile, after the event, his mother was not permitted to mourn for her son, but compelled to rejoice by Caracalla who ensured all her words and gestures were closely watched.

Shortly afterwards, Papinianus was beheaded and his body dragged through the streets of Rome. A new 'terror' then followed in the imperial capital, with 20,000 viewed as aligned with either Severus or Geta executed. Notable unfortunates included Publius Helvius Pertinax, the son of Severus' old mentor Pertinax. Here, Publius completely misread Caracalla's mood after the murder of Geta, thinking it safe to make a joke at the emperor's expense in court. As earlier detailed, by this time Caracalla had gathered several honorific titles, including *Germanicus*, *Parthicus*, and *Arabicus* to reflect earlier triumphs over the enemies of Rome with his father. Publius now suggested the emperor add *Geticus* to the list. This was a play on words, referencing the Getae, a Thracian people on the Lower Danube. However, the 'joke' backfired spectacularly as Caracalla had him executed immediately, despite him being a *suffected* consul for the year. Meanwhile, Commodus' surviving sister, and a cousin of Caracalla called Septimius Severus, were also killed.

Caracalla next ensured Geta officially 'disappeared' by ordering a cowed Senate to declare a *damnatio memoriae* against him. This led to all of the images of Geta across the empire being defaced, and inscriptions mentioning him similarly destroyed. The brutality of

Geta's *damnatio memoriae* is evident everywhere in the Roman world. Thus, in Rome his image and name were removed from the Arch of Septimius Severus in the *forum Romanum* in Rome (this act still visible today), while similarly they were removed from the *Arcus Argentariorum* in the *forum Boarium*. Here, the images and names of Plautianus and Plautilla were also chiselled away. Elsewhere, Henig and Soffe detail another example, this time in Britain where a slighted marble bust of Geta, now in the Getty Museum in Malibu, California, was found in the River Thames[44]. Meanwhile, in Leptis Magna, Severus' hometown, the head of Geta was removed from the quadrifrons Severan arch there, and its nose broken off. It was then hastily buried nearby. Now, with Geta cancelled, Caracalla looked to build on his father's martial legacy. However, for him, a sad end awaited, too.

Conclusion

The Severan Legacy

Most Roman emperors didn't die in their beds of natural causes, but Severus most likely did. In that regard, he could count his reign a success. A usurper himself, who grabbed the throne at the point of a sword, he'd then seen off challenger after challenger, until the aristocracy and military had been cauterised of all potential opposition. In so doing, Severus created his reset of the empire, or hostile take-over as some see it. This established the Severan Dynasty which lasted until AD 235. In this conclusion, I now consider the Severan legacy, first narrating the fortunes of the dynasty which carried his name, then examining the impact his reset had on Rome and the empire's leading families, before finally looking at the fortunes of the wider empire itself.

SEVERAN RESET – DYNASTY

Severus' brother Publius Septimius Geta died in Italy in AD 204 of natural causes, the emperor outliving his elder brother by nine years. It is unclear when his sister Septimia Octavilla died, though she may also have predeceased him. However, as emperor his success ensured the family name's longevity through the establishment of his own dynasty. Here, I focus primarily on the fortunes of Caracalla and Julia Domna, and also Marcus Opellius Macrinus given the role this only non-Severan member of the dynasty played in the downfall of the former two.

Caracalla became sole emperor after the murder of his brother, Geta, and then reigned until his own assassination in AD 217. Some argue he has had a bad press and that, at least as a military leader, he was in the same league as his father. However, all our primary sources are clear about his ill-favoured character. The *Historia Augusta* sums this up best, saying:[1]

> 'His mode of life was evil and he was more brutal even than his cruel father. He was gluttonous in his use of food and addicted to wine, hated by his household and detested in every camp save that of the praetorian guard; and between him and his brother there was no resemblance whatever.'

Caracalla's first focus after the savage round of proscriptions that followed Geta's demise was domestic. Here, at the start of his reign, he secured his own legacy through instituting the AD 212 *constitutio Antoniniana* for which he is best remembered today. This legal edict made all freemen of the empire citizens. Prior to this only those born in Italy could become Roman citizens, with freemen in the provinces called *perigrini*. This gave them a slightly different, inferior legal status, important given they made up over 80 per cent of the empire's population. Therefore, Caracalla's move to broaden the citizen base to include all freemen anywhere in the empire had enormous implications. For example, it broadened the legal recruiting base for elite military units, the soldiery always a central focus of Severan thinking, and crucially gave the emperor even greater control over how his subjects were taxed. We are fortunate here to have a surviving portion of this historic edict, preserved on a badly damaged papyrus document found in Egypt:[2]

> 'I give thanks to the immortal Gods, because they preserved me, thus I think I should be able magnificently to make a suitable response to their majesty if I were able to lead all who are presently my people and others who should join my people to the sanctuaries of the Gods.

I give to all of those who are under my rule throughout the whole world Roman citizenship, with the provision that the just claims of communities should remain, with the exception of the dediticii. The whole population should already have been included in my victories. My edict will expand the majesty of the Roman people.'

However, as soon as his ground-breaking edict had been enacted, Caracalla lost all interest in administering his empire. Bored with life in Rome, which now came with a daily round of responsibilities he found mind-numbing, he was soon relying on Julia Domna to run the imperial administration. Indeed, it was she who quickly took responsibility for receiving petitions and answering imperial correspondence.

Instead, Caracalla began to look around for more foreign adventure. He found it on the northern frontier, where the Germanic Alamanni had breached the *limes* in Raetia in a mass raid on imperial territory. The emperor left Rome in AD 213 never to return, even missing the inauguration ceremony for the baths there which carry his name to this day. Once in Raetia, he mounted a two-year campaign where he defeated the Germans comprehensively and chased them back over the frontier. He then ordered a refortification programme along the *limes* not only in Raetia but also Germania Superior to ensure their resilience against future threats. Finally, he signed new treaties with allied German tribes to provide a buffer against future Alamannic invasions.

By Spring AD 214, Caracalla was ready to move on again, this time with a tour of his eastern provinces. Travelling along the Danubian frontier, he soon crossed into Asia in late summer and overwintered in Nicomedia in Bithynia et Pontus. While there one of his obsessions manifested in an unexpected way, with Dio detailing that:[3]

'He was so enthusiastic about Alexander the Great [not unusual for a Roman emperor] that he used certain weapons and cups which he believed had once been his, and had earlier set up many likenesses of him both in the camps and in Rome itself. Now, he went further, organising a phalanx, composed entirely of Macedonians, 16,000 strong. He named it "Alexander's phalanx," and equipped it with the arms that warriors had used in the great conqueror's day; these consisted of a helmet of raw ox-hide, a three-ply linen breastplate, a bronze shield, long pike, short spear, high boots, and sword.'

Of note, the Hellenistic way of war was far different to that of the Romans, the former using sixteen-deep *sarissa* pike phalanxes with the first five ranks setting their weapons at the charge. As such, compared to the far more flexible Principate Roman system with its legionaries and auxilia, this was antique indeed.

Caracalla left Nicomedia on 4 April AD 215, and by the summer was back in Antioch-on-the-Orontes. There he stayed for a few months, and then left for Alexandria, where another dark chapter in his reign took place. Here, as he travelled to the Egyptian provincial capital, he learned of a popular satire in the city attracting large audiences which mocked his assassination of his brother, and his other pretences. Again, his sense of humour failed him, though this time more sanguineous and on a large scale. When a deputation of leading Alexandrians arrived to greet him on arrival in December, he had them slaughtered on the spot. He then set his troops loose sacking the city for several days, looting and plundering. Thousands were killed. Here his Alexander fixation came to the fore again, with Dio once more adding the detail:[4]

'Toward the philosophers who were called Aristotelians he showed bitter hatred in every way, even going so far as to desire to burn their books, and in particular he abolished their common messes in Alexandria and all the other privileges that they had enjoyed there; his grievance against them was that Aristotle was supposed to have been involved in the death of Alexander.'

Caracalla stayed in Alexandria until April AD 216. He then left to seek more martial glory, this time against the Parthians. The emperor knew this was a sure-fire way of bolstering his support back in Rome. Opportunity was presented by the civil war that followed Vologases V's earlier death in AD 208, between his two sons Vologases VI and Artabanus V. By the time Caracalla had earlier arrived in Alexandria, the brothers had already split the empire in two, with support from the Parthian nobility divided between them. For Caracalla, this was too good an opportunity to miss. Soon he was in Antioch again, amassing a huge army. This included ten cohorts of the Praetorian Guard, his *equites singulares Augusti* imperial guard cavalry, three full legions, vexillations from five others' legions, and large numbers of supporting auxiliary cavalry and foot.

His first action, as with his father two decades earlier, was to secure the eastern frontier region. This included awarding *colonia* status to Homs, his mother's hometown, and to the important desert trading city of Palmyra. He next turned his attention to Osrhoene, the eastern province created by his father and home to *legio* III *Parthica*. There, a survivor of the royal line which had ruled the region prior to Rome's annexation was styling himself Abgarus IX and trying to claim some level of independence again. Caracalla's solution was simple. He lured him and his son to the governor's palace in Antioch and had them killed. However, the emperor then overplayed his hand trying a similar trick with king Khosrov of Armenia, a recent Parthian appointee. Though the latter was captured and would remain imprisoned by the Romans until his death two years later, his country rose in revolt and would remain a problem for the Romans for a decade. This forced Caracalla to deploy some of his troops on the Armenian border for security, which he then claimed as a victory.

Caracalla was now ready to intervene in Parthia and had to choose who to back. At least ostensibly, he chose Artabanus V, the brother with the most support in the Parthian west. This was after intelligence reached him that the Parthian king was losing the loyalty of the nobles closest to him, making him vulnerable to diplomatic intrigue. However, as always with this emperor, all was not what it seemed.

Caracalla now sent an unprecedented offer to Artabanus, suggesting he marry one of the Persian co-monarch's daughters, uniting their empires. As detailed earlier, the emperor was a free agent in that regard, having disposed of his first wife Fulvia Plautilla as soon as his father had died. After first demurring, Artabanus accepted, knowing this was the best way to secure the Parthian throne for himself alone.

Delighted, Caracalla set off eastwards with his entire army excepting the troops on the Armenian border and soon crossed the Euphrates. A formal rendezvous was then arranged by the Romans for Caracalla to meet his future Parthian wife and father-in-law, the location unknown. The event took the form of a lavish reception, with leading members of the Parthian nobility in attendance. However, it proved a deadly trap. At a given moment, Caracalla ordered the Romans present to attack their Parthian guests with concealed weapons. A massacre ensued, with Herodian saying Artabanus only narrowly escaped with the help of his close guard.[5]

Caracalla then launched a rampage across the region which came to a head in late summer AD 216 when the Romans captured the key Parthian religious city of Arbela near the old Assyrian capital Nineveh. This was brutally sacked, with Caracalla ordering the Parthian royal tombs desecrated and the bones of their former kings scattered. With the campaigning season now coming to an end, Caracalla then declared victory over the Parthians and led his army back to Syria with huge amounts of loot.[6]

However, he had unfinished business in the east. His father had famously sacked the Parthian capital Ctesiphon, but he hadn't. In fact, he'd failed to force a single major engagement with the Parthians. His martial honour at stake, he now determined to launch another offensive in the Spring of AD 217. This time, his army was even bigger.

Crossing the Euphrates once more, Caracalla set up a forward headquarters in the Osrhoene provincial capital Edessa, modern Urfa. While there, as his command team worked on a detailed plan for the

Romans to advance down the Tigris valley to Ctesiphon, the emperor decided to visit the famous Temple of the Moon near Carrhae, planning to say prayers for Crassus who had lost his life there fighting the Parthians in 53 BC. However, on 8 April, he met one of the most incongruous ends of any Roman emperor. After stopping briefly to urinate on the roadside and unwisely sending his bodyguards away so he had some privacy, he was killed by a guard officer called Julius Martialis, who stabbed him from behind.

This was the result of a plot that had been in the planning for months, led by the ambitious *praefectus praetorio* Macrinus who had accompanied the emperor east. At some stage Macrinus began to fear his loyalty to Caracalla was under suspicion. This then became a self-fulfilling prophecy when he began a conspiracy against the emperor to save himself. He now became a traitor in the system, looking for any opportunity to remove Caracalla. However, the emperor was almost warned of the plot by Materianus, his *praefectus urbi* back in Rome commanding the urban cohorts. Crucially, this post gave Materianus responsibility for the *frumentarii* imperial secret service when the emperor was away on campaign. In that capacity his agents got wind of the plot and soon a sealed message was on its way to the emperor using the *cursus publicus*. However, in a crucial error, the courier was not made aware of the key dispatch being carried among the emperor's normal post. Therefore, when Caracalla received the mail in Edessa on the eastern frontier at the beginning of April, instead of reading it himself he gave the dispatches to Macrinus to deal with, including the warning from Materianus. One can imagine Macrinus' terror as he read it, and he quickly disposed of the incriminating note.

Unsurprisingly, his plot now went into overdrive, and he quickly recruited Martialis who was furious that Caracalla had earlier executed his brother. The assassin struck soon afterwards, killing the emperor with a single blow. Here, Macrinus was taken completely by surprise at the speed of the deed, and he hastily silenced Martialis by executing him on the spot.

The assassination of Caracalla put the Roman army in a very difficult position. This was because word now reached them that an enraged Artabanus was approaching with an enormous army of his own, determined to avenge Caracalla's treachery at the wedding gathering and the desecration of the royal tombs. Far from undermining Artabanus, Caracalla's actions had bolstered his support among the Parthian nobility. They now demanded revenge.

The senior Roman officers present panicked and quickly appointed Macrinus emperor given his position as *praefectus praetorio*, despite it being obvious to all he was behind Caracalla's assassination. Here, the *Historia Augusta* is insightful, having the Roman commanders declare their hatred for the deceased Caracalla:[7]

> 'Anyone as emperor rather than the fratricide [Caracalla], anyone rather than the incestuous one, anyone rather than the filthy one, anyone rather than the slayer of the Senate and people.'

Some officers present did argue Macrinus was unsuitable to become emperor given he was an equestrian and not a Senator. However, as with most of the high command he was a North African, and this won the day for him. Sadly for his posthumous reputation, all the primary sources are highly critical of his tenure in power, particularly the *Historia Augusta* which portrays him as a classic pantomime villain, saying he was hated by all.[8] Cassius Dio[9] and Herodian[10] are more benign, though not much. It is they who detail he acted against Caracalla through self-preservation rather than any desire to become emperor. However, both agree Macrinus was an ineffectual emperor who made a series of dramatic missteps from the beginning of his short reign. This made him particularly unpopular with the rank and file in the army. Realising this, and knowing battle was likely given Artabanus' proximity, he tried to inspire his army with a stirring address. Sadly, for him he was too honest about the jeopardy they faced, with the Parthians hell bent on revenge and no quarter likely to be given.

To compound things, he then proved a poor war leader, perhaps displaying cowardice given that instead of arraying his army for battle he tried to placate Artabanus, releasing his Parthian captives to show good faith. Artabanus rejected this out of hand, demanding the Romans relinquish the whole of northern Mesopotamia to the Parthians, rebuild the towns and cities they had destroyed, and pay huge amounts in compensation. Unsurprisingly, the terms were unacceptable to the Romans and Macrinus quickly rejected them. Battle would now be joined. Note here that all the primary sources say that for some reason Artabanus was unaware Caracalla had been assassinated, believing he was still emperor.

The only choice Macrinus now had was the type of battle he would fight. By this point the two armies were camped opposite each other at Nisibis, still a key border city under Roman control. Macrinus had three options. First, to lead his army into the city and prepare for a Parthian siege, hoping a relief force would arrive from elsewhere in the east. Second, to withdraw west towards Antioch where the regional defences would give a greater degree of protection. Finally, to give open battle. The first wasn't an option given Nisibis was too small to accommodate his large army. The second wasn't either given he knew his huge column would be harried the whole way by Parthian horse archers. Therefore, he prepared for open battle.

We don't have the exact date of the engagement in AD 217, but as dawn broke on the day of the battle both sides deployed ready to fight, the Romans in their classic *triplex acies* formation of three lines. Each comprised legionaries in the centre, with auxiliaries on the flanks, and *lanciarii* light legionaries and other skirmishes deployed forward of the first line to deter the Parthian horse archers. The legionary artillery was deployed behind the third line to fire over the heads of those to the front. Meanwhile, the auxiliary cavalry was deployed on the flanks.

Opposite, the Parthians deployed in five large divisions, reflecting the feudal structure of their society. Each contained a mass of horse archers around a core of fully armoured cataphract noble lancers. On the flanks they also deployed camel-mounted cataphracts, these aiming to deter the Roman mounted troops opposite.

The Parthians opened the battle in the early morning, their horse archers circling in front of the Roman skirmishers, firing volley after volley of arrows. Here, the Parthian missile troops outnumbered the Romans, and soon the latter's light troops were driven back through the heavy infantry to the rear. The horse archers now closed with the legionaries and auxilia who locked shields to protect themselves from the barrage. However, the volume of fire eventually told, and here and there gaps began to open in the Roman shield wall. When it did, Parthian cataphracts charged home to try and break the Roman line. The Roman heavy foot countered by throwing showers of spiked caltrops to their front which disrupted the Parthian charge. The Roman line held. Just. The Parthians then suffered heavy casualties as their cavalry withdrew.

This set a pattern which continued for the entire first day of the battle, with the Parthians launching several assaults until night fell. All failed. Both sides then withdrew to their camps for the night. The second day was then a complete repeat of the first, with the Parthians charging weak points in the Roman lines but failing to achieve a breakthrough.

However, on the third day, Artabanus tried a new stratagem to break the deadlock. He ordered his cavalry to use their greater numbers to outflank the Roman line. The Romans, with superior battlefield training, responded by abandoning the *triplex acies*, instead deploying into one line of battle. This extended their frontage to match that of the Parthians. Even then, they were still in danger of being encircled until in a final desperate gambit Macrinus ordered the non-combatant drivers and shield bearers out of the Roman camp to extend their line one last time. The Parthians feared this might be a pre-planned trap given Caracalla's devious reputation, and so Artabanus finally ordered his army to disengage, ready to resume combat the next day. By this time, after three days of fighting, Herodian says casualties on both sides were so great that:[11]

'... the entire plain was covered with the dead; bodies were piled up in huge mounds, and the dromedaries especially fell in heaps.'

Macrinus knew that, to this point, he'd had a lucky escape. Therefore, in this lull in the fighting, he sent word to Artabanus that Caracalla was dead. He then offered substantial compensation if allowed to retire from the field. The Parthian king, his feudal army restive after the short campaign, agreed. The two sides settled on a price of 200 million *sesterces* to recompense the Parthians, with the Roman army then retiring westwards in good order. However, given the Parthians remained on the field of battle, they claimed one final victory over the Romans. At best, Macrinus could claim a draw. As it proved, that was not enough.

Neither protagonist at the Battle of Nisibis lasted long in power. For Macrinus, the revenge of the Severans followed swiftly. As soon as he arrived back in Antioch, Caracalla's mother, Julia Domna, and her sister, the by now fabulously wealthy Julia Maesa, began to plot against him. He quickly found out and banished both, though the ill Julia Domna chose to starve herself to death instead. This was a truly sad end for the former empress, who had outlived not only her husband but both sons.

Julia Maesa did leave, heading to her native Emesa, taking her children Julia Soaemias and Julia Mamaea with her. There they joined the former's son Heliogabalus, who, even though only fourteen, was the chief priest of the Levantine sun deity of the same name. Once in Emesa, Julia Maesa took advantage of a visit by some legionaries of the nearby Raphanea-based *legio* III *Gallica* to convince them her grandson was the illegitimate son of Caracalla, and so the true heir to the throne. The soldiers proclaimed him emperor there and then.

Things now moved quickly against Macrinus. An attempt to defeat Heliogabalus at Raphanea failed. This led to an engagement outside Antioch on 8 June AD 218 where Macrinus fled the field and headed for Rome. However, he was soon captured in Chalcedon in Bithynia before he could cross to Europe. Before fleeing, he'd also sent his son Marcus Opellius Diadumenianus, recently made his co-emperor, to the care of Artabanus in Parthia. However, the boy was captured in transit at Zeugma and executed in late June. When Macrinus heard the terrible news, he tried to escape captivity but was injured and then executed in Cappadocia. His head was sent to Heliogabalus in Antioch, where it joined that of his son. Artabanus fell next, though I tell his final story in the context of the Severan legacy of the wider empire.

Heliogabalus proved a disaster for the Severans. Clearly a troubled young man, he had been raised amid the high-level, high stakes manoeuvring of an imperial family reeling from the death of their founder in York, and Caracalla's subsequent blundering unpredictability. His grandmother and mother clearly thought they could wrest back power for the Severans through his appointment as emperor, which they did. However, when they then tried to rule the empire through him, their plans spectacularly failed.

Heliogabalus' short reign is notorious for religious controversy and sex scandals, ensuring his reputation is one of the most salacious of any Roman emperor. For example, he replaced Jupiter, the traditional head of the Roman pantheon, with the Emesan sun deity by which he himself came to be known, Heliogabalas. Once in Rome, he then forced leading members of the Senate and military to participate in religious rites celebrating their new chief God at events he presided over in person. Meanwhile, he married four women (one a vestal virgin), and eventually his private life descended to a level of debauchery that would have shamed Commodus. Quickly, this shocking behaviour estranged the Praetorian Guard and Senate, and, amidst growing public opposition, he and his mother were assassinated on 12 March AD 222. Here, having been summoned to the *Castra Praetoria* Praetorian camp under duress, the guard turned on him. As he tried to flee, he and his mother were then savagely cut down, beheaded and their torsos stripped naked. The latter were dragged through the city, after which they were cast in the Tiber. We do not know the fate of the heads. It later transpired his assassination was the result of Severan family realpolitik when it became known it had been arranged by his grandmother Julia Maesa, keen to remove a grandson she thought threatened the dynasty.

Heliogabalus was quickly replaced by his younger nephew, the thirteen-year-old Severus Alexander, son of Julia Mamaea. His reign began well, with Rome prospering in a time of peace for almost a decade. However, when he was later militarily challenged, he proved wanting. His first test was against the new Sassanid Persian Empire, which had replaced the Parthians in the east. Here, the first Sassanid monarch Ardashir I raided the border province of Mesopotamia in AD 230, punching through the Roman defences there to reach Syria. He then demanded the return of all the former territories of the Achaemenid Persian Empire now under Roman control, including Anatolia. This was clearly not going to happen, and after fruitless negotiations the emperor launched an invasion of the east in AD 232. However, of his three columns of march, only that through Armenia achieved any success, while the two to the south failed to recapture any Persian-occupied territory. An uneasy stalemate followed, allowing the Romans to turn their attention to the Rhine frontier. There, various Germanic tribes had begun raiding Roman territory in large numbers. Alexander headed back west in person and was soon on the northern *limes*, with his mother alongside. Having stopped the initial incursions, he then tried to secure peace through diplomacy and bribery. This alienated many in his military leadership, with a conspiracy following which led to the murder of both emperor and mother while in the Roman camp. Maximinus Thrax then became the emperor with the support of the army, ending the Severan dynasty. Thus, sadly for Septimius Severus, his reign proved the most successful of the entire dynasty, with all his successors proving failures to a greater or lesser extent.

SEVERAN RESET – ROME

The Severan legacy proved far longer lasting in Rome, both in terms of the built environment and wealth. In the first case, much of ancient Rome visible today is Severan in date. This includes significant parts of the imperial palace on the Palatine Hill, the Temple of Vesta in the *forum Romanum*, the Arch of Septimius Severus below the Capitoline Hill, the *Arcus Argentariorum* in the *forum Boarium*, the Severan *propylaeum* entrance to the *Porticus Octaviae*, the foundations of his grand *Septizodium*, the remains of the Temple of Fortuna Muliebris, the remains of the *Forma Urbis Romae* map of the Severan city, the enormous Baths of Caracalla, and the remains of the Temple of Heliogabalus on the Palatine Hill.

Meanwhile, Severus' three savage rounds of proscriptions against the empire's elites, first in the east after defeating Niger, next in Gaul after defeating Albinus, and finally in Rome itself, permanently changed the very top of Roman society. This was unsurprising given over 100 Senators were brutally dragged from office, often to their execution without trial. Shockingly, this was over one sixth of the entire Senate, their family wealth then confiscated into the coffers of the Severan family or the imperial *fiscus* treasury. Such wealth redistribution at the point of a sword then gave rise to a new prominence for North Africans in Rome at the expense (literally) of Italians, a key aspect of the Severan reset.

Further, the equestrian order also received a boost under Severus. This lasted long into the Dominate phase of empire, and was one of the key ways he moved to check the power of the Senate. His appointment of equestrians to command his three new Parthian legions was so unusual it is noted by all the primary sources, as is his appointment of equestrian governors, particular in the east. Here, again, we see the rise to prominence of the North Africans, with Birley highlighting that over 60 per cent of all the procurators Severus appointed across the empire were North African.[12]

SEVERAN RESET - EMPIRE

Perhaps Severus' most visible legacy was his geographical reset of the empire. This had enormous long-term implications for the Roman world lasting way beyond the end of the empire in the west. Here, I consider how this impacted the east, North Africa and Europe, and finally how the collapse of the Severan dynasty set in train the demise of the Principate and the onset of the Dominate.

In the east, Severus played a key role in the downfall of the Parthian dynasty, along with Caracalla and Macrinus. The success of Severus' second eastern campaign against Vologases V, and particularly the ease with which he captured and sacked the Parthian capital Ctesiphon, significantly undermined the support of the Parthian nobility for their Arsacid rulers. Notably, the Parthians were still recovering from their defeat at the hands of Lucius Verus' Roman-Parthian war campaign when Severus attacked, and Vologases' ineffectual defence of Parthian territory only added to the reputational damage already inflicted in the early AD 160s. Then, after Vologases' death in AD 208, the civil war between his two sons Vologases VI and Artabanus V did nothing to stabilise the regime. Further, the inability to follow up any success the Parthians may have claimed at Nisibis in AD 217 highlighted a fundamental structural weakness that had emerged within the empire. This allowed Ardashir I, the ruler of Parthian satrapy of Persis, to usurp Artabanus V in AD 224. Ardashir then established the Sassanid Persian Empire, though any Roman claim to success in the downfall of the Arsacids proved double-edged to say the least. This was because, while the Parthians were a near-symmetrical threat to the Romans, the Sassanids were truly symmetrical, and defeated the Romans as often as they lost. The ongoing conflict between the Romans and Persians then endured on and off for four centuries until both exhausted each other in the lengthy Byzantine-Sassanian War at the beginning of the seventh century AD. This set the scene for the Arab Conquest in the region which by the beginning of the eighth century AD had conquered the whole of North Africa, with Spain to follow from AD 710.

More specifically, Severus also reordered the provincial make-up of the eastern frontier, such that by the time he died in York in AD 211, it was significantly different to that he inherited in AD 193.

First, he divided the original province of Syria into Coele-Syria in the north and Syro-Phoenicia in the south. Then, later, after defeating the Parthians, he added two new provinces in the east. These were Mesopotamia and Osrhoene, both acting as buffer regions for Roman urban and agricultural heartlands nearer the Mediterranean coast. Finally, before he left the east never to return, Severus reorganised the frontier zone there. This included expanding the *limes Cappadocia* and the northern section of the *limes Arabicus* to include Mesopotamia and Osrhoene and similarly expanding the southern section of the *limes* in the region by transferring a large part of Syro-Phoenicia to Arabia Petraea. Thus, by the end of his rule, the Romans controlled more territory in the east than at any time previously, excepting perhaps a brief spell under Trajan after his campaigns there.

Moving on to North Africa, Severus' home region also received his close attention as he reset the empire. Most visibly, while travelling through the region in AD 202–AD 203, he formally separated Numidia from Africa Proconsularis, making the legionary fortress and *canaba* at Lambaesis its new capital, with the civilian settlement then becoming a *colonia*. Additionally, in the eastern Maghreb, the success of his Spring AD 203 campaign against the Garamantes resulted in much of their territory south of Tripolitania being incorporated into Africa Pronconsularis. The *limes Tripolitanus* in the Fezzān were then expanded to take in this newly conquered land. Finally, before heading back to Rome from Carthage, Severus also added several key settlements beyond the Numidian *limes* to Roman territory. Thus, by the time he arrived back in the imperial capital, Roman territory in North Africa had matched the east in being greatly expanded, much of this new land to remain under Roman control until the Vandal conquest in AD 429–AD 435.

Next, the Severan reset of imperial territory was also very evident in Europe, particularly the frontier regions. For example, the northern *limes* along the Rhine and Danube were significantly refortified after Severus' AD 197 campaign against Albinus in Gaul. However, Severus' biggest European legacy was in Britain.

First, in the aftermath of the defeat of Albinus, he ordered the construction of the 3.2km land wall around the provincial capital London. Given this was later rebuilt as the medieval land wall, it still defines the modern City of London. Thus, today's Square Mile, one of the world's leading financial centres, is still defined by a fortification built at the end of the second century AD by a Roman emperor born in North Africa.

Second, it was Severus who initiated the division of the original province of Britannia into two. This replicated his earlier division of Syria and Africa Proconsularis, though in this case it was completed later under Caracalla. Here, after the change, imperial territory on the main island of Britain now featured two new provinces. These were Britannia Superior in the south, with its capital in London, and Britannia Inferior in the north, with its capital in York.

However, far more important was the abandonment by Caracalla and Geta of their father's conquests in the far north after his death. This was the last time the Romans attempted to conquer significant territory in the region of modern Scotland. If Severus had lived there is a good chance the Scottish Borders, Fife and the upper Midland Valley would have joined the imperial territory in the south as part of an expanded northern province. This would have featured a classically Mediterranean stone-built Roman urban environment with towns or larger, a significant trunk road system and busy Roman harbours. However, as the Romans left almost as soon as Severus passed away in York, with the northern frontier again dropping down to the line of Hadrian's Wall, this did not happen. Indeed, from that point the political, economic and social development of the far north of Britain went in its own direction, leading to the political settlement between the far north and south which still exists today. This a true Severan legacy which resonates in our modern world.

Finally, in Britain, we have one last, truly brutal legacy to consider. This is the effect on the campaigning region of the two Severan assaults there in AD 209 and AD 210. Here, though Severus failed to achieve his main aim with the final conquest of the far north, he succeeded in his short-term goal of pacifying the Maeatae and Caledonians. This is not surprising given the numbers butchered or captured in the final genocidal campaign.

A variety of factors have been used to show this to be the case. For example, Hodgson says there is a long historical tradition of viewing Severus' *expeditio felicissima Brittannica* as successful given the evident peaceful state of the British provinces through the rest of the third century AD,[13] with Frere earlier highlighting the fact the northern frontier remained at peace until at least AD 296 after the fall of the usurping North Sea Empire of Carausius and Allectus.[14] This is probably the longest period of peace in the region until the immediate pre-modern era.

Meanwhile, other hard evidence also supports the general view that lowland Scotland was significantly depopulated after the campaigns of AD 209 and 210, particularly the latter. For example, under the terms of the settlement Caracalla forced on the natives of the far north after his father's death both the Maeatae and Caledonians were compelled to supply recruits to the Roman military through enforced conscription. These were then formed into auxiliary units for deployment to the northern frontier on the continent. Evidence of this is seen in an inscription dated AD 232 at the Roman fort at Walldürn near Frankurt in western Germany, then Germania Superior. This mentions a unit of *Brit(tones) dediticii* serving there during Caracalla's campaign against the Alamanni. Meanwhile, a Caledonian named Lossio Veda, grandson of Vepogenus, appears in a dedication in Colchester far to the south in the reign of Severus Alexander. This man is usually interpreted as an officer given the inscription which details his presence there is on a fine bronze plaque (RIB 191). Specifically, it says, 'To the God Mars Medocius of the Campeses and to the Victory of our Emperor Alexander Pius felix, Lossio Veda, grandson of Vepogenus, a Caledonian, set up this gift from his own resources.'

Further, significant woodland regeneration in the Severan battlespace in the far north has now been definitively identified through pollen analysis. Here, it is now evident that much of the agricultural land in the Scottish Borders, Fife and the upper Midland Valley went uncultivated for a number of generations, indicating a significant depopulation event. Further, recent archaeological research between 1996 and 2005 by the Ben Lawers Project (published by the Society of Antiquaries of Scotland) may show physical evidence of this depopulation. This work was carried out around Loch Tay in the Central Highlands and shows that a healthy iron age settlement pattern of hut circles, homesteads and crannogs flourished until the end of the second century AD, after which all the sites were abandoned with no trace at all of human activity for another 250 years, except perhaps one crannog that might have been reoccupied by AD 420. This location is on the western periphery of the campaigning area and would certainly have supplied troops to fight with the Maeatae or Caledonians, they then clearly not returning given this level of abandonment.

Taken all together, the above evidence does indicate strongly that the genocide suggested by Dio did indeed take place, with the campaigning region ravaged. As Southern suggests, this indicates the 'slash and burn' policy of the AD 210 campaign clearly led to severe levels of depopulation, which took several generations of peaceful coexistence to overcome.[15]

A last comment regarding Severus' legacy for the wider empire concerns his role in the end of the Principate. This is because, sadly, we must consider his dynasty a failure given its demise led directly to the shattering 'Crisis of the Third Century'. Lasting from AD 235 with the assassination of Severus Alexander through to the accession of Diocletian in AD 284, this was an event that almost destroyed the Roman world. The crisis was a time of deeply penetrating incursions of Germans and Goths across the Rhine and Danube into Roman territory, the emergence of Sassanid Persia as the new eastern superpower, economic chaos, multiple usurpations and civil war, and plague. Indeed, such was the strain placed on the Roman system that Diocletian was forced to initiate a series of major reforms

THE AFRICAN EMPEROR

across the entirety of Roman society that ended the Principate and initiated the Dominate. Thus, while the Severans were the last great imperial project of the first phase of the Roman empire, Severus himself proved the only emperor of real note, in his case immensely so. From the point of his death in York in AD 211, everything went downhill as far as his lineage was concerned. Geta, then Caracalla, then Julia Domna, next Heliogabalus and finally Severus Alexander all met sad ends, all apart from the empress at the point of a sword. Perhaps a fitting end for a dynasty initiated by that most martial of Roman emperors, Septimius Severus.

List of References

INTRODUCTION
1. Homer, *Iliad*, 6.57
2. Cassius Dio, *Roman History*, 76.15
3. Cassius Dio, *Roman History*, 77.15

CHAPTER 1 – IDENTITY AND RACE IN THE ROMAN WORLD
1. Snowden, *Before Colour Prejudice*, vii
2. Snowden, *Before Colour Prejudice*, vii
3. Hornblower and Spawforth, *The Oxford Classical Dictionary*, 1,293
4. Bede, *Ecclesiastical History of the English People*, 2.1
5. Homer, *The Iliad*, 2.867
6. Aeschylus, *The Persians*, 433
7. Aristotle, *The Politics*, 1.1252b
8. Cicero, *Speach in Defence of Marcus Aemius Scauro*, 2.7
9. Diodorus Siculus, *Library of History* he says, 5.26.3
10. Sidebottom, *The Mad Emperor*, 99
11. St Paul, *1 Corinthians*, 14.11
12. Lucian of Samosata, *Works*, 5.1
13. Williams, *Lost Realms*, 2
14. Heather, *The Fall of the Roman Empire*, 49
15. Dodgeon and Lieu, *The Roman Eastern Frontier and the Persian Wars AD 226–363: A Documentary History*, 124
16. Cassius Dio, *Roman History*, 78.1.1
17. *Historia Augusta*, Clodius Albinus, 4.10
18. *Historia Augusta*, Pescennius Niger, 6.6

CHAPTER 2 – THE WORLD OF SEPTIMIUS SEVERUS
1. Matyszak, *Roman Conquests: Macedonia and Greece*, 60
2. Strabo, *The Geography*, 3.3.3

3. Pollard and Berry, *The Complete Roman Legions*, 161
4. Pollard and Berry, *The Complete Roman Legions*, 130
5. Cornell and Matthews, *Atlas of the Roman World*, 164
6. D'Amato, *Roman Army Units in the Western Provinces*, 38
7. Birley, *The Roman Government of Britain*, 300
8. Jones and Mattingly, *An Atlas of Roman Britain*, 175
9. Hornblower and Spawforth, *The Oxford Classical Dictionary*, 1,258
10. Potter, *Rome in the Ancient World: From Romulus to Justinian*, 223
11. Cassius Dio, *Roman History*, 5.40

CHAPTER 3 – EARLY LIFE AND THE RISE TO POWER

1. Herodotus, *The Histories*, 4.183
2. Herodotus, *The Histories*, 4.183
3. Silius Italicus, *Punica*, 1.39
4. Silius Italicus, *Punica*, 1.39
5. Matyszak, *Forgotten Peoples of the Ancient World*, 169
6. Nikita, *Activity Patterns in the Sahara Desert: An Interpretation Based on Cross-Sectional Geometric Properties*, 423
7. Polybius, *The Rise of the Roman Empire*, 1.19
8. Appian, *Punic Wars*, 2.11
9. Strabo, *The Geography*, 17.3.2
10. Cassius Dio, *Roman History*, 59.29
11. Cassius Dio, *Roman History*, 76.16.1
12. Herodian, *History of the Roman Empire*, 2.9.2
13. *Historia Augusta*, Septimius Severus, 19.7
14. Birley, *Septimius Severus*, 37
15. Kean and Frey, *The Complete Chronicle of the Emperors of Rome*, 111
16. Birley, *Septimius Severus*, 52
17. Birley, *Septimius Severus*, 69
18. Levick, *Julia Domna: Syrian Empress*, 124
19. Cassius Dio, *Roman History*, 59.30
20. Scott, *Cassius Dio's Julia Domna: Character Development and Narrative Function*, 413
21. Herodian, *History of the Roman Empire*, 1.10.1
22. Herodian, *History of the Roman Empire*, 1.10.2

LIST OF REFERENCES

23. Herodian, *History of the Roman Empire*, 1.10.3
24. Birley, *Septimius Severus*, 77

CHAPTER 4 – AD 193: THE YEAR OF THE FIVE EMPERORS

1. Cassius Dio, *Roman History*, 74.11
2. Cassius Dio, *Roman History*, 73.1
3. Herodian, *History of the Roman Empire*, 1.13.3
4. Cassius Dio, *Roman History*, 73.24
5. Cassius Dio, *Roman History*, 73.24
6. Cassius Dio, *Roman History*, 73.21
7. Cassius Dio, *Roman History*, 73.22
8. Herodian, *History of the Roman Empire*, 1.17.1
9. Cassius Dio, *Roman History*, 73.22
10. *Historia Augusta*, Pertinax, 4.3
11. Herodian, *History of the Roman Empire*, 2.1.4
12. *Historia Augusta*, Pertinax, 4.4
13. *Historia Augusta*, Pertinax, 4.5
14. Cassius Dio, *Roman History*, 74.1
15. Herodian, *History of the Roman Empire*, 2.1.7
16. Herodian, *History of the Roman Empire*, 2.1.7
17. Cassius Dio, *Roman History*, 74.1
18. Cassius Dio, *Roman History*, 74.2
19. Herodian, *History of the Roman Empire*, 2.1.1
20. Herodian, *History of the Roman Empire*, 2.1.1
21. *Historia Augusta*, Commodus, 20.1
22. Cassius Dio, *Roman History*, 74.2
23. Herodian, *History of the Roman Empire*, 2.9.5
24. Cassius Dio, *Roman History*, 74.5
25. Herodian, *History of the Roman Empire*, 2.2.1
26. Herodian, *History of the Roman Empire*, 2.4.4
27. Herodian, *History of the Roman Empire*, 2.4.7
28. *Historia Augusta*, Pertinax, 8.4
29. *Historia Augusta*, Pertinax, 8.4
30. *Historia Augusta*, Pertinax, 7.8
31. Birley, *Septimius Severus*, 91
32. *Historia Augusta*, Pertinax, 7.8

33. *Historia Augusta*, Pertinax, 8.9
34. *Historia Augusta*, Pertinax, 9.9
35. *Historia Augusta*, Pertinax, 15.7
36. Herodian, *History of the Roman Empire*, 2.5.1
37. *Historia Augusta*, Pertinax, 10.1
38. Cassius Dio, *Roman History*, 74.8
39. *Historia Augusta*, Pertinax, 10.9
40. *Historia Augusta*, Pertinax, 10.10
41. Cassius Dio, *Roman History*, 74.9
42. *Historia Augusta*, Pertinax, 10.8
43. *Historia Augusta*, Pertinax, 14.1
44. *Historia Augusta*, Pertinax, 11.2
45. Cassius Dio, *Roman History*, 74.11
46. *Historia Augusta*, Pertinax, 11.1
47. Cassius Dio, *Roman History*, 74.9
48. *Historia Augusta*, Pertinax, 11.1
49. Cassius Dio, *Roman History*, 74.9
50. Cassius Dio, *Roman History*, 74.9
51. Herodian, *History of the Roman Empire*, 2.5.3
52. Cassius Dio, *Roman History*, 74.9
53. *Historia Augusta*, Pertinax, 11.5
54. Herodian, *History of the Roman Empire*, 2.5.3
55. *Historia Augusta*, Pertinax, 11.7
56. Cassius Dio, *Roman History*, 74.9
57. Cassius Dio, *Roman History*, 74.9
58. Herodian, *History of the Roman Empire*, 2.5.4
59. *Historia Augusta*, Pertinax, 11.8
60. Cassius Dio, *Roman History*, 74.10
61. Cassius Dio, *Roman History*, 74.10
62. *Historia Augusta*, Pertinax, 14.7
63. *Historia Augusta*, Pertinax, 14.7
64. *Historia Augusta*, Julianus, 2.5
65. Herodian, *History of the Roman Empire*, 2.7.7
66. Cassius Dio, *Roman History*, 74.11
67. Cassius Dio, *Roman History*, 74.12
68. *Historia Augusta*, Julianus, 7.1

LIST OF REFERENCES

69. Cassius Dio, *Roman History*, 74.13
70. *Historia Augusta*, Julianus, 7.3
71. *Historia Augusta*, Julianus, 6.8
72. Cassius Dio, *Roman History*, 74.16
73. Cassius Dio, *Roman History*, 74.16
74. Cassius Dio, *Roman History*, 74.16
75. Herodian, *History of the Roman Empire*, 2.12.1
76. Cassius Dio, *Roman History*, 74.17
77. Cassius Dio, *Roman History*, 74.16
78. *Historia Augusta*, Septimius Severus, 7.1
79. Cassius Dio, *Roman History*, 75.2
80. *Historia Augusta*, Pertinax, 14.10
81. Cassius Dio, *Roman History*, 75.4
82. *Historia Augusta*, Septimius Severus, 7.8
83. Cassius Dio, *Roman History*, 75.4

CHAPTER 5 – IMPERATOR: CIVIL WAR

1. *Historia Augusta*, Pescennius Niger, 6.6
2. Kean and Frey, *The Complete Chronicle of the Emperors of Rome*, 104
3. Hornblower and Spawforth, *The Oxford Classical Dictionary*, 1,148
4. Kean and Frey, *The Complete Chronicle of the Emperors of Rome*, 104
5. Kean and Frey, *The Complete Chronicle of the Emperors of Rome*, 105
6. Herodian, *History of the Roman Empire*, 2.8.6
7. Mennen, *Power and Status in the Roman Empire*, 197
8. Cassius Dio, *Roman History*, 75.6
9. Elliott, *Ancient Greeks at War*, 156
10. De Bruin, *From the Hague to Britannia – Severan Military Activities Along the North Sea Coast (AD 193–AD 235)*, 137
11. Moorhead, *The History of Roman Coinage in Britain*, 109
12. Birley, *Septimius Severus*, 110
13. Birley, *Septimius Severus: The African Emperor*, 114
14. Herodian, *History of the Roman Empire*, 2.15.1
15. Herodian, *History of the Roman Empire*, 3.7.1
16. Kean and Frey, *The Complete Chronicle of the Emperors of Rome*, 106
17. *Historia Augusta*, Clodius Albinus, 4.9
18. *Historia Augusta*, Clodius Albinus, 4.1

19. *Historia Augusta*, Clodius Albinus, 4.6
20. Kean and Frey, *The Complete Chronicle of the Emperors of Rome*, 107
21. *Historia Augusta*, Clodius Albinus, 13.1
22. Cassius Dio, *Roman History*, 74.15
23. *Historia Augusta*, Clodius Albinus, 12.1
24. *Historia Augusta*, Clodius Albinus, 12.6
25. Cassius Dio, *Roman History*, 76.1
26. Herodian, *History of the Roman Empire*, 3.6.10
27. Herodian, *History of the Roman Empire*, 3.7.2
28. Cassius Dio, *Roman History*, 74.16
29. Moorhead, *The History of Roman Coinage in Britain*, 105
30. *Historia Augusta*, Clodius Albinus, 10.7
31. *Historia Augusta*, Clodius Albinus, 10.8
32. Cassius Dio, *Roman History*, 76.1
33. Herodian, *History of the Roman Empire*, 3.7.1
34. *Historia Augusta*, Clodius Albinus, 10.11
35. *Historia Augusta*, Clodius Albinus, 10.11
36. Cassius Dio, *Roman History*, 76.6
37. Pollard and Berry, *The Complete Roman Legions*, 206
38. Herodian, *History of the Roman Empire*, 3.7.3
39. *Historia Augusta*, Clodius Albinus, 8.4
40. Herodian, *History of the Roman Empire*, 3.7.2
41. Cassius Dio, *Roman History*, 76.6
42. Cassius Dio, *Roman History*, 76.6
43. Cassius Dio, *Roman History*, 76.6
44. Cassius Dio, *Roman History*, 76.6
45. Herodian, *History of the Roman Empire*, 3.7.3
46. Cassius Dio, *Roman History*, 76.7
47. Cassius Dio, *Roman History*, 76.7
48. Cassius Dio, *Roman History*, 76.3
49. *Historia Augusta*, Clodius Albinus, 9.3
50. *Historia Augusta*, Clodius Albinus, 9.4
51. *Historia Augusta*, Septimius Severus, 12.2
52. Birley, *Septimius Severus*, 126
53. Cassius Dio, *Roman History*, 77.12

LIST OF REFERENCES

54. Frere, *Britannia: A History of Roman Britain*, 172
55. Birley, *Septimius Severus*, 126

CHAPTER 6 – IMPERATOR: SEVERUS IN THE EAST AND EGYPT

1. Goldsworthy, *The Eagle of the Lion*, 238
2. Birley, *Septimius Severus*, 127
3. Cassius Dio, *Roman History*, 75.8
4. *Historia Augusta*, Septimius Severus, 12.13
5. Potter, *Rome in the Ancient World: From Romulus to Justinian*, 262
6. *Historia Augusta*, Septimius Severus, 12.13
7. Campbell, *The Frumentarii*, 55
8. Tenney, *An Economic Survey of Ancient Rome: Volume V, Rome and Italy of the Empire*, 85
9. Horace, *Odes*, 3.5
10. *Historia Augusta*, Septimius Severus, 15.2
11. Cassius Dio, *Roman History*, 76.9
12. *Historia Augusta*, Septimius Severus, 15.3
13. Cassius Dio, *Roman History*, 76.9
14. *Historia Augusta*, Septimius Severus, 15.3
15. Cassius Dio, *Roman History*, 76.9
16. Cassius Dio, *Roman History*, 76.3
17. Cassius Dio, *Roman History*, 76.10
18. Birley, *Septimius Severus*, 131
19. *Historia Augusta*, Septimius Severus, 16.1
20. Birley, *Septimius Severus*, 131
21. Cassius Dio, *Roman History*, 76.11
22. Cassius Dio, *Roman History*, 76.13
23. *Historia Augusta*, Septimius Severus, 17.4
24. Cassius Dio, *Roman History*, 76.13
25. Cassius Dio, *Roman History*, 76.15

CHAPTER 7 – IMPERATOR: SEVERUS IN ROME AND NORTH AFRICA

1. Cassius Dio, *Roman History*, 77.16
2. Cassius Dio, *Roman History*, 77.17

3. Birley, *Septimius Severus*, 145
4. Cassius Dio, *Roman History*, 76.1
5. Syvanne, *Caracalla: A Military Biography*, 83
6. Cassius Dio, *Roman History*, 76.1
7. *Historia Augusta*, Septimius Severus, 16.1
8. Kean and Frey, *The Complete Chronicle of the Emperors of Rome*, 113
9. Birley, *Septimius Severus*, 146
10. Blas de Roblès, Sintes and Kenrick, *Classical Antquities of Algeria*, 169
11. Noreña, *Imperial Ideals in the Roman West*, 225
12. Blas de Roblès, Sintes and Kenrick, *Classical Antquities of Algeria*, 185
13. Blas de Roblès, Sintes and Kenrick, *Classical Antquities of Algeria*, 271
14. Birley, *Septimius Severus*, 148
15. Golvin, *Ancient Cities Brought to Life*, 106
16. Golvin, *Ancient Cities Brought to Life*, 106
17. Birley, *Septimius Severus*, 151
18. Philostratus, *Lives of the Sophists*, 188
19. Cassius Dio, *Roman History*, 75.16
20. *Historia Augusta*, Septimius Severus, 14.7
21. Cassius Dio, *Roman History*, 77.3
22. Herodian, *History of the Roman Empire*, 3.10.8
23. de la Bédoyère, *Praetorian*, 217
24. Cassius Dio, *Roman History*, 77.7
25. Cassius Dio, *Roman History*, 76.10
26. Birley, *Septimius Severus*, 169

CHAPTER 8 – IMPERATOR: ARRIVAL IN BRITAIN

1. Birley, *The Roman Government of Britain*, 186
2. Birley, *Septimius Severus*, 160
3. Birley, *The Roman Government of Britain*, 192
4. Cassius Dio, *Roman History*, 76.10
5. Cassius Dio, *Roman History*, 76.10
6. Herodian, *History of the Roman Empire*, 3.14.1
7. Paulus Orosius, *Seven Books of History Against the Pagans*, 7.17
8. Birley, *Septimius Severus*, 175

LIST OF REFERENCES

9. Upex, *The Roman Villas of the Lower Nene Valley and the Praetorium at Castor*, 61
10. Avery, *The Story of York*, 6
11. Tacitus, *The Agricola*, 17.1
12. Mattingly, *An Imperial Possession: Britain in the Roman Empire*, 147
13. Tacitus, *The Agricola*, 33.1
14. Tacitus, *The Agricola*, 12.1
15. Strabo, *The Geography*, 4.5.1
16. Mattingly, *An Imperial Possession: Britain in the Roman Empire*, 423
17. Cassius Dio, *Roman History*, 77.12
18. Moffat, *A Marvellous Plant: The Place of the Heath Pea in Scottish Botanical Tradition*, 13
19. Breeze, *Roman Scotland*, 111

CHAPTER 9 – IMPERATOR: THE SEVERAN CAMPAIGNS IN BRITAIN

1. Birley, *Septimius Severus*, 200
2. Moorhead and Stuttard, *The Romans Who Shaped Britain*, 162
3. Moorhead and Stuttard, *The Romans Who Shaped Britain*, 93
4. Cassius Dio, *Roman History*, 77.12
5. De Bruin, *From the Hague to Britannia – Severan Military Activities Along the North Sea Coast (AD 193–AD 235)*, 137
6. Herodian, *History of the Roman Empire*, 3.14.4
7. Jones, *Roman Camps in Scotland*, 103
8. Reed, *The Scottish Campaigns of Septimius Severus*, 95
9. Jones, *Roman Camps in Scotland*, 113
10. Cassius Dio, *Roman History*, 77.40
11. Cassius Dio, *Roman History*, 77.40
12. Kamm, *The Last Frontier: The Roman Invasions of Scotland*, 126
13. Faulkner, *The Decline and Fall of Roman Britain*, 120
14. Cassius Dio, *Roman History*, 76.13
15. Herodian, *History of the Roman Empire*, 3.14.4
16. Paulus Orosius, *Seven Books of History Against the Pagans*, 7.17
17. Herodian, *History of the Roman Empire*, 3.14.4
18. Reid, *Bullets, Ballistas and Burnswark: A Roman Assault on a Hillfort in Scotland*, 22

19. Reid, *Bullets, Ballistas and Burnswark: A Roman Assault on a Hillfort in Scotland*, 23
20. Cassius Dio, *Roman History*, 76.13
21. Hodgson, *The British Expeditions of Septimius Severus*, 35
22. Cassius Dio, *Roman History*, 76.14
23. Cassius Dio, *Roman History*, 76.16
24. *Historia Augusta*, Septimius Severus, 18.1
25. Aurelius Victor, *De Caesaribus*, 20
26. Paulus Orosius, *Seven Books of History Against the Pagans*, 7.17
27. *Historia Augusta*, Septimius Severus, 22.4
28. Birley, *Septimius Severus*, 184
29. *Historia Augusta*, Septimius Severus, 22.4
30. Hilts, *Major Roman Bath House Revealed in Carlisle*, 11
31. Birley, *Septimius Severus*, 185
32. Southern, *Roman Britain*, 248
33. Cassius Dio, *Roman History*, 77.15
34. *Historia Augusta*, Septimius Severus, 19.1
35. Herodian, *History of the Roman Empire*, 3.15.1
36. Cassius Dio, *Roman History*, 76.15
37. Cassius Dio, *Roman History*, 76.15
38. Kean and Frey, *The Complete Chronicle of the Emperors of Rome*, 115
39. Kean and Frey, *The Complete Chronicle of the Emperors of Rome*, 115
40. Scarre, *Chronicle of the Roman Emperors*, 139
41. Birley, *Septimius Severus*, 187
42. Birley, *Septimius Severus*, 189
43. Cassius Dio, *Roman History*, 78.2
44. Henig and Soffe, *Lullingstone Roman Villa*, 266

CONCLUSION

1. *Historia Augusta*, Caracalla, 9.3
2. *Giessen Papyrus*, in *Die Giessener literarischen Papyri und die Caracalla-Erlasse*, 40.1.1-12
3. Cassius Dio, *Roman History*, 77.7
4. Cassius Dio, *Roman History*, 77.7
5. Herodian, *History of the Roman Empire*, 4.11.7
6. Herodian, *History of the Roman Empire*, 4.11.8

LIST OF REFERENCES

7. *Historia Augusta*, Macrinus, 2.4
8. *Historia Augusta*, Macrinus, 2.5
9. Cassius Dio, *Roman History*, 10.31
10. Herodian, *History of the Roman Empire*, 4.12.8
11. Herodian, *History of the Roman Empire*, 4.15.5
12. Birley, *Septimius Severus*, 196
13. Hodgson, *The British Expeditions of Septimius Severus*, 48
14. Frere, *Britannia: A History of Roman Britain*, 176
15. Southern, *Roman Britain*, 251

Bibliography

ANCIENT SOURCES

Aeschylus, *Persians and Other Plays*. 2009. Collard, C., Oxford: Oxford World Classics.
Apuleius, *The Golden Ass*. 2008. Walsh, P.G. Oxford: Oxford World Classics.
Aristotle, *The Politics*. 2009. Barker, E., Oxford: Oxford World Classics.
Marcus Aurelius, *Meditations*. 1964. Staniforth, M. London: Penguin.
Bede, *Ecclestaistical History of the English People*.1995. Sherley-Price, L., London: Penguin.
Julius Caesar, *The Conquest of Gaul*. 1951. Handford, S.A., London: Penguin.
Marcus Cato, *De Agri Cultura*. 1934. Ash, H.B. and Hooper, W.D., Harvard: Loeb Classical Library.
Cicero, *Selected Works*. 2004. Grant, M., London: Penguin.
Cassius Dio, *Roman History*. 1925. Cary, E., Harvard: Loeb Classical Library.
Diodorus Siculus, *Library of History*. 1952. Sherman, C. L., Harvard: Loeb Classical Library.
Flavius Eutropius, *Breviarium*, 1993. Bird, H.W. Liverpool: Liverpool University Press.
Quintus Horatius Flaccus (Horace), *The Complete 'Odes' and 'Epodes'*. 2008. West, D., Oxford: Oxford Paperbacks.
Gaius, *Institutiones*. 1946. De Zulueta, F., Oxford: Oxford University Press.
Historia Augusta, Life of Pertinax (1921, Maggie, D., Harvard, Loeb Classical Library).
Sextus Julius Frontinus, *Strategemata*, 1969, Bennett, C.E., Portsmouth, New Hampshire: Heinemann.
Herodian, *History of the Roman Empire*. 1989. Whittaker, C. R., Harvard: Loeb Classical Library.
The Holy Bible, King James Version.
Homer, *The Iliad*, 1950. Rieu, E.V., London: Penguin.
Livy, *The History of Rome*, 1989. Foster, B. O. Cambridge, MA: Harvard University Press/Loeb Classical Library.
Lucian of Samosata, *Works*. 2016. Harmon, A. M., St Albans: Wentworth Press.
Paulus Orosius, *Seven Books of History Against the Pagans*. 1936. Woodworth, R. I., New York: Columbia University.

Pausanias, *Guide Greece: Central Greece*. 1979. Levi, P., London: Penguin.
Flavius Philostratus, *Lives of the Sophists*. 1992. Miles, G., Cambridge, MA: Harvard University Press/Loeb Classical Library.
Pliny the Elder, *Natural History*. 1940. Rackham, H., Harvard: Harvard University Press.
Plutarch. *Lives of the Noble Greeks and Romans*. 2013. Clough, A. H. Oxford. Benediction Classics.
Pliny the Younger, *Epistularum Libri Decem*. 1963, Mynors, R.A.B., Oxford: Oxford Classical Texts - Clarendon Press.
Polybius, *The Rise of the Roman Empire*. 1979, Scott-Kilvert, I., London: Penguin.
Quintilian, *Institutes of Oratory*. 2015, Selby Watson, J., Scotts Valley, California: Create Space Independent Publishing Platform.
Silius Italicus, *Punica*. 1989. Duff, J. D., Harvard: Loeb Classical Library.
Suetonius, *The Twelve Caesars*, 1957. Graves, R. London: Penguin.
Cornelius Tacitus, *The Agricola*. 1970, Mattingly, H., London: Penguin.
Cornelius Tacitus, *The Annals*. 2003, Grant, M., London: Penguin.
Cornelius Tacitus, *The Histories*. 2008, Fyfe, W. H., Oxford: Oxford Paperbacks.
Strabo, *The Geography*. 2014, Roler, D.W., Cambridge: Cambridge University Press.
Aurelius Victor, *De Caesaribus*. 1994. Bird, H.W. Liverpool: Liverpool University Press.

MODERN SOURCES

Applebaum, A. 2007. Another Look at the Assassination of Pertinax and the Accession of Junianus. *Classical Philology*, No.2, 198-207.
Avery, A. 2007. *The Story of York*. Pickering: Blackthorn Press.
Barker, P. 1981. *The Armies and Enemies of Imperial Rome*. Cambridge: Wargames Research Group.
de la Bédoyère, G. 2017. *Praetorian: The Rise and Fall of Rome's Imperial Bodyguard*. New Haven: Yale University Press.
de la Bédoyère, G. 2017. The Emperors' Fatal Servants. *History Today*. March 2017 Issue, 58-62.
Bentley, P. 1984. A Recently Identified Valley in the City. *London Archaeologist*, V.5 Number 1, 13-16.
Bidwell, P. 2007. *Roman Forts in Britain*. Stroud: Tempus.
Birley, A. R. 1981. *The Fasti of Roman Britain*. Oxford: Clarendon Press.
Birley, A. R. 1993. *Marcus Aurelius: A Biography*. London: Routledge.
Birley, A. R. 1999. *Septimius Severus: The African Emperor*. London: Routledge.
Birley, A. R. 2005. *The Roman Government of Britain*. Oxford: Oxford University Press.

BIBLIOGRAPHY

Birley, A. R. 2007. The Frontier Zone in Britain: Hadrian to Caracalla. In: de Blois, L. and Lo Cascio, E. eds. *The Impact of the Roman Army (200 BC-AD476)*. Leiden: Brill. 355-370.

Bishop, M.C. 2016. *The Gladius*. Oxford: Osprey Publishing Ltd.

Bishop, M. C. Lucius Verus and the Roman Defence of the East. Barnsley: Pen & Sword.

Bradley, K. 1998. *Slavery and Society at Rome*. Cambridge: Cambridge University Press.

Breeze, D. J. 2000. *Roman Scotland*. London: Batsford Ltd/ Historic Scotland.

Brooks, N. P. 1994. Rochester Bridge AD43 to 1381. In: Yates, N. and Gibson, J. H. ed. *Traffic and Politics – The Construction and Management of Rochester Bridge AD 42-1993*. Woodbridge: The Boydell Press, 1-35.

Burgess, R. W. 1993. Principes cum Tyrannis: Two Studies on the Kaisergeschichte and Its Tradition. *The Classical Quarterly*. V.43, 491-500.

Campbell, B. 2011. *Rivers and the Power of Ancient Rome*. Chapel Hill: University of North Carolina Press.

Campbell, D. B. 2020. The Frumentarii. *Ancient Warfare*. XIII-4, 52-55.

Connolly, P. 1988. *Greece and Rome at War*. London: Macdonald & Co (Publishers) Ltd.

Cornell, T. J. 1993. The End of Roman Imperial Expansion. In: Rich, J. and Shipley, G. eds. *War and Society in the Roman World*. London: Routledge, 139-170.

Cornell, T. J. and Matthews, J. 2006. *Atlas of the Roman World*. Oxford: Phaidon Press Ltd.

Cowan, R. 2002. *Aspects of the Roman Field Army: The Praetorian Guard, Legio II Parthica and legionary vexillations – PhD Thesis*. Unpublished: University of Glasgow.

Cowan, R. 2003. *Roman Legionary, 58 BC – AD 69*. Oxford: Osprey Publishing.

Cowan, R. 2003. *Imperial Roman Legionary, AD 161 – 284*. Oxford: Osprey Publishing.

Cowan, R. 2007. *Roman Battle Tactics 109 BC – AD 313*. Oxford: Osprey Publishing.

Cowan, R. 2015. *Roman Legionary AD 284-337*. Oxford: Osprey Publishing.

Cunliffe, B. 1988. *Greeks, Romans and Barbarians. Spheres of Interaction*. London: Batsford Ltd.

D'Amato, R. and Sumner, G. 2009. *Arms and Armour of the Imperial Roman Soldier*. Barnsley: Frontline Books.

D'Amato, R. 2009. *Imperial Roman Naval Forces 31BC – AD500*. Oxford: Osprey Publishing.

D'Amato, R. 2016. *Roman Army Units in the Western Provinces (1)*. Oxford: Osprey Publishing.
D'Amato, R. 2018. *Roman Heavy Cavalry (1)*. Oxford: Osprey Publishing.
D'Amato, R. 2019. *Roman Army Units in the Western Provinces (2)*. Oxford: Osprey Publishing.
De Bruin, J. 2019: From The Hague to Britannia: Severan military activities along the North Sea coast (193–235 AD), in van Zoolingen, J. (ed.), *AB HARENIS INCVLTIS*. Artikelen voor Ab Waasdorp, The Hague, 137–53.
Dodgeon, M. H. and Lieu, S. N. C. 1994. *The Roman Eastern Frontier and the Persian Wars AD 226-363: A Documentary History*. London: Routledge.
Dowley, T. 1997. *The Atlas of the Bible and Christianity*. Oxford: Candle Books.
Elliott, P. 2014. *Legions in Crisis*. Stroud: Fonthill Media ltd.
Elliott, S. 2016. *Sea Eagles of Empire: The Classis Britannica and the Battles for Britain*. Stroud: The History Press.
Elliott, S. 2017. *Empire State: How the Roman Military Built an Empire*. Oxford: Oxbow Books.
Elliott, S. 2018. *Septimius Severus in Scotland: The Northern Campaigns of the First Hammer of the Scots*. Barnsley: Greenhill Books.
Elliott, S. 2018. *Roman Legionaries*. Oxford: Casemate Publishers.
Elliott, S. 2019. *Julius Caesar: Rome's Greatest Warlord*. Oxford: Casemate Publishers.
Elliott, S. 2020. Clash of the Titans: The Battle of Lugdunum, AD 197. *Ancient Warfare*, XIII-3, 27-35.
Elliott, S. 2020, *Romans at War*. Oxford: Casemate Publishers.
Elliott, S. 2020. *Pertinax: The Son of a Slave Who Became Roman Emperor*. Barnsley: Greenhill Books.
Elliott, S. 2021. *Roman Britain's Missing Legion*. Barnsley: Pen & Sword.
Elliott, S. 2021. *Roman Conquests: Britain*. Barnsley: Pen & Sword.
Elliott, S. 2021, *Old Testament Warriors*. Oxford: Casemate Publishers.
Elliott, S. 2021, *Ancient Greeks at War*. Oxford: Casemate Publishers.
Erdkamp, P. ed. 2013. *The Cambridge Companion to Ancient Rome*. Cambridge. Cambridge University Press.
Faulkner, N. 2001. *The Decline and Fall of Roman Britain*. Stroud: Tempus.
Frank, T. 1940. *An Economic Survey of Ancient Rome: Volume V, Rome and Italy of the Empire*. Baltimore: John Hopkins University Press.
Frere, S. 1974. *Britannia: A History of Roman Britain* (3rd edn). London: Routledge.
Golvin, J. C. 2003. *Ancient Cities Brought to Life*. Ludlow: Thalamus Publishing.
Goldsworthy, A. 2000. *Roman Warfare*. London: Cassell.
Goldsworthy, A. 2003. *The Complete Roman Army*. London: Thames and Hudson.

Goldsworthy, A. 2023. *The Eagle and the Lion*. London: Head of Zeus.

Graafstaal, E. 2018. What Happened in the Summer of AD 122. Hadrian on the British Frontier – Archaeology, Epigraphy and Historical Agency. *Britannia*. V.48, 76 - 111.

Heather, P. 2005. *The Fall of the Roman Empire*. London: Macmillan.

Heather, P. 2009. *Empires and Barbarians*. New York: Macmillan.

Heather, P. 2018. *Rome Resurgent*. Oxford. Oxford University Press.

Hekster, O. 2002. Commodus: An Emperor at the Crossroads. Leiden: Brill.

Henig, M. 'The victory gem from Lullingstone Roman villa', *Journal of the British Archaeological Association*, 160 (2007), 1–7.

Henig M. and Soffe. G. 2022. Lullingstone Roman Villa. In: Henig, M., Soffe, G., Adcock, K., and King, A. eds. *Villas, Sanctaries and Settlement in the Romano-British Countryside*. Oxford: Archaeopress Publishing Ltd, 261-280.

Herrmann-Otto, Elizabeth. 2013. Slaves and Freedmen. In: Erdkamp, P. eds. *The Cambridge Companion to Ancient Rome*. Cambridge: Cambridge University Press. 60-76.

Hilts, Major Roman Bath House Revealed in Carlisle, *Current Archaeology*, Issue 399, 11.

Hingley, R. 1982. Roman Britain: The structure of Roman imperialism and the consequences of imperialism on the development of a peripheral province. In: Miles, D. ed. *The Romano-British Countryside: Studies in Rural Settlement and Economy*. Oxford: BAR/ Archaeological and Historical Associates Ltd, 17-52.

Hingley, R. 2005. *Globalizing Roman Culture – Unity, Diversity and Empire*. London: Routledge.

Hingley, R. 2018. *Londinium: A Biography*. London: Bloomsbury Acadamic.

Hodgson, N. 2007. Arbeia Roman Fort – South Shields. *Current Archaeology*, Issue 133, V.18, 24-42.

Hodgson, N. 2014. The British Expeditions of Septimius Severus. *Britannia*, V.45, 31-51.

Holland, T. 2019. *Dominion*. London: Little, Brown.

Hornblower, S. and Spawforth, A. 1996. *The Oxford Classical Dictionary*. Oxford: Oxford University Press.

Horsted, W. 2021. *The Numidians*. Oxford: Osprey Publishing.

James, S. 2011. *Rome and the Sword*. London: Thames and Hudson.

Jones, G. D. B. 1980. The Roman Mines at Rio Tinto. *The Journal of Roman Studies*, V.70, 146-164.

Jones, B. and Mattingly, D. 1990. *An Atlas of Roman Britain*. Oxford: Oxbow Books.

Jones, R. 2011. *Roman Camps in Scotland*. Edinburgh: Society of Antiquaries of Scotland.

Jones, R. 2012. *Roman Marching Camps in Britain*. Stroud: Amberley Publishing.

Kamm, A. 2011. *The Last Frontier: The Roman Invasions of Scotland*. Glasgow: Tempus.

Kean, R. M. and Frey, O. 2005. *The Complete Chronicle of the Emperors of Rome*. Ludlow: Thalamus Publishing.

Keppie, L. 2015. *The Legacy of Rome: Scotland's Roman Remains*. Edinburgh: Berlin.

Kiley, K. F. 2012. *The Uniforms of the Roman World*. Wigston: Lorenz Books.

de Kind, R. 'The Roman portraits from the villa of Lullingstone: Pertinax and his father P Helvius Successus', in *Otium. Festschrift für Volker Michael Strocka*, ed. T Ganschow, M Steinhard, D Berges and T Frölich (Remshalden, 2005), 47–52.

Kolb, A. 2001. The Cursus Publicus. In: Adams, C. and Laurence, R. eds. *Travel and Geography in the Roman Empire*. London: Routledge, 95–106.

Kulikowski, M. 2016. *Imperial Triumph: The Roman World From Hadrian to Constantine*. London: Profile Books.

Kuhlmann, P. A. 1994. *Die Giessener literarischen Papyri und die Caracalla-Erlasse*. Giessen: Giessen Universitatsbibliothek.

Lambert, M. 2010. *Christians and Pagans*. New Haven: Yale University Press.

Le Bohec, Y. 2000. *The Imperial Roman Army*. London: Routledge.

Levick, B. 2007. *Julia Domna: Syrian Empress*. London: Routledge.

Matyszak, P. 2009. *Roman Conquests: Macedonia and Greece*. Barnsley: Pen & Sword.

Matyszak, P. 2022. *Forgotten Peoples of the Ancient World*. London: Thames & Hudson.

Mattingly, D. 1995. *Tripolitania*. Ann Arbor, Michigan: University of Michigan Press.

Mattingly, D. 2006. *An Imperial Possession, Britain in the Roman Empire*. London: Penguin.

Mattingly, D. 2006. The Garamantes: The First Libyan State. In: Mattingly, D., McLaren, S., Gadgood, K., Savage, E., and Al-Fasatwi, Y. eds. *The Libyan Desert: Natural Resources and Cultural Heritage*. London: Society for Libyan Studies, 1–10.

Mattingly, D. 2011. *Imperialism, Power and Identity – Experiencing the Roman Empire*. Princeton: Princeton University Press.

McHugh, J. S. 2015. *Commodus: God and Gladiator*. Barnsley: Pen & Sword.

McLynn, F. 2010. *Marcus Aurelius: Warrior, Philosopher, Emperor*. New York: Vintage.

Mennen, I. 2011. *Power and Status in the Roman Empire, AD 193–284*. Leiden: Brill.

Millett, M. 1990. *The Romanization of Britain*. Cambridge: Cambridge University Press.
Millett, M. 1995. *Roman Britain*. London: Batsford.
Moffat, B. 2000. A Marvellous Plant: The Place of the Heath Pea in Scottish Botanical Tradition. *Folio*. Issue 1. 13-15.
Moorhead, S. 2013. *The History of Roman Coinage in Britain*. Witham, Essex: Greenlight Publishing.
Moorhead, S. and Stuttard, D. 2012. *The Romans Who Shaped Britain*. London: Thames and Hudson.
Mouritsen, H. 2015. *The Freedmen of the Roman World*. Cambridge. Cambridge University Press.
Nikita, E. 2011. Activity Patterns in the Sahara Desert: An Interpretation Based on Cross-Sectional Geometric Properties. *American Journal of Physical Anthropology*. V.146. 423–434.
Noreña, C. 2016. *Imperial Ideals in the Roman West*. Cambridge: Cambridge University Press.
Oleson, J. P. 2009. *The Oxford Handbook of Engineering and Technology in the Classical World*. Oxford: Oxford University Press.
Ottaway, P. 2013. *Roman Yorkshire*. Pickering: Blackthorn Press.
Parfitt, K. 2013. Folkestone During the Roman Period. In: Coulson, I. ed. *Folkestone to 1500, A Town Unearthed*. Canterbury: Canterbury Archaeological Trust, pp. 31-54.
Parker, A. 2019. *The Archaeology of Roman York*. Stroud: Amberley Books.
Parker, P. 2009. *The Empire Stops Here*. London: Jonathan Cape.
Parry, D. 2005. *Engineering in the Ancient World*. Stroud: Sutton Publishing Ltd.
Pausche, D. 2009. Unreliable Narration in the Historia Augusta. V. 8. 115-135.
Perring, D, 2017. London's Hadrianic War. *Britannia*, V.41, 127-147.
Pitassi, M. 2012. *The Roman Navy*. Barnsley: Seaforth.
Pollard, N. and Berry, J. 2012. *The Complete Roman Legions*. London: Thames & Hudson.
Potter, D. 2004. *The Roman Empire at Bay, AD 180–395*. London, Routledge.
Potter, D. 2009. *Rome in the Ancient World: From Romulus to Justinian*. London: Thames & Hudson.
Poulter, J. and Entwhistle, R. 2016. Charting the Roads. *Current Archaeology*, Issue 314, V.27, 12–18.
Rankov, B. 2009. A Secret of Empire (imperii Arcanum): an unacknowledged factor in Roman imperial expansion. In: Hanson, W. S. ed. *The Army and Frontiers of Rome: Papers offered to David J. Breeze on the occasion of his sixty-fifth birthday and his retirement from Historic Scotland*. Portsmouth, Rhode Island: Journal of Roman Archaeology Supplementary Series, no. 74, 163-172.

Reed, N. 1975. The Scottish Campaigns of Septimius Severus. *Proceedings of the Royal Society of Antiquaries of Scotland*, PSAS 107 (1975-76), 92-102.

Reid, R. 2016. Bullets, Ballistas and Burnswark: A Roman Assault on a Hillfort in Scotland. *Current Archaeology*, Issue 316, V.27, 20-26.

Robertson, A. S. 1974. Romano-British Coin Hoards: Their Numismatic, Archaeological and Historical Significance. In: Casey, J. and Reece, R. eds. *Coins and the Archaeologist*. Oxford: BAR/ Archaeological and Historical Associates Ltd, 12-36.

Robertson, A. S. 1980. The Bridges on the Severan Coins of AD 208 and 209. In: Hanson, W. S. and Keppie, L. J. F, eds. *Roman Frontier Studies*. Oxford: BAR/ Archaeological and Historical Associates Ltd, 12-36.

Rodgerds, N. and Dodge, H. 2009. *The History and Conquests of Ancient Rome*. London: Hermes House.

Rubin, Z. 1980. *Civil-War Propaganda and Historiography*. Leuven: Peeters.

Russell, B. 2013. *The Economics of the Roman Stone Trade*. Oxford: Oxford University Press.

Sage, M. *Septimius Severus & The Roman Army*. Barnsley: Pen & Sword.

Salway, P. 1981. *Roman Britain*. Oxford: Oxford University Press.

Scarre, C. 1995. *The Penguin Historical Atlas of Ancient Rome*. London: Penguin.

Scarre, C. 1995. *Chronicle of the Roman Emperors*: London: Thames and Hudson.

Schmitz, M. and Sumner, G. *Roman Conquests: The Danube Frontier*. Barnsley: Pen & Sword.

Scott, A. G. 2017. Cassius Dio's Julia Domna: Character Development and Narrative Function. *TAPA*, V.147, No. 2, 413-33.

Selkirk, R. 1995. *On the Trail of the Legions*. Ipswich: Anglia Publishing.

Sheppard, S. 2020. *Roman Soldier versus Parthian Warrior*. Oxford: Osprey Publishing.

Sidebottom, H. 2022. *The Mad Emperor*. London: Oneworld.

Southern, P. 2001. *The Roman Empire from Severus to Constantine*. London. Routledge.

Southern, P. 2013. *Roman Britain*. Stroud: Amberley Publishing.

Snowden, F. M. 1983. *Before colour Prejudice*. Cambridge, Massachusetts: Harvard University Press.

Starr, C. G. 1941. *The Roman Imperial Navy 31BC–AD 324*. New York: Cornell University Press.

Syvanne, I. 2017. *Caracalla: A Military Biography*. Barnsley: Pen & Sword.

Toner, J. 2015. *The Day Commodus Killed a Rhino: Understanding the Roman Games*. Baltimore: John Hopkins University Press.

Upex, S. G. 2022. The Roman Villas of the Lower Nene Valley and the *Praetorium* at Castor. In: Henig, M., Soffe, G., Adcock, K., and King,

A. eds. *Villas, Sanctaries and Settlement in the Romano-British Countryside.* Oxford: Archaeopress Publishing Ltd, 42-64.

Wallace-Hadrill, A. ed. 1989. *'Patronage in the Ancient World'*. Routledge: London.

Wilcox, P. 1986. *Rome's Enemies (3): Parthians and Sassanid Persians.* Oxford: Osprey Publishing.

Wilkes, J.J. 2005. Provinces and Frontiers. In: Bowman. A. K., Garnsey, P. and Cameron, A. eds. *The Cambridge Ancient History Vol. XII, The Crisis of Empire, AD 193-337.* Cambridge: Cambridge University Press, 212-268.

Williams, T. 2022. *Lost Realms.* London: William Collins.

Wilson, I. 1999. *The Bible of History.* London: Weidenfeld & Nicholson.

Windrow, M. and McBride, A. 1996. *Imperial Rome at War.* Hong Kong: Concord Publications.

Index

Abgar 137
Adiabene 34, 134, 136, 137
Aethiop 3
Africa Proconsularis 37, 41, 42, 44, 65, 84
Agricola, Gnaeus Julius 218
Agricola, Sextus Calpurnius 70
Aldborough 217
Alexandria 260
Amenhophis III, statues 171
Antioch-on-the-Orontes 77, 81, 117, 129, 260
Antonine Wall 9, 19, 20
Antonine Dynasty 17, 82, 89
Antonine Itinerary 217
Antoninus Pius 17
Arbela 137
Arch of Caracalla 188, 189
Arch of Constantine 228, 229
Arch of Hadrian 30
Arch of Septimius Severus 179, 180, 181, 228
Arcus Argentariorum 179
Ardoch 237,
Atlas Mountains 42
Augustus, Emperor xii, 17
Aures Mountains 42, 43
Auxilia xiv
Avidius Cassius 37, 76

Bainbridge 203
Ballista 230
Barbagia 7
barbaricum 7
Bastarnae 28

Baths of Caracalla xi, 182
Battledykes 237
Bay of Naples 29
bellum desertorum 83
beneficiarii consularis 47
beneficiarii procuratoris 47
Berbers 38
Bervie Water 238
Binchester 217
Birdoswald 204
birrus 22
Biskra 43
Bosra 34
Boulogne-Sur-Mer 22, 79, 144, 212
Brigantes 204, 214, 217
Britannia 18, 19, 23, 213
Britannia Inferior 23, 157, 213
Britannia Superior 23, 213
Brough-on-Humber 213
Budapest 27
Burgh-on-Sand 247
Byzantium 31, 130, 131
Byzantine Empire xiii

Caerleon 21
Caistor St Edmunds 231
Caledonians 237
Caligula, Emperor 20, 42, 63
Capitoline Hill 160
Capitoline Triad 49
Caratacus 20
Caracalla, Emperor x, xi, 11, 21, 71, 138, 146, 190
    Assassinates brother 253, 254
    Born 81

Campaign in Scotland 237
Death 263, 264
Names xiv
Carlisle 246, 247
Carnuntum 129
Carpow 220, 226, 233
Carthage 39, 40, 42, 44
Castleford 213
Castra Praetoria 87
Catterick 217
Cherchell 44
Chester 21, 22
Chesters 204
Cirencester 3
Classis Alexandrina Augusta 37
Classis Britannica 21, 144
Classis Flavia Moesica 210
Classis Germanica 210
Classis Misenensis 29
Classis Pannonica 210
Classis Ravennas 29
Claudius, Emperor 20
Cleander 89
Clodius Albinus, Governor xi, 14, 22, 80, 87, 88, 102, 157
Coele-Syria 135
cohors I Flavia urbana 79
cohors V Gallorum 226
cohort xiv
Column of Marcus Aurelius 228
Commodus, Emperor 59, 87, 88, 92
Constantine I 30
Constantine, city 42
Consilium Principis 46
constitutio Antoniniana 5
Corbridge 217
Cramond 220, 233
Crannog 275
Cripplegate fort 47
Crisis of the Third Century x, xiii, 9, 18
Ctesiphon 136
cura annonae 41

Curial class 2
cursus honorum 74
cursus publicus 48, 101
Cyrenaica 38
Cyrenaica et Creta 37

Dacia 13, 27, 28
damnatio memoriae 11, 190
Danube, river 18, 84
Dere Street 21, 203, 206
Diocletian 30
Djemila 135, 188, 203
Dominate xiii
Domitian, Emperor 52, 175
domus Augustana 175
domus Tiberiana 177
Dover 22
Dura-Europos 229

Ebchester 217
equites singulares Augusti 91, 110, 123
Equestrian class 2
Ermine Street 21, 213, 218
Euphrates, river 9, 33, 77, 165
expeditio felicissima Brittannica 27, 201, 212, 220
    Logistics 209, 218
    Size of force 225
equites Dromedarii 34

fabricae 24
Firth of Forth 216
fiscus 46, 73, 103, 105
Fosse Way 21
Flavian Dynasty 17
Forma Urbis Romae 177
Forum Romanum x, 176
Frontinus, Governor 289
Fulvia Pia 63
Fulvia Plautilla 185, 262

Gaius Claudius Septimius Aper 68
Gallia Lugdunensis 24, 78, 80, 83

INDEX

Garamantes 40, 58
Gask Ridge 237
Gebel el Akbar 37
Gemellae 43
Geta, Emperor x, xi, 11, 21, 76, 146, 193
    Born 81, 83
    Death 71, 253, 254
Geta, Publius Septimius, brother 70, 74, 84
Geta, Publius Septimius, father 63
Gholaia 40
Ghoufi 43
gladius 109, 151
Gordian III 9, 167
Governor xi, 9, 19, 21
Grampians 221, 222, 234
Grassy Walls 237
Great Estuary 231
Guelma 187
Guerilla warfare xiv

Hadrian, Emperor 18, 52
Hadrian's Wall 9, 18, 19, 217
Hatra 34, 134, 136, 137
Heath pea 223
Heliogabalus 182
High Cross 21
Hispania Baetica 25
Hispania Tarraconensis 168
Highland Boundary Fault 221, 222
Highland Line 221, 222
Hippo Regis 187
Homer ix
Homs 80
Househill Dunipace 237
Housesteads 204

Iazyges 76
Iceni 231
Iliad ix
imperator destinatus 163
Innerpeffray East 237

Isle of Arran 221
Issus, Battle of 127, 133

Julia Domna 11, 89, 146, 190
    Marries Severus 24, 80, 81
    Rebuilds temple of Vesta 176
Julio-Claudian Dynasty 17
Julius Caesar x, 20
Juthingi 28

Kair House 237

Laetus 81, 91, 93
Lambaesis 42, 188
lancea 109
legate xiv
legio I *Italica* 28
legio I *Parthica* 167
legio II *Adiutrix* 28
legio II *Augusta* 21, 47, 202, 238
legio II *Parthica* 29, 163, 167
legio III *Augusta* 44, 64, 67
legio III *Cyrenaica* 34
legio III *Parthica* 167
legio IV *Scythica* 34
legio V *Macedonia* 28
legio VI *Victrix* 21, 202
legio VII *Gemina* 144
legio IX *Hispana* 21
legio XIV *Gemina Martia Victrix* 84
legio XX *Valeria Victrix* 21, 202, 226
Legion xiv
Legionaries xiv
Legionary *lanciarii* 230
Leicester 213
Leptis Magna ix, 38
limes Arabicus 169
limes Cappadocia 169
limes Tripolitanus 43
limes Germanicus 24
Loch Leven 238

[301]

Loch Tay 275
London xi, 21, 157, 212
lorica hamata 229
lorica segmentata 109, 227, 229
lorica squamata 229
Lucilla, sister of Commodus 89
Lucius Septimius Severus 63, 180
Lucius Verus, Emperor 45, 72
Lugdunum, Battle of 88, 127, 139
Lupus, Governor 145
Lupus Magnas 93
Lyon 24, 79, 81

Macrinus, Emperor 10
Maeatae 237
Maghreb 38, 41
Marching Camps 220, 237
Marcomanni 28, 106
Marcomannic Wars 76
Marcus Aurelius, Emperor xi, 37, 45, 52, 72, 75
Mauri 38, 44, 57
Mesopotamia 166
Milan 83
Moesia Inferior 27, 28, 95, 118
Moesia Superior 27, 28. 95
Muiryfold 238

Narcissus 94
Nero, Emperor 17, 52, 59, 92
Nerva, Emperor 17
Nervo-Trajanic Dynasty 17
Newstead 219, 235
Nicomedia 260
Nile, River 37
Nisibis 157
Nubia 12
Numidia 42
Numidians 9, 12, 38

Oea 38
officium consularis 47
Osrhoene 134, 136, 137

Paccia Marciana 75, 76
    Death 80
Palatine Hill 160
Pannonia Inferior 27, 28
Pannonia Superior 27, 28, 84, 87, 97
Papinianus 197, 209, 226, 245
Parthia 13, 40, 72
Parthicus Adiabenicus 137
Parthicus Arabicus 137
Parthicus Maximus 166
Paulinus, Governor 20
Pelesium 170
Pentapolis 37
Petra 34
perigrini 5
Persepolis 13
Pertinax, Emperor 45, 106, 123, 125
Pescennius Niger xi, 14, 87, 88, 102
Philae 171
Philip the Arab, Emperor 9
Piercebridge 217
pilum 109, 151, 228
Plautianus 71, 129, 130
Plautilla 71
Plautius, Governor 20
praefectus classis 210
praefectus urbi, Rome 84
Praetorian Guard xi, 29, 46, 87, 91, 102, 106, 108
Principate xiii
Procurator 45, 46
procurator metallorum 47
Publius Papinius Statius 66
Publius Septimius Aper 64, 73
Pudens, Governor 155, 202

quaestorship 73, 74
Quadi 28, 106
Quintilian 65
Quintus Aemilius Saturninus 171

Rhine, river 7, 18, 23, 25
Richborough 20

INDEX

Risingham 203
Rochester 212
Roman-Parthian War 72
Rome x, 4, 10, 27, 29, 174
    campus Martius 177
    Circus Maximus 123, 175
    Severan buildings 175
    Temple of Vesta 176
    'Terror' under Caracalla 254
Romulus Augustulus,
    Emperor xiii

Sabratha 38
Sahara Desert 43
Saldae 42
Sardinia 7
Sarmatians 28
Sassanid Persia 13
Scorpian 230
Scottish Borders 21, 155
Scotland ix, 209, 214, 216, 219
Scottish Highlands 155, 221
scutum 109
Seleucia-on-Tigris 33
Senate xii, 29, 38, 41, 74, 119
Senatorial class 1
Senecio, Governor 203, 204, 207
Septimius Flaccus 64
Septimius Macer 12, 64
Septimia Octavilla 68
Septimia Polla 68
Septimius Severus – Emperor ix, x,
    15, 18, 29, 101
    Birth 63
    Burial 253
    Celebrates his *decennalia* 17
    cursus honorum 73, 74
    Death ix, 250, 252
    Family background 11
    First eastern campaign 127
    First marriage 75, 76
    Genocidal order ix
    Gout 184, 185, 212

    Legionary *legate* 78
    Rise to power 70
    Second eastern campaign 127,
        164, 166
    Second marriage 24, 801, 81
Septizodium, Rome 176
Severan Buildings, Palatine
    Hill 175
Severan Dynasty xiii, 18
Severan Tondo 11
Severus Alexander xiii
Sicily 29
Solway Firth 9, 35
South Shields 22, 231
spatha 228
Springhead 212
St Alban 22
St Albans 21
St Leonards Hill 235
St Patrick 22
St Paul 7
Stanegate 19, 21
Stonehaven 221, 238

Tacfarinas 40
Tangiers 44
Tarquin the Proud 212
Tay, river 220
Tébessa 189
Temple of Jupiter Optimus
    Maximus 160
tetrarchy 30
Thrace 13
Tiberius, Emperor 40
Tidis 20
Tigris, river 33
Timgad 42, 189
Titus Quinctius Flaminius 153
Trajan's Column 228
Trajan, Emperor 17, 52
Tripolitania 41
Tyne, river 9, 19
Tyrrhenian Sea 29

Urbicus, Governor 9
Utica 187

Vespasian, Emperor 20, 37, 39
vexillation xv, 21, 47, 149, 159, 191, 202
Vexillation fortress 47
via Appia 175, 176
via Egnatia 30
via Nova 176
via Sacra 176
Vindolanda 21
Vologases V 135, 136

Wallsend 231
Watling Street 20, 21, 212
Welsh Marches 21

Year of the Five Emperors x, 18
Year of the Four Emperors 17
York ix, xi, 21
    Imperial capital 233

Zanticus, Iazyges King 76